In the Service of my People

In the Service of my People

Reflections of a Jewish Educator

Dr. Norman Schanin

gefen
publishing house בית הוצאה לאור
JERUSALEM ♦ NEW YORK

Typesetting: Marzel A.S. – Jerusalem
Cover Design: Studio Paz, Jerusalem

1   3   5   7   9   8   6   4   2

Gefen Publishing House
POB 36004, Jerusalem 91360, Israel
972-2-538-0247 • isragefe@netvision.net.il

Gefen Books
12 New Street Hewlett, NY 11557, USA
516-295-2805 • gefenbooks@compuserve.com

www.israelbooks.com

Printed in Israel   *Send for our free catalogue*

ISBN 965-229-242-7

Library of Congress Cataloging-in-Publication Data:

Schanin, Norman 1922-
In The Service of My People: Reflections of a Jewish Educator/ Norman Schanin.
Includes bibliographical references.
1. Schanin, Norman, 1922- 2. Jewish educators—United States—Biography.
3. Jewish educators—Israel—Biography. 4. Jews—Education. 5. Jewish religious education.
6. Judaism—Study and teaching. I. Title.
BM102.S34 A3 2000 • 296.6'8'092—dc21 [B] • CIP Number: 00-064633

Contents

Preface 7

Part I: Memoirs of a Jewish Educator

Chapter 1 On Developing a Jewish Consciousness and Commitments . . . 10

My Formative Years **10** • Zionism and the Holocaust **17** • The Kvutza Experience **19** • Form and Substance **22**

Chapter 2 Service In The United States Army (1944-1946) 27

The 547 Signal Base Depot Company **30** • Going Overseas **32** • England, France and Belgium **33** • Aboard the U.S.S. Sea Flyer **41** • Manila, Philippine Islands **46** • As Chaplain's Assistant **49** • Rebuilding the Manila Synagogue **51** • The Protest Movement **54** • Kvutzat Chaverim **56**

Chapter 3 Young Judaea 71

My First Professional Steps **72** • The Reconstructionist Institute for Jewish Youth Leadership **73** • Young Judaea National Director **75** • Senior Young Judaea **78** • Camp Tel Yehudah **86** • The Camp Program **89** • The Winds of Change **93**

Chapter 4 The Forest Hills Jewish Center (1952-1968) 98

The School **102** • The Youth Activities Program **105** • Developing a New Curriculum Design **106** • Working with Pre-Service Teachers and Teenagers **114** • Professional Growth and Development **116** • Our Hearts are in the East **119** • The Association of Americans and Canadians for Aliyah **126**

Chapter 5 The David Yellin Teachers College (1968-1988) 132

First Steps **132** • A Two-Year Seminary **134** • The Mechina Pedagogic High School **135** • The Early Childhood Center **138** • The Board of Directors **141** • Presenting a Long-Range Plan **143** • The Drive Toward Academization — From Seminary to College **146** • The Yom Kippur War **150** • The Hebrew University **152** • Innovative Programs **157** • Developing New Models **159** • Jewish Identity and Judaic Studies **162** • Campus Development **164** • Friends of the College **166** • Retirement and Continuity **168** • After Twenty Years of Service **170**

Part II: Reflections on What I Believe

Chapter 6 The Meanings of Jewishness 174

Jewish Identity **176** • In Pursuit of Meaning **182** • Values and Ideals as "Pacemakers" **184** • The Still Small Voice of Conscience **186** • Loyalty **188** • Some Educational Implications **190** • The Meanings of Jewishness **192** • The Challenge of Zionism **194** • Jewish Commitment, Loyalty and Service **195** • The Process of Education — Formal and Informal **197** • Curriculum Issues **199** • Community Responsibility **203** • Needed: A Moral Dimension for Jewish Education **205** • The School's Role as a Moral Authority **206** • Moral Imperatives (To Believe or not to Believe) **207** • This is my God **210** • Good and Evil; Reward and Punishment **212** • Prayer **213** • Educational Significance **215**

Chapter 7 Postscript: Retirement and Kehillat Mevakshei Derech 220

War and Peace **220** • In Retrospect **226** • On Retirement **230** • Kehillat Mevakshei Derech **231** • By Way of Conclusion **246**

Index 249

לנכדי

אלעד, ארז, יעל, עינת, עמרי ורוני

For my grandchildren
Elad, Erez, Yael, Einat, Omri and Roni

עֲטֶרֶת זְקֵנִים בְּנֵי בָנִים, וְתִפְאֶרֶת בָּנִים אֲבוֹתָם.
משלי י"ז, ו

"Children's children are the crown of old men,
and the glory of children are their parents."

Proverbs 17, 6

Preface

This book contains a message that was initially written as part of a legacy for my children and in particular my grandchildren. It then developed into a program of educational action for colleagues and those interested in its methodology. It records the story of a lifelong personal dedication to the meanings of my Jewishness and the ideal formed in my youth of giving service to the Jewish people. As I look about me and evaluate the current condition of the Jewish people, I marvel at the unending struggle for our spiritual fulfillment as a people. Our original covenant with the One God — as understood by each of us privately — has to be discovered anew by each individual, as he or she proceeds in search of truth and understanding. Such is the real meaning of life which is born out of the love between two individuals who choose to create a third. And so it goes on.

This is a tale that will take us across oceans and seas as it unfolds in several major areas around the world: in the United States where it all began and was formed; in Europe and the Far East as part of the experiences of an American soldier during World War II; as a returnee to the United States as a Jewish educator; concluding in the State of Israel — the place where it all began historically, when the original covenant was formed; and finally in retirement.

I am extremely grateful to so many people who have played an intimate part in forming the content of this book and its production. Above all, there is my continuing love and partnership with my wife Roslyn (Rahel), for her responsiveness and understanding, and for serving as my primary source of strength and determination to succeed in the fulfillment of our dreams. My thanks to my sons David, Jonathan and Hillel for their loving support and thoughtfulness as they shared with us feelings of family unity.

My indebtness and appreciation to my dear friends Sanford L. Batkin, Henry and Lottie Burger, and their son and daughter-in-law Paul and Asnat Burger, for making possible the publication of this book.

I am especially grateful to my life-long friend and mentor, Rabbi Dr. Jack J. Cohen for his valuable suggestions towards improving the clarity of the text. Thanks to Gefen Publishers, Ilan and Dror Greenfield for their belief in its significance, my admiration for Alex Auswaks, Emma Corney and Esther Herskovics, whose editorial assistance has made this book more readable and better understood.

May the reader enjoy the fruits of my labors.

Jerusalem in the year 2000 — ה'תש"ס

Dr. Norman Schanin

Part I

Memoirs of a Jewish Educator

Chapter 1

On Developing a Jewish Consciousness and Commitments

The process of my becoming an educator in the service of the Jewish people was a gradual but continuing life experience. It developed out of avocational interests, which in time, after appropriate training and some vital experiences, became vocational. As a young teenager, I began step by step to develop a strong Jewish awareness, which fashioned my identity and directed my evolving conscience and loyalties as a person.

My Formative Years

My family background provided the basic elements of being Jewish, but lacked some of the specific commitments essential to the meaning of our Jewishness. There was recognition and some observance of Jewish customs, holidays and traditions. Both my parents were born abroad, mother in Poland and father in Russia. My mother, Jeane, arrived in America as a child with her parents before World War I, while my father, Charles, emigrated to the United States as a teenager together with his two older brothers, Harry and Jack, during that war. Mother was educated in the public schools of New York; father was self-educated. After the premature death of my grandfather, Nisan, my father and his brothers were apprenticed at a very early age to learn the upholstery trade. This enabled them to aid the survival of their widowed mother, Sarah Breyner Schanin, as well as their sisters and younger brother, in the small village of Samentevich, now Byelorus (formerly Byelorussia). As apprentices, my father and his brothers lived with a rich Jewish family in a neighboring large city.

In 1912, when Dad was fourteen years old, the three brothers came to the

My mother Jeane during the 1920's

My father Charles during the 1920's

Norman at age 4

United States and were taken in by their Aunt Dora (my grandmother's sister) and her husband Nathan. The plan then was to bring their mother and other siblings to America, by which time they would have saved up enough for the boat trip from Russia to America. This plan never materialized due to the upheavals in Russia and in Germany (the country of embarkation). However, the brothers continued to send money to their mother whenever possible throughout the years, until the outbreak of World War II, when all contacts were severed. My father's mother, Sarah Breyner, died some two years later in 1942; some reports indicate she might have been killed by the Nazi invaders. The rest of the family remaining in the U.S.S.R. were living in Novozybkov, Byelorussia. They fled to Siberia in the wake of the advancing German armies.

In our small nuclear family, my sister Evelyn and I were always surrounded by and in the company of the extended Fishman and Schanin families. My mother's parents, Rose and Jacob Fishman, and their other children, Sam (Jimmy), Lilly and Yetta (Bobby), were a close-knit group and shared all family experiences, such as getting together on religious holidays and celebrating special occasions and accomplishments. A similar situation existed with my father's family, during the early years. In the absence of parents, his mother's sister Dora and her husband Nathan looked after the three teenage brothers until they were eventually able to take care of themselves as young men. The entire Schanin family in the United States were in the furniture business, sometimes together, but ultimately in two separate firms. My father and his brothers worked at one, and Dora's husband and their two sons, Hyman and Joseph, worked at the other.

My wife Roslyn's family, the Fleischers, were not as close-knit. Both of her parents, Sophie and Louis, had been married previously and Roslyn was the only child born of this marriage. There were two half-brothers Harry and Murray, and a half-sister May, all much older than Roslyn, and not as close to each other as we would have liked. Over the years, we tried to be a cohesive force within the Fleischer, Rosenwald and Rothbaum families.

Both of our extended families were hard-working, middle class people. I was privileged to be the firstborn child on both sides of my parents' families, the Fishmans and the Schanins. I was treated royally by all the members of these families. In my later years, as the oldest cousin on both sides, I tried, not always successfully, to maintain an ongoing relationship with my relatives. This concept of being part of a warm and close family is something that Roslyn and I have sought to share and transmit to our children and grandchildren.

My memories of growing up in a warm and loving family in Brooklyn, New York, are filled with much nostalgia and appreciation. I have been blessed with these memories, and Roslyn and I continue to enjoy similar experiences with our children and grandchildren.

At the age of six, my formal Jewish education in the neighborhood Orthodox synagogue began. As best I can remember, the class which I attended was typical of a "Heder." I learned how to read the Siddur and the Bible in Ashkenazic Hebrew and received information about Jewish holidays and religious observances.

My Jewish education took a giant leap forward with our move to the Flatbush area in Brooklyn, and my enrollment in the East Midwood Jewish Center Religious School. This was a well organized afternoon school with trained and experienced teachers, and a professional educator as its principal. The Rabbi of the Congregation, Harry Halpern, and the Religious School Principal, Azriel Eisenberg, and later Henry R. Goldberg, were outstanding Jewish personalities who became role models and major influences for me during these crucial early teen years. It was during these years that I rediscovered the meaning of my Jewishness which was to shape and direct my life and development.

The Junior Congregation in the EMJC, and other related informal activities, presented a very strong and positive Jewish influence and social experience for me and those young people who became involved in the program. The Synagogue and its officials were part of the Conservative religious movement. I became a cantor in the Junior Congregation, occasionally led services, and was eventually elected an officer.

The availability of an actively functioning Junior Congregation for children and youth between the ages of seven-eight until thirteen-fourteen, can serve as a significant educational instrument. This is especially important for young people whose parents might not attend religious services with any regularity. My Junior Congregation experiences, as a young participant in the one at the East Midwood Jewish Center, and later as the educator in charge of the Forest

Hills Jewish Center Junior Congregation, were extremely positive and reinforcing. This can be duplicated elsewhere. In order to do so, it is necessary to create an atmosphere that is informal, friendly and cohesive, where the functioning leaders are cantors, rabbis and Torah readers who are members of the group. The officers of the group are chosen by the membership. In such an instrument, it is important to develop a membership with which the young person can identify and be expected to participate in regularly. The educator or parent in charge of the program provides the guidance, assistance, instruction and supervision. Such a person should serve as a model as well as ensure the continuity of the program.

As my Bar Mitzvah ceremony and celebration approached, the question arose in the family as to whether I was to continue in the religious school beyond this time when most boys in our circle dropped out. During this questioning period, there was a change in the school administration. Henry R. Goldberg replaced Azriel Eisenberg, who became a Bureau of Jewish Education Director in another city. Eisenberg prepared for Goldberg a list of candidates for continuing their Jewish education in the Hebrew High School of the Congregation and of those functioning in leadership roles in the Junior Congregation. My name was on that list.

As another step toward cementing my continuing ties with the school and Junior Congregation, Goldberg obtained for me a three-week "cantors" scholarship at Camp Achvah. This eye-opening experience in a Jewish summer camp and my continuing participation in the Junior Congregation as a cantor, officer and later a leader of younger cantors, influenced me to continue on in the Hebrew High School. Goldberg was instrumental in my obtaining a tuition scholarship, which helped my parents accept the idea of my continuing to receive a formal Jewish education.

My short stay at Camp Achvah introduced me to a very different but emotionally and intellectually stimulating environment, with a strong Zionist and Hebraic emphasis. The camp was directed by Samson Benderly and assisted by such outstanding American Jewish educators as Judah Lapson, Abraham P. Gannes, and their actively involved wives. The impact on me of this first such experience was very strong and something I could identify with. I was able to carry this experience over to my continuing work in the Junior Congregation and my later involvements, with the Palestine Song and Dance Group and Kvutza in the United States and then in the Philippine Islands.

At this point in time, my developing Jewish consciousness was ready for intellectual stimulation and direction. I found this through contact with personalities additional to those described above. Jack J. Cohen, a local neighbor and friend, became a surrogate older brother to me. He served as a young teacher on the faculty of the religious school. Then, together with Jacob Rosenfeld, my Young Judaea club leader, Cohen introduced me to the teachings of Rabbi Mordecai M. Kaplan and the Reconstructionist movement. These mentors, together with Henry Goldberg and Rabbi Harry Halpern, provided the encouragement and intellectual stimulation I was seeking. I was introduced to the Kaplanian concept of Jewish peoplehood and the understanding that Judaism was the product of Jewish cultural development over the centuries. The idea of Jews being a people led, of course, to Zionism and Israel as the homeland of the Jewish people.

My developing intellectual framework was enriched and given direction by the philosophy of Rabbi Dr. Mordecai M. Kaplan. I studied seriously and repeatedly the basic thoughts in his monumental and profound volume, *Judaism as a Civilization*. I accepted the challenge he presented in these words: "The quality and quantity of life that spell Judaism must be rediscovered and reemphasized. It must be recognized as nothing less than a civilization. It must figure in the consciousness of the Jew as the *tout ensemble* of all that is included in a civilization, the social framework of national unity centering in a particular land, a continuing history, a living language and literature, religious folkways, mores, laws and art."[1] Rabbi Kaplan was a highly respected faculty member of the Jewish Theological Seminary of America and Dean of its Teachers Institute. Later on, I was privileged to sit in his class as a student in the latter Institute.

Reconstructionism provided me with the knowledge and understanding that being Jewish meant, primarily, belonging to the Jewish people. It was this meaning of peoplehood that provided Jews with a rich and unique culture, whose central component was a religious philosophy and way of life, all of

---

1. Kaplan Mordecai M., *Judaism as a Civilization* (enlarged edition) The Reconstructionist Press, New York 1957, p. 513. (First published by Macmillan, N.Y. 1934).

which are bound up with Israel as the Jewish homeland. Peoplehood, religion and culture, and the land of Israel, became the cornerstones of my search for meaning and provided me with the intellectual understandings necessary to develop direction and purpose in life. These are the basic ideas which enabled me to become a devoted Jew and Zionist, prepared to dedicate my life in the service of the Jewish people.

During these formative years, I was introduced to the importance of good educational administration as an office helper to my principal, Henry R. Goldberg, who remained a lifelong friend and mentor. It was also during this time that I became involved in helping to catalogue the extensive Judaic and general library in the home of Rabbi Harry Halpern. Both these experiences served to enrich my life and to help me choose a career in Jewish education.

Henry R. Goldberg — or H.R.G. as we fondly called him among ourselves — was a short man, a bachelor, and basically a shy person, but with an unexpected sense of humor. He had the wonderful ability to be friendly with people in a quiet and unassuming manner. Henry built a first-rate model afternoon Hebrew school, with both early childhood and high school programs. He was able to assemble an outstanding group of teachers, many of whom were both Roslyn's and my elementary and high school teachers. Goldberg organized an active Parents Association and, of course, the Junior Congregation. His crowning achievement was the successful establishment of one of the first and finest day schools in the Conservative movement. This school, later known as the Rabbi Harry Halpern Day School, became one of the key branches of the newly established Solomon Schechter Day Schools in the United States and Canada.

Henry became the founding President of the Educators Assembly of the Conservative movement. We continued our personal friendship when my career assignments took me out of the East Midwood Jewish Center and Brooklyn; we added the dimension of a professional relationship. I was privileged to follow in his footsteps and, in later years, also become the President of the Educators Assembly.

Throughout my lifetime I seem to have had the good fortune to be in the right place at the right time. This has enabled me to make some of the momentous decisions which have affected my life's direction. A seemingly insignificant strike for higher wages by the teachers of the East Midwood Jewish Center Religious School delayed the opening of the 1938-1939 school year by two to three months. I was now eager and impatient to pursue my Jewish studies more seriously, since I was very much aware of my inadequate Judaic background. I was especially weak in the knowledge of the Hebrew language and the classical Jewish texts, which are at the heart of Jewish culture and religion. Consequently, due to the long delay in opening the Hebrew High School, and though still a teenager attending a public high school during the day, I decided to enroll in the Israel Friedlander adult education courses. These were held twice a week at the Jewish Theological Seminary of America on 122nd Street in Manhattan, New York City. This important decision led to my continuing studies at the Seminary for many years. It provided me with the opportunity to meet with like-minded people and participate in the enriching informal cultural and social activities initiated by the student council, then known as the Hebrew Arts Committee.

I had difficulty in passing the entrance examinations to the Teachers Institute of the Seminary, but after two attempts I was finally admitted for the 1941-1942 academic year. My difficulty in learning foreign languages has remained a problem throughout my life. I grew up in a monolingual environment which did not help my foreign language development. However, I finally received my Bachelor of Religious Education degree from the Teachers Institute in 1948. My studies at the Seminary were interrupted for two and a half years during World War II, when I served in the United States Army. After my demobilization I resumed my studies in 1946 to complete the five-year program. But more of this later on.

Zionism and the Holocaust

During my early teen years, I became an active member of the Zionist youth movement, Young Judaea. As mentioned above, our club was led by a challenging older man, Jacob Rosenfeld, who contributed greatly to my understanding of and commitment to the struggle of the Jewish people to restore its ancient homeland in Eretz Yisrael. As a Reconstructionist, he taught me about the centrality of the Jewish people and the ideal of peoplehood by

making Zionism meaningful for Diaspora Jewry. Reconstructionism enabled me
to understand that being Jewish meant, first and foremost, membership in the
Jewish people. This meaning of peoplehood provides Jews with a rich and
unique culture — one whose central component is a religious philosophy and a
way of life that are bound up with Israel as the Jewish homeland.

As an outgrowth of my work with the Junior Congregation, together with
my good friend Sheldon Feinberg, I helped organize a Palestine Song and Dance
Group. Sheldon was also a product of the East Midwood Jewish Center
Religious School and its Junior Congregation. We were encouraged in this
activity by the quiet and supportive efforts of Henry R. Goldberg, the new
principal of the East Midwood Jewish Center Religious School.

Sheldon and I became close friends and active Zionists. Together we traveled
on the subway to and from Brooklyn and Manhattan, to collect money for the
Jewish National Fund. Sheldon, who has a lovely singing voice, would sing
Zionist songs and say a few words about Palestine. We would then pass among
the passengers with a blue and white Jewish National Fund box to collect
donations. For me this task was not easy, since I was more reserved and self-
conscious than Sheldon. He was far more outgoing and seemed to enjoy the
challenge and the experience.

The Palestine Song and Dance Group, which initially comprised pre-
teenagers (Sheldon and I were then older teenagers by some four or five years),
continued to meet between 1939 and 1941. The group would appear
occasionally before Zionist and other groups at the East Midwood Jewish
Center, and elsewhere in Brooklyn. When the terrible early stories of Nazi
horrors in Germany began to become known, filling the newspapers and radio,
we reacted strongly and wanted to do something more helpful as a group than
singing and dancing.

I remember a meeting held by the group following a Friday night teenage
service that we conducted in the Bet Hamidrash ("Little Synagogue") of the
Center. We were upset about the terrible news from Nazi Germany and had a
discussion about what we could do on our own level. The decision was taken
that Shabbat to organize a more formal group dedicated to the survival and
advancement of the Jewish people wherever Jews lived. We were also especially
concerned about what was happening in Palestine, where, at that time, the Jews

were in conflict with the British Mandatory authorities, as well as with Arabs living in the region. And so, in 1941, the group to be called "Kvutza" was born. Sheldon and I served as organizers of the group. However, Sheldon was drafted into the United States Army shortly thereafter, while I continued to work directly and alone with the group.

The Kvutza Experience

The Kvutza experience was a milestone for me. It came at a time when I was sufficiently mature to begin to put things together in my life, intellectually and emotionally. It marked my transition into young manhood and awakened my Jewish consciousness to the point where I felt the strong desire and need to express it in actions. I was prepared to make commitments.

The real experience of establishing and working with Kvutza left an indelible impression upon my life, both personally and professionally. From then on, there was no question that I would become an educator in the service of the Jewish people. For me, this meant transmitting to young people what it meant to be a member of the Jewish people; creating a dynamic Jewish community in America, and being involved in establishing an independent and vibrant Jewish homeland in Palestine (later Israel), both needed for the creative survival of the Jewish people.

In a very personal sense, Kvutza provided me with the greatest blessing of all — finding a beloved wife and life companion. Rahel (Roslyn to old friends), was one of the indigenous leaders among her peers in the group. And so, we had a continuing opportunity of sharing activities for several years within the framework of Kvutza. Here our personal relationship gradually deepened and blossomed, until our decision was made some years later to marry. Working with Kvutza was a very significant educational and vocational experience in my preparations to become a professional educator. I became convinced then of the importance of blending informal and formal education, and became aware of some of the methodology and principles involved in working in both spheres.

The success of merging formal and informal educational programs has been proven to me, as a result of both my avocational and vocational experiences. The class in formal education is a group, or several smaller groups, which consists of participating individuals, who are dealing with subject matter in an environment shared by others, and the resulting interrelation between them with the assistance of a teacher. A club — or any other informal group structure — is a unit engaged in social relationships and interaction, for a stated purpose, function or cause. Both the formal class and informal groups can progress in accordance with their acknowledged goals when there is positive human interaction between teacher or group leader and the students or group members. This is the basis of an educational methodology that is to be developed around a particular subject to be taught or learned and activated in some individual internalized way. These are some of the principles experienced in Kvutza and my later work in teacher education.

The founding members of Kvutza adopted, the proclamation, "The People of Israel Lives" (עַם יִשְׂרָאֵל חַי), as its motto and goal. For several months the members considered the question of how to experience the ideal of living a creative Jewish life. Sometimes we were able to grasp some of the meaning and magnitude of our strivings, only to lose sight of them in the confusion of our thinking and lack of experience.

From the beginning, we attempted to establish a community of Jewish interests for ourselves and for those around us. We hoped that this would enable those who so desired to find a pattern of Jewish living that would provide them with happiness and creative expression, along with fulfillment of their needs and wants. The goal was to create the environment necessary for the flourishing of a creative Judaism as we understood it.

The plan was to develop a program of group activities to function within the normal framework of Jewish communal life. The members did not want to cut themselves off from either their homes or the community at large. The hope was to find personal satisfaction and fulfillment, but also to assist in the ultimate reorganization and revitalization of Jewish living within the local community. I wrote about this in an explanatory article about Kvutza entitled "Youth in Quest of a Living Judaism."[1]

The idea that Kvutza was a community of interests developed by and for its members, was also reflected in the choice of name for the group — Kvutza. The

---

1. "The Reconstructionist," June 15, 1945, Vol. XI, No. 9.

Israeli Kibbutz served as the model for our organizational and philosophical development. The group had no formal leaders or officers. Though Sheldon Feinberg and I were older than the other members, we established our formal place as members, who were expected to share their larger experiences and knowledge with the group. As a youth community, Kvutza attempted to provide its members with much of their social, spiritual, cultural and intellectual needs as teenagers. A strong feeling of belonging, of being special, was developed among its members, who in turn expressed a lasting loyalty to the group, and a commitment to its ideals. For many of the founding members, the ideas and ideals of Kvutza were to serve as lifetime goals, directions and commitments.

This idea of creating a teenage youth community within the larger adult community was somewhat unique for its time. The group was separate, independent, self-sufficient, yet an integral part of a larger whole — the local Jewish community and the Jewish people. This was an idea that some youth movements in America, Europe and Israel began to develop and experience in their desire to pursue meaningful goals, and implement them while retaining their independence. Others set themselves apart from the community, sometimes even from home and family, in their desire to achieve independence and to be different.

Looking back at my work with Kvutza, I am sometimes amazed at the realization that what was created, organized and developed with the group was accomplished despite my limited experiences. My intuition enabled me to work with others, particularly teenagers, in a group setting. Only during later years, when I formally studied the theories and methodology of group work, did I begin fully to understand the dynamics of what had been achieved.

As already indicated, Kvutza grew out of the Palestine Song and Dance Group organized earlier. The original Kvutza functioned as a social group with a cultural-Zionist orientation. The process of becoming an enduring group was fortified by the effective communication of ideas, the coordination of efforts in an atmosphere of friendliness and feelings of pride within the group.

This successful attempt to create a community of interests for teenagers was based on the development of a cohesive group. Our members worked together and took responsibility for all the chores, programmatically and organizationally. There were positive relations among the members and a minimalization of individual competitiveness. An interesting development within the group was its ability to build a structure consisting of distinguishable parts or positions that engendered respect among the members for one another. These parts were different when viewed in terms of responsibility, friendship and communication. Each individual was able to occupy different positions in the group, often on a rotating basis, depending upon his or her personal interests.

Form and Substance

It is interesting to recall the oath of membership and statement of principles adopted by Kvutza. Actually, they represented a kind of philosophy of Jewish life combined with commitments and an action program for young people. This oath contained a declaration of aims and purposes. There were three parts to the oath. The first was a statement indicating that the group was dedicated to the "development of a creative and vital Jewish life in America"; the second goal was the "upbuilding of Eretz Yisrael as the Jewish National Home," and, finally, the aim of the "furtherance of democracy and world peace."

To achieve these aims and purposes, the members were called upon to obligate themselves to attend all meetings of Kvutza and to participate in all its activities. This oath of membership also defined the specific obligations of each member. These included the pledge to live one's life "publicly and privately as a Jew," to seek "fellowship and cooperation with other Jews in order to ensure the survival of the Jewish people and the advancement of Jewish civilization." The choice of language in defining the oath and obligations reflected many of the concepts developed by Mordecai M. Kaplan in his philosophy of Reconstructionism. The oath then concluded with a series of nine commitments which members were expected to fulfill.

I believe, in retrospect, that this Oath of Membership was an indication of the depth of commitment that was expected of the teenagers. It was something very special and quite extraordinary when the group was established as part of the American Jewish community in the early 1940's.

It is unlikely that there were many other teenage youth programs with such an oath and list of obligations to be freely accepted on an individual basis by each member. Many members, as adults, continued to develop and live their lives as Jewish lay leaders, teachers, rabbis, or as enlightened and committed laymen. Most continued their Jewish lives in the United States, while others emigrated to Israel.

Kvutza had a very original and unique organizational structure. Reflecting on my work with Kvutza, I can now see the connection between what was developed then and my early interest in and limited understanding of the process of group dynamics and group methodology. This interest and understanding were later enriched and strengthened when I majored in group work as part of my studies toward a Master of Education Degree.

As indicated earlier, Kvutza did not have any formal leaders or officers. Although Sheldon Feinberg and I were the group organizers, we nevertheless considered ourselves and encouraged the others to look upon us as fellow members and not as "leaders." Each member was considered equal to any other in the group. Everyone was expected to select some subject or activity for which he was to assume responsibility as a program chairman. This ensured equality among the members of the group; one did not have to compete against others for leadership roles.

The subjects and activities reflected what the group considered to be an aspect of the totality of the Judaism the members had accepted. An interesting work pattern was thus developed. The chairman of each activity or project was expected to work with others in presenting this field of interest at one or more of the full group's meetings. In order to deal with issues of initiative, responsibility and scheduling, a Va'ad (Executive Committee) was elected by majority vote each year. Its function was to organize and delegate tasks, and then supervise the presentation of the programs for each meeting. It then reviewed the work of these committees, established a schedule of activities, and determined whether standards were being maintained by individual members and the committees.

Another innovative programming idea was that of dividing the meetings into two parts; the fixed and the variable. The fixed elements included opening each meeting with an inspirational reading from the Bible or other relevant material. During the year, the group conducted the Havdalah ceremony marking the end of the Shabbat, since meetings were held Saturday night. A short business session was followed by the cultural part of the program. This was the variable part, which took several forms, as determined by the program committee scheduling that evening: a book review; discussion of a current affairs issue; a report or an activity; music, dance or dramatics, art; a guest speaker; or a film.

An interesting and somewhat original development was the establishment of a Keren Tarbut (Cultural Fund) to finance the programs presented by the group. Members contributed a monthly sum, which was used not only to support group activities, but also to help individual members fund their commitment to engage in some Jewish cultural pursuit.

On the occasion of the first anniversary of Kvutza, the group presented two Onegei Shabbat (Sabbath afternoon programs). One was devoted to Jewish folk songs and the second to folk dance. The culmination of the anniversary celebration was a large public presentation of Jewish arts on the theme of our motto — The People of Israel Lives (עַם יִשְׂרָאֵל חַי). The program was a major effort conducted by the members on as high a professional level as was then possible for amateurs. It featured a biblical pageant and two original sketches of modern Palestine (pre-Israel), written and presented by the members, and the performance of the stirring cantata, "What is Torah?" by Judith and Ira Eisenstein, leaders in the Reconstructionist movement. For me, the experience of this latter presentation was of great significance, fulfillment and happiness; Roslyn accompanied the group on the piano and I conducted the cantata.

Over the next five years, Kvutza produced two similar evenings on the same theme of Am Yisrael Hai. Each featured original works by members of the group and different cantatas written by the Eisensteins, "Our Bialik" and a Hassidic tale, "The Seven Golden Buttons." The second Am Yisrael program was conducted without the participation of Sheldon Feinberg or myself, since both of us were then serving in the United States Army. During our absence, a parents group, chaired by Henry R. Goldberg, filled in as advisors to the group.

Later on, some of the original members of Kvutza organized younger groups; the first was called Junior Kvutza and later on Kvutza Bet. These were comprised of small groups of younger teens between the ages of thirteen and fifteen. By 1947, the original members of Kvutza began to go off to colleges and universities in different part of the city, the country and even abroad to Switzerland. Some married, while others became engaged or were on their way to marrying partners from outside the group. Thus the senior group came to a formal ending.

Many of the members continued to be in contact with one another over the years (Roslyn and I became engaged in 1944, and married in 1946). But the Kvutza idea and ideal continued on for several additional years. Roslyn organized and led a third group in later years known as Kvutza Gimmel. The female members who comprised this group were all pre-teens. As will be reported later on, the Kvutza program also took root in Manila, the Philippine Islands, where I was stationed while in the American army between 1945 and 1946.

It is important to note that in fulfillment of its stated goals, the Kvutza members provided special services to the local Jewish community in Brooklyn, New York. They took part in programs sponsored by community organizations, and many of the activities conducted by local schools and organizations at the East Midwood Jewish Center. Much of the participation by members was in the form of volunteer service. To complete its communal and ideological commitments, Kvutza eventually affiliated with three organizations: Senior Judaea and the Young Judaea leadership organization, the Jewish Reconstructionist Foundation as its only youth group, and the Brooklyn Jewish Youth Council.

Since we were dealing with teenagers, the earlier years for each in his or her family setting and inter-relationships, as well as their formal and informal educational experiences, must all be considered when trying to evaluate the permanent influence the Kvutza encounter had on each member. Then too, what came after this period in the life of a teenager, the college education received, the career choice, and most important of all, the marriage partner, greatly influenced the next step each took. I have kept in contact with many of the original members and have also been able to gather information about the post-Kvutza experiences of others. I feel very content with that which was achieved by Kvutza as a group and the lasting impact it had on its members.

For me, personally, it was one of the most exhilarating, exciting and

meaningful experiences of my young life, one in which I found myself
consciously believing. It enabled me to determine the directions I was prepared
to dedicate my life to in the future. To this must be added the important fact
that it was the time and place in which my love for Roslyn developed and
blossomed.

Chapter 2

Service In The United States Army (1944-1946)

When World War II erupted, I was a student at New York University, Washington Square College of Arts and Sciences. I majored in History and took Biology as a minor. At the same time, I was enrolled as a full-time student in the Teachers Institute of the Jewish Theological Seminary of America. As was the practice in those days, most college students eligible for the draft during wartime were permitted to continue their schooling until they received their academic degree. I began my undergraduate studies in September 1939 and received my Bachelor of Arts (B.A.) degree in June 1943. After the war, I continued my education at the School of Education of New York University, completing the requirements for the Master of Arts (M.A.) degree in February 1948. During that same year I was awarded the Bachelor of Religious Education (B.R.E) degree from the Teachers Institute of the Jewish Theological Seminary of America.

I received my first order to report for induction into the United States Army on April 14th, 1943. I reported as required but did not pass the physical examination administered, due to poor eyesight. I was thus classified as physically unfit. However, as the war needs became more critical, the army created a limited service category in order to accept for military service those with physical limitations such as mine. And so, in January 1944, I was ordered to appear for a medical reexamination. When this was completed, the doctor who reviewed my physical profile and saw that I was on the border line between passing and failing, asked me whether or not I wanted to enter the army. My immediate response was — yes. I felt deeply the need to become a soldier in the cause of defending those things I felt strongly about as an American and as a Jew.

An interesting incident, in connection with this question as to whether or not to enter the army during the war, occurred shortly before my induction into the army became a reality. I was invited by the Registrar of the Rabbinical School, Rabbi Moshe Davis, to consider entering the Rabbinical School of the Seminary. Such an action would, of course, grant me an army deferment until I became a Rabbi, and then I would be eligible for a Chaplain's position. I declined the invitation. I was not ready to make such a commitment to become a Rabbi. Along with this, the moral issue of whether to enter the military service during the war or much later after its termination were the immediate reasons for my declining this important and kind invitation. On January 4th, 1944, I took the oath of allegiance and was inducted into the United States Army. I reported for active service on January 25th, 1944.

At the Reception Center in Fort Dix, New Jersey, I underwent several interviews and aptitude tests; the army had a problem classifying me for specific duties. Since I was not to be a combat soldier, I was subject to the policy of sending soldiers with limited service profiles to one of its schools for a two-month training course in whatever field it needed candidates, or where there were openings for new inductees. I attended two such service schools: one for cooks and bakers, and after my basic training and much argument from me before the classification officers, a Signal Corps Clerical School. Fortunately, I had taken an extra typing course during my senior high school year, enabling me to prove my typing ability and convince the classification officer of my qualifications for the Clerical School. I did not want to spend my army service as a cook and baker. This assignment to the Signal Corps Clerical School was most fortunate, since it was very much related to what occurred during the thirteen months I served abroad in the European and Asian theaters of war. It set into motion very important and meaningful experiences, which could not have been predicted for someone classified by the military as a cook and baker, or a Signal Corps clerk. But more about this later on.

The Cooks and Bakers School experience had its advantages. For the two-month course, I was stationed on Governor's Island in New York Bay, and so I was able to come home several evenings a week. Some interesting anecdotes can be told about this experience. Our instructional courses were on the island, but our practical training was held at the large army induction center on Lexington

Avenue, located in the heart of central Manhattan. The poor new recruits were to be the victims of cooks and bakers-in-training. I remember, too, the several occasions when Roslyn and I met for a date in Manhattan, and the problem I had with saluting officers. As a new recruit still without basic training, I knew officers had to be saluted, but I was not very certain when and under what circumstances. Manhattan was, of course, filled with thousands of officers and enlisted men on leave, and so the saluting business became a problem because of my uncertainties. To solve, or rather avoid the problem, we took to walking on the side streets rather than the main boulevards, thus reducing the need for saluting.

The crowning anecdote concerns my contact with pork chops (non-kosher of course). Toward the end of our two-month cooks and bakers training course, I was surprised to be called into the office of our unit's Commanding Officer at the Induction Center. After permitting me to stand at ease, the officer proceeded to tell me it had been reported to him that I was seen breading pork chops with a fork so as not to touch the meat. I was, of course, astonished by the statement, firstly since I knew the matter not to be true, and secondly, because I realized subconsciously (and later on consciously) that this was a test of some kind related to my being Jewish. The officer had my personnel file open before him which had recorded my studies at the Jewish Theological Seminary, and my being Jewish. I indicated to him that the information he had received was incorrect. The interview ended after a few minutes with my saluting the officer and returning to my duties. Some days later, I was told that I was to be in charge of the group of soldiers in the course who were about to be transferred back to Fort Dix, New Jersey, for reassignment. My task was to lead the march of our group down Lexington Avenue to nearby Grand Central Station, where we were to entrain for Fort Dix. I was entrusted with all the sealed personnel files of the group which were to be turned over to the officer who was to receive us. In retrospect, the unusual interview was a kind of test set up by the officer, who was probably Jewish himself.

The group returned to Fort Dix for reassignment to a basic training camp, where we were to be attached to a more permanent unit for army duty. The stay at Fort Dix was short and uneventful. On Shabbat, I attended religious services, as I did whenever possible during my army career. A large group of us were then transported by train to Camp Crowder, Missouri, for basic training and assignment to a regular unit in the Signal Corps.

Camp Crowder was a huge army encampment situated on the plains of Missouri. The nearest city was Joplin, which was where most soldiers visited while on weekend leave. Most of us were not close enough to reach home for short leaves. Conditions at the camp were quite good. This was a new, or perhaps an expanded older, military installation. Our living quarters were fairly new and in good order. Each barrack was divided into squads. Soon we began our six-week general basic training.

The training program was intense and grueling, at least for me. We were up early and returned exhausted to our beds late in the evening; occasionally we bivouacked out at night in tents after training operations. We ate "K" rations in the field, and participated in all types of army maneuvers designed to teach us to fight, to protect ourselves and to be able to cope with a variety of unknown situations that could occur during wartime. To my great surprise, while on the rifle range, I fired a perfect score with the U.S. Enfield rifle in the standing to sitting position. For this I was awarded the certificate of membership in the exclusive Forty-Five club. (In each firing position there were nine shots each worth up to five points; a perfect score added up to forty-five.) On weekends I usually stayed on the base, attended Sabbath services and spent time at the Base Red Cross PX, usually listening to music, and writing letters. I became friendly with several of the soldiers who lived in our two-floor barracks building. Most of them were Jewish and from the New York area. I visited Joplin once or twice, but found the place unexciting and not too appealing.

The 547ᵗʰ Signal Base Depot Company

Upon completing the basic training program, we were reclassified and then assigned either to a new Signal Corps unit that was about to be formed, or as replacements to already existing units. It was at this point that I strongly requested not to be appointed as a cook and baker. When my touch-typing skill was considered, I was sent to the Signal Corps Clerk School at Camp Crowder for additional training. After completing the two-month course, I was sent to the 547ᵗʰ Signal Corps Depot Company that was then being formed.

The 547th was activated on September 15th, 1944, at Camp Edison, Sea Girt, New Jersey. The Camp was part of the Fort Monmouth, New Jersey, Signal Corps complex and was situated near the Atlantic Ocean, some two hours train ride from New York City. All the enlisted men in this unit, or at least most of them, were in the limited service physical category described above. We were a collection of older and younger recruits, some married and with children, others single and fresh out of high school or college. (I believe that the number of college graduates was very small indeed.)

There was only a small handful of Jewish men among approximately 115 soldiers in the Company. Some soldiers became friendly, while others avoided us. I can't recall any overt actions or words which could be considered anti-Semitic. However, I did feel uncomfortable on some occasions, whether for reasons real or imagined I can't say at this point. The only official acknowledgement of our existence as Jews was made at Christmas time, when the First Sergeant mentioned to us that it was customary for the Jewish soldiers to volunteer for kitchen and guard duty on Christmas Day, and in return we would be replaced by non-Jews for similar duties later on Yom Kippur. We, of course, gladly accepted this arrangement.

After a series of classroom lectures we were assigned to the operation of the Avon, New Jersey, Signal Corps Warehouse as a miniature depot. Our task as a company was to set up a complete Signal Corps Depot that was to receive equipment and supplies for storage and transshipment to the armies in the field. We had to organize a complete inventory of all that we received and stored, and maintain the equipment and supplies in good condition for immediate use. I was to report for duty at the shipping section of the depot. While in New Jersey, we printed our company mimeographed newspaper, "The Depot Digest." I became a member of its staff. We were only able to print two issues because of the company's movements from one base to another.

By Thanksgiving Day, November 30th, 1944, we had been transferred to the huge Holabird Army Signal Depot in Baltimore, Maryland. This was one of the largest such depots in the country. Here we experienced working in a real functioning depot. After several weeks, we returned to our original base in Camp Edison, New Jersey, where we concluded our training by holding many outdoor bivouacs in the field. These took place during the dead of night in winter, when it was very cold and snowy. We were now ready for our overseas assignment in one of the war zones.

Going Overseas

On November 25th, the Saturday night before Thanksgiving, I gave Roslyn an engagement ring. It was a tremendously happy and significant occasion in our lives.

We left Camp Edison on January 30th, 1945, and arrived at Camp Kilmer, New Jersey, which was a staging area for those going overseas to the European Theater of Operations. Here we were checked and issued appropriate clothing and equipment, and our medical records were reviewed. Those who needed additional or updated immunization injections for service abroad in foreign countries were duly attended to. Some eight days later we left Camp Kilmer and proceeded to a Jersey City port. There we boarded a ferryboat called the Red Bank, fittingly named after the town located next to Fort Monmouth, the large Signal Corps base in the area. We sailed up the Hudson River (New York Bay) to a pier located at about 21st Street in Manhattan. As we disembarked from the ferry, we were greeted by music from a W.A.C (Women's Army Corps) band. We all collapsed on our duffel bags on the pier awaiting orders to board our new home, the converted American luxury liner originally called the S.S. Washington and now named the U.S.S. Mount Vernon. The Red Cross ladies were on hand to give us some welcome hot coffee and doughnuts.

At this point I should tell you about my duffel bag. As well as all the clothing and other supplies issued by the army (including a rifle and ammunition), I carried a small library of Judaica, pictures, and a box camera contained in a wooden box to protect it from abuse. The weight of my duffel bag was, for me, horrendous. I did not heed the warnings given by other more experienced soldiers to travel light. Every time the Company moved from one place to another, we were required to carry the duffel bag for a distance until we reached the vehicle assigned to carry the Company's baggage. And so here I was, worn out, sitting on the wooden floor of the vehicle, and tingling with anticipation at the prospect of crossing the Atlantic Ocean in an army transport ship to destinations unknown in the European war zone.

After a short while we were ordered to board the ship with our duffel bags and rifles. We immediately moved into the bowels of this huge ship, each soldier assigned to a hammock which served as a bed. The hammocks were arranged in layers of three or four, from floor to ceiling. There were several thousand soldiers aboard this former luxury liner. The physical conditions were cramped, though very tolerable considering the number of men located in each area, and in contrast to stories by others who had traveled on smaller army/navy transports. We left New York on February 7th, 1945, and since we were on a large and fast ship, we did not travel in a convoy. This, too, added somewhat to the tension. At the first signs of darkness, the entire ship was blacked out so as to avoid possible detection by enemy submarines and warships. There was little to do but retire to one's hammock bed and read by flashlight.

Life aboard ship was neither very difficult nor unpleasant. We ate three hot meals a day in shifts, watched movies, read books from the library, and played on the basketball court. If you had the patience to sweat out the lines, malt beer and cokes were available throughout the day. I volunteered and conducted Kabbalat Shabbat services on the ship for the one Sabbath we were aboard. I don't remember any of the details of the services other than that they did take place, since I reported them in one of my letters to Roslyn which she still has today.

England, France and Belgium

A week later, we finally saw the hilly shores of Scotland and Northern Ireland as we steamed down between them to Liverpool, England. We landed there for our first stop in the European Theater of Operations on February 16th, 1945. My first impressions of England were not very favorable. This was a first visit for me. After disembarking, we marched through the streets of Liverpool to the train station. The port area was not the most flourishing part of the city. What we could see was much desolation, dirt and squalor. We were probably passing through a depressed slum area. This was wartime and Great Britain suffered as a frontline battle area. The people, especially the children, were dressed shabbily and scantily. I was quite moved by the poor appearance of the children. They wore wooden shoes, which apparently were then quite common, no coats or sweaters, and it was cold outside during the month of February. Wherever we could on such occasions, whether in England, France or Belgium, we gave to passers-by the chocolates, gum and cigarettes we had received from the army.

When visiting other parts of England, we found the general situation much better and even impressive, considering that these people had been experiencing the hardships of war since 1939. The civilian population continued to suffer greatly from the nightly indiscriminate German rocket bombing of the large cities and ports. By train we sped southward to Andover and encamped at Barton Stacey, Hants, awaiting further orders. We spent two weeks there, during which time we engaged in athletics and occasionally received twenty-four hour passes for visiting London.

France was next. We crossed the English Channel from Southampton to Le Havre aboard the liberty ship Marine Wolf on March 4th, 1945. The overnight Channel crossing was probably the only time that the danger and risk factors were very high for us. The Channel was heavily mined and enemy submarines were on the prowl. When the coast of France appeared on the horizon at daybreak, I was quite excited. We landed at Le Havre. This signaled the beginning of our European experience, which took us through the winter, spring and part of the summer of 1945.

This was Europe, the place where history had been written down for more than 2,000 years. This was the Europe of Jewish history, of the rise and fall of many Jewish communities and their manifold contributions to civilization, only to culminate in the death camps of Nazi Europe. My first pictures of France and Europe were difficult and very upsetting; death and destruction were to be seen on all sides. It was a frightful sight repeated many times during our travels through France and Belgium. We were quartered in a transient army camp outside Le Havre where we lived in tents.

At the end of two weeks we again boarded trains, this time for Paris, which was to be our transfer point for going to Belgium. We had lunch in a Parisian restaurant called Café Margarite which had probably been a beautiful and fashionable café at one time. To get to the restaurant and then later back to the railway station, we had to march through several streets in Paris. After returning to the station, we were ordered to store our equipment and rifles. Then the company personnel were granted several hours leave to visit Paris. I, together with a few others, was "elected" to serve on guard duty to protect our personal gear, company equipment and weapons. I spent the next few hours in the railway station. I believe that this was the Gare d'Orsay, which has since been converted into the beautiful Musée d'Orsay, a very impressive museum which displays the old and the new in its architectural reconstruction. Roslyn and I visited this museum during one of our more recent trips to Paris. Structurally, it looked to me to be that very same railway station where I stood on guard duty in March 1945.

My first views of Belgium were seen through the open door of a boxcar, a 40×8 railroad car of World War I vintage. It was a very rough and bumpy trip. We stood most of the time during the few hours it took to cross the French border into Belgium, in order to see something of the countryside and the small towns through which we passed. Belgium had not been damaged as badly as the parts of France we had passed through. Those sections bordering on Germany were wrecked, indicative of the hard fighting that was still going on around the borders and in Germany itself.

This was also the time of the attempted breakthrough by the encircled German armies during the Battle of the Bulge in the Ardennes Forest of Belgium. It was one of the last attempts by the Germans to push back the Allied armies. For many days and nights during March and April, the Allied air armada sent a constant stream of thousands of airplanes over our heads in Belgium on their way into Germany. It was an awesome display of might, sight and sound. The noise volume of these continuous air sorties by this huge number of planes was tremendous and even frightening, though we knew they were ours. During the Battle of the Bulge, we could sometimes hear the echoes of the distant bombings and artillery fire.

Our Belgian destination was a small village called Courcelles, where there existed a huge factory warehouse, formerly owned and operated by the Pittsburgh Glass company of the United States. Until the German retreat and pullback, it served as a German Army supply warehouse. The village of Courcelles bordered on an artery of the main railway line that transverses Belgium from the French border to all parts of Belgium, then on to the Netherlands or to Germany. The warehouse had its own spur line which linked up with the artery and the main railway line.

Upon arriving in Courcelles on March 12th, 1945, we marched from the railroad station to our new home in a schoolhouse located a few kilometers from the warehouse. At the time, this operated as one of the world's largest Signal Corps Depots, known as S-858. This depot supplied the 1st, 3rd, 7th, 9th, and 15th Allied army groups, as well as units of the 9th Air Force. This period, between the final elimination of the German Bulge to V-E Day on May 7th, 1945, was a hectic time, when carloads of Signal Corps equipment rolled in and out of the depot, day and night. I was assigned to the Shipping Section of the depot. We received, inventoried, stored and then transshipped the Signal Corps equipment and supplies as requested. It was for this work that the officers and soldiers of the Company were awarded a Battle Star, which was an honor and privilege for us to add to the overseas ribbons we were entitled to wear.

When we took over the schoolhouse as our living quarters, there were still traces of children's classes and physical signs of the German occupation before our arrival. The school buildings were old, not very large, but with a nice small yard for athletics and relaxation, weather permitting. However, the school building was heated only by large pot-belly coal and wood burning stoves located in the center of each classroom. That winter was cold, with lots of rain and some snow. To make matters more uncomfortable, the toilets were outside the building and across the yard. It was quite an ordeal to go to the bathroom during the night in the freezing cold, often only in long underwear or with some additional inadequate covering. I found the lack of adequate heating and the outside latrines very difficult to bear physically. In fact, after about two months of this cold and wet living, I contracted pneumonia and had to be admitted to an army hospital.

The central hospital was located in Charleroi, the nearest large city to Courcelles, also on the main railway line. That's where I was on V-E Day. I was released for rest and relaxation (no army duties) just in time to participate in the local celebrations honoring this historic moment. Incidentally, opposite the hospital and my window, there was a Russian prisoner of war facility, a series of buildings surrounded by a wall. The Russians there were waiting for repatriation and entertained us with songs, shouting and bodily movements, as they sat outside on the slanted roofs of their buildings.

The festival of Passover during the year 1945 began on March 29th, and some of the Jewish men in the Company expressed interest in finding out whether anything special was being arranged in the Charleroi United Service Organization (U.S.O.) facility for those interested. The U.S.O., manned and operated by the Red Cross for servicemen and women, provided many fine services for all soldiers. While in the city and at the U.S.O. building, some of us saw a notice on the bulletin board indicating that arrangements were being made with some local Jewish families, who were inviting interested Jewish servicemen and women to join them for the Passover Seder. We, of course, signed up and were told where and when to assemble in order to meet our hosts. My friend Sammy Ginsburg from Detroit, Michigan, and I were invited to share the Seder with the Gothelf family of Charleroi. The Gothelf family was comprised then of Marja and her husband Joseph, and their lovely little two year old daughter, Jeanine.

The Gothelf family with Norman; Charleroi, Belgium, 1945

The senior Gothelfs were originally from Poland. Somehow, before the German occupation of Belgium, the Gothelfs managed to get to that country. They survived the occupation, and their daughter was born during the war years. They were a lovely, warm and caring family, and both Sammy and I struck up a really close relationship with them. We visited them often, bringing with us many fruits and vegetables as well as canned foods from the army, not usually available at the local market. The trip from Courcelles to Charleroi took about half an hour by trolley car; thus we were able to visit them frequently during our off-duty free hours. Jeanine loved the attention and the gifts we often brought with us.

For me, this encounter was extremely positive. I missed my family and friends and the Jewish components in my life. This contact with a real Jewish family and the opportunity to be able to share experiences was extremely rewarding. Their life story as fugitives from the Nazi regimes in Europe and as refugees was difficult to listen to. Still, they were the lucky ones who had managed to survive the Shoah (Holocaust) and to begin rebuilding their family life as free people without the threat of the Nazi presence.

After many years of occasional correspondence, Roslyn and I visited Marja and Jeanine in June 1990, on our trip to meet relatives in the Soviet Union. Joseph had died in 1967 and later on Jeanine married and had a son, Nicolas. The family had moved from Charleroi to Brussels, where we visited with them. They then took us on a trip back to Courcelles, so that I could recount my experiences there for them and Roslyn. After much difficulty, we finally located the schoolhouse and the warehouse factory which had served as a Signal Corps depot during World War II. The schoolhouse had been rebuilt and expanded, and the depot was now being used as a multi-purpose factory for several large companies engaged in various enterprises. The town of Courcelles had changed considerably during the forty-five years that had passed since my last visit. It was large enough to be considered a small city. The trolley rails were still to be seen in the streets, though the trolley cars had been replaced by buses.

But now to return to my everyday army experiences as part of the 547th Signal Corps Company in Courcelles, Belgium. Two anecdotes come to mind as I write these memoirs of that period. The first concerns the disposal of items of equipment which had an expiration date limiting their use. We had thousands upon thousands of large nine-volt batteries which had reached or passed their expiration date. The orders were very clear and specific. Such equipment was not to be shipped or stored, but had to be discarded and destroyed. And so these thousands upon thousands of large batteries were used to pave the roads servicing the Depot. The German P.O.W.'s assigned to us as a labor force worked tedious days setting by hand the rows of batteries which were then covered over by asphalt.

The second event was not pleasant and reflected my very strong emotional and intellectual reaction to the news that was beginning to appear in the press about the horrors of the Nazi atrocities primarily against our Jewish people. As the Allied armies progressed into all parts of the German occupation areas, the first documented details and pictures of the concentration camps and their victims were circulated and printed. I remember reading about it in an issue of the Stars and Stripes, the American army newspaper for military personnel. My revulsion at reading and seeing these horrible revelations left me extremely agitated. Still carrying the copy of the newspaper, I left my office in the depot in order to check on some shipment that I was responsible for. As I passed one of the empty boxcars sitting on the tracks within the depot, I noticed several of the German P.O.W.'s sitting on the floor and eating the army rations that they had apparently found while unloading the boxcar. I ran over to them and in my very broken Yiddish and agitated state shouted at them, waving the pictures from the newspaper in front of their faces. I tried to tell them about the inhuman treatment afforded the concentration camp victims by their compatriots, while they were experiencing a very humane situation as prisoners of the Allied forces. Judging by the expression on their faces, and their silence, I left with the feeling that they thought I had either gone completely mad, or that they had no understanding at all of what I was saying.

With the war now over in the European Theater of Operations, the tensions and pressures subsided somewhat. A six-day week work schedule now became standard, with the P.O.W.'s doing the only real physical work. The Charleroi PX and U.S.O. facilities and activities were expanded, and there was talk of three-day passes to Paris and Brussels and extended furloughs to London. Until now we had only occasional day passes to Brussels, which was some two-three hours away by train. The open question for all of us in the Company was whether we would remain at the Depot in Courcelles or be sent elsewhere. With the exception of one or two men in the company, especially among the officers and some of the non-commissioned officers, most of us were relatively new recruits and recent arrivals overseas. We understood it was doubtful that we would be returning home in the near future, once the process of rotating veteran soldiers back to the United States had begun.

On June 13th, 1945, we were again carrying our duffel bags to a new destination. Once more, we boarded the 40×8 boxcars in a fleeting visit to Paris where we changed engines. We then continued down to the Marseilles Staging Area for redeployment, our destination still unknown. We lived in tents. It was

On the way to the Far East via the port of Marseilles, France, 1945

already the beginning of summer, so the tent city was not too difficult to take. The Staging Area was somewhat northwest of Marseilles near the interesting city of Lyon. We were able to visit that old Roman city and also received occasional passes to go down to Marseilles. Rumors galore were flying as to our next destination. Gradually it became clear, without any official announcements, that we were probably going to be transshipped to the Pacific Theater of Operations, now that the war in Europe and Africa had ended. The war against the Japanese was still being fought. Our proximity to a major port in southern France, the exchange of our winter clothing for summer wear, and the checking and updating of our medical records for immunization shots already received all pointed to the Far East as our next direction.

Aboard the U.S.S. Sea Flyer

We left the staging area in huge open trucks and headed for the port city of Marseilles where we boarded a liberty ship, the U.S.S. Sea Flyer, destination formally still unknown. We left Europe on the July 31st, 1945. The Sea Flyer was hardly a fast-moving luxury ship. It was one of the "Liberty Ship" class, a war-designed and produced ocean-going vessel for transporting army personnel and equipment. It carried some two thousand soldiers and military cargo. It lacked all the special comforts we enjoyed in our last Atlantic Ocean crossing. The tiered sleeping quarters were impossible to take for any length of time, so we availed ourselves of the open top deck in our free time for recreational activities. Fortunately it was summer and the weather was quite pleasant. Many of us even slept on the open deck to avoid the unpleasantness of the cramped, smelly and noisy conditions in the sleeping areas in the decks below where we had also stored our duffel bags and personal belongings.

We headed due west toward the American continent. When the atom bombs were dropped, forcing the Japanese to surrender, we were still on the high seas in the Atlantic Ocean. Rumors again began to fly, probably reflecting more of hopes and wishes than reality, that we would be returning to the United States, now that World War II had ended. We continued to cross the Atlantic. It was then that our first destination became known, the Panama Canal.

As luck would have it, a Protestant Navy Chaplain, Thomas M. Gibson, was aboard the ship. He was very accommodating and interested in providing the Jewish servicemen with a program. After settling into life aboard the Sea Flyer — our home for at least two or more weeks (we still did not know our final destination) — I became aware of the Chaplain's presence and activity. Announcements periodically came across the P.A. system indicating the availability of the Chaplain for consultation and listing the schedule of Christian religious services. I decided to seek him out and ascertain whether it was possible to organize Shabbat services for the Jewish servicemen aboard. He responded with much interest and accepted my volunteering to organize the program.

I called together a few friends and new acquaintances made aboard the ship, and we organized Friday night Kabbalat Shabbat Services. One of the new friends, Abe Ellenbogen, was familiar with conducting services, and he also had a very good voice. He became the cantor and I served as the "Leader" at the services. My job was to announce pages and distribute assignments for conducting the services. I usually delivered a short talk and then led a discussion based on the Torah reading for each Shabbat. During the month of August, while crossing the Pacific Ocean, I gave a series of short talks about the history of European Jewry and led a discussion about Palestine and Zionism that continued following several of the services. Circumstances aboard ship only permitted a short service, usually about an hour. The Friday night service was conducted in a room that doubled as a chapel.

One of the new friends I found among the shipmates was Leo Laufer. He and I shared many ideas, especially about Zionism and a Jewish homeland. He came from a more left-wing, non-religious HaShomer Hatzair background. We had a number of discussions and intellectual arguments, especially on the subject of religion and the nature of Judaism for modern man. This made life aboard the ship more tolerable and stimulating. I introduced him to Reconstructionism and the teachings of Mordecai M. Kaplan, and he taught me how to play chess. After much debate, he agreed to become part of the group that conducted and participated in the weekly services we held aboard the ship. We have remained close friends to this very day.

After sailing for about a week, we realized that our ship was not being diverted to the United States, but would continue on towards a Far East destination. Our first stop en route was the Panama Canal. We arrived in the Canal Zone on August 11th, 1945. There we stopped at a Naval Base, where we had a one-day layover as we took on fresh food supplies, water, fuel and sundries. I was unique in that I was the only army enlisted man aboard the ship to receive permission to go on land.

Since we now knew that we would probably be on the high seas of the Pacific Ocean for the coming High Holidays, we had to find suitable material for the occasion. Once again, Chaplain Gibson showed his consideration of the needs of the Jewish servicemen aboard the Sea Flyer. He obtained permission for me to leave the ship to visit the Jewish Chaplain at the Naval Base to locate various Jewish artifacts. I particularly wanted to find a Shofar. The Jewish Welfare Board army prayer book we had available included some prayers for the High Holy Days, and several of us had our own complete prayer books for all occasions. Gibson had arranged for me to be picked up on the dock by a driver and jeep. He took me to the base chapel where I met with the Jewish Chaplain. He was only able to give me a bottle of kosher wine but no Shofar. The driver then returned me to the ship. The land visit was an exciting and interesting interlude for me after having spent two weeks sailing aboard ship. We, of course, already knew that several weeks of sea travel remained before we would arrive at our Far Eastern destination.

Crossing through the Panama Canal was an educational experience. From the deck of the ship we watched as we went through the various locks until we reached the correct water height for passage from the Atlantic Ocean to the Pacific Ocean. The weather was hot and humid, and most of us stood at the rails of the ship without our shirts, some with army fatigue caps, as we crossed through the Canal. Upon entering the Pacific Ocean, we were informed that our next destination was to be New Guinea where we were to join a convoy of ships going up to the Philippine Islands and Japan. In order to reach New Guinea from Panama, we had to travel south-west and cross the equator. The weather continued to be hot but comfortable. As we approached the equator, we learned of the naval custom of dousing all those who crossed the line for the first time with water. The navy personnel were delighted to pour buckets of seawater over us, and we responded with much laughter and mutual kibitzing. To mark the occasion, each of us first-timers received a certificate testifying that we had undergone this maritime experience as called for by naval tradition.

Our next stop was Hollandia, New Guinea, where we arrived on September 2nd, 1945. Once again we took on fresh supplies, but we were not permitted to disembark at this port. In the pictures taken of me aboard ship and at this port, I look rather emaciated. As a young man I was quite tall and thin; my weight at that point in time had remained at about 135 pounds (some 60 kg). I ate very selectively in the army due to Kashrut restrictions, but generally I did not go hungry; there were usually additional portions of bread, jam and potatoes for those who wanted them. From Hollandia, New Guinea, we steamed north toward the Philippine Islands. Since the war with Japan had recently ended, there was no longer any need to travel in a convoy. After loading up with supplies, we sailed on toward our next destination, Manila, the capital city of the Philippine Islands. But first to look back and report about Rosh HaShanah aboard the U.S.S. Sea Flyer on the Pacific high seas.

Rosh HaShanah in 1945 took place on September 8th and 9th. We already knew that we would be aboard ship on those days; we were scheduled to arrive in Manila between Rosh HaShanah and Yom Kippur. Plans had to be made for that very important occasion in the Jewish calendar. Once again Chaplain Gibson extended a helping hand with suggestions and arrangements.

An explanation is needed here before detailing the Rosh HaShanah services. What will be said about the High Holy Days applies equally to other religious ceremonies and occasions, such as the Shabbat and the yearly holiday cycle, as experienced under military service conditions. The pluralistic approach reported on here had overtones for such issues as the observance of Kashrut in the military services and living in foreign countries where we were stationed. Each individual had the right to choose, act, feel and think privately and personally within the framework of military law and order. Whenever possible, attempts were made by the military establishment, or by some of us on our own initiative, to provide for the differing religious needs of most servicemen, and especially those participating in the public events and occasions that mark the Jewish calendar.

Some religiously observant servicemen preferred to make their own way and perform their religious duties and practices privately in a manner appropriate to their needs. Others sought out those who could share some or all of their religious needs and sensibilities. I, generally, was part of this latter group. However, whenever called upon, I tried to assist those who could not accept this pluralistic and free choice approach to public religious observances and practices. Occasionally, there were individuals who would choose to be present at religious occasions requiring a Minyan (a group of at least ten male worshippers), but they would then continue to do what their religious preferences required them to do.

I had no hesitation or problem in maintaining my Jewishness under the difficult conditions of being part of a non-Jewish environment while wearing the United States Army uniform. I always managed to find other Jewish servicemen with whom I could share my feelings and thoughts, and who were prepared to join me in trying to organize some expression of our Jewishness. Whenever possible, I tried to involve the non-Jews who were somewhat connected with the religious conduct of our military lives, to be part of the Jewish experience, at least in understanding if not in direct participation. There were some Jewish servicemen who had severe problems of adjustment as religious Jews and hence voluntarily gave up completely their Jewish practices and religious commitments; others may have reached a point of crisis in their lives and sought or required severance from the military service. Most Jewish servicemen who had no specific religious orientation or commitment, seem to have had few problems in adjusting to their military service, except perhaps those who might have experienced overt manifestations of anti-Semitism.

I have gone into the above detailed explanation to establish an understanding of the basis for whatever decisions were made concerning the holding of Rosh HaShanah services aboard the Sea Flyer. We planned and conducted a non-orthodox service in an unorthodox fashion, in keeping with the unusual circumstances imposed on us aboard a troop transport ship on the high seas in the Pacific Ocean.

Since we did not have a Torah or a Shofar, we were missing two major components for the Rosh HaShanah service. We therefore had to make do with what was available — an abbreviated prayer book and readings in Hebrew and English of appropriate portions of the Bible. For a simulated Shofar we called upon the ship's bugler, non-Jewish, to use his bugle mouthpiece to make some artificial sounds resembling those of a Shofar. We also invited the Protestant Chaplain to read an appropriate portion of the Bible which was normally read on this special occasion. Abe Ellenbogen served as the Cantor, and I gave a short talk based on several discussions held aboard the ship from the time we left Marseilles, France, to our approaching arrival on the shores of the Philippine Islands, which we were expected to reach shortly.

As best I can recall, the services were well received by all who participated in them. We were able to conduct three Rosh HaShanah services, one indoors on the first evening, which was also Shabbat, and two day services outdoors on the top deck. We printed a program describing the services and the significance of the occasion on a very attractive leaflet made available by the Chaplain. Three days later, on September 12th, 1945, we arrived in Manila, the Philippine Islands, our final destination for this part of our military assignment. We had been afloat on the Sea Flyer some forty-seven days and traveled over 16,000 nautical miles.

Manila, Philippine Islands

The first view of Manila from the ship and on the way via landing barges to the shore, was one of destruction. Many shorefront buildings had been bombed into rubble. A similar sight greeted us on Taft Avenue, a main street crossing Manila. The Manila Synagogue was among the public buildings on that avenue destroyed by the Japanese when they retreated before the returning American armed forces in February 1945. The Synagogue was erected in 1922 and housed the Temple Emil Congregation. In addition, in 1940, just before the Japanese invasion, the Bachrach Wing was added to the Synagogue, containing a Jewish Community Social Hall and meeting rooms for educational programs. The Japanese used the Manila Synagogue as a munitions dump, and when their retreat began, they blew up the building, leaving only the outer walls standing. It was reported afterwards that this was the only Synagogue under the American flag which suffered destruction at the hands of the enemy. But more about the Manila Synagogue later on.

After our landing in Manila, the 547th Signal Corps Depot Company was assigned quarters in an open field on which was located a very large tent city. There were dozens upon dozens, if not hundreds of tents which housed the many soldiers arriving in Manila at the end of the war with Japan. All were awaiting reassignment in the area or to be moved to Japan. The tent city contained all the basic facilities needed for army personnel living in an open field; these included outside latrines, kitchen and mess hall facilities, a medical corps tent for doctor's visits and first-aid, a special tent for Company office use, and a temporary PX with supplies for purchase by soldiers living in the tent city for their immediate personal needs.

Children, teenagers and adults from the local civilian population circulated freely among the tent dwellers. They were looking for handouts of food, chocolate, gum and cigarettes, offering all kinds of small objects to buy, and providing personal services to those willing to pay for them. The daytime heat was oppressive and the nights cool. The area was infested with flies, mosquitoes, and various kinds of rodents. The days were spent in housekeeping duties within the Company and general areas. Day passes to visit the city center were readily available; occasionally we were called upon to provide labor for other army maintenance tasks. There was plenty of time for letter writing, reading, card and chess playing.

All in all not a very interesting or stimulating situation — except for the frequent visits to Manila proper. Mail had not yet caught up with us. Only a trickle of letters and packages arrived at first, and later on most of us were inundated with the large backlog of parcels and correspondence that had been following us around from Europe, during the long sea voyage and finally to Manila. The food packages — some of which arrived in usable condition — were shared by all tent mates and other friends, for the very short period that the contents endured.

A few days after we settled in to our tent city quarters, those of us concerned made arrangements and received permission to attend Yom Kippur services which were conducted in an open-air stadium in Manila proper. It was a moving experience to see this large stadium filled with thousands of Jewish army and navy personnel, officers and enlisted men and women praying together on Yom Kippur. As I became more familiar with the local situation, I began to look about for whatever organized Jewish connections were available in the Manila area. I presented myself before the local Jewish Chaplain, Rabbi Dudley Weinberg from New England, and to his assistant. They sponsored some centralized activities and conducted Erev Shabbat services in The United Church of Manila on Azcarraga and Lepanto Streets. In addition, I learned of a U.S.O. building on Perez Street, which contained a J.W.B. (Jewish Welfare Board) Club for Jewish servicemen and women. It offered an informal social and cultural program. The building provided space for a Sabbath morning, more traditional religious service for those interested and available.

The U.S.O.-J.W.B. building provided a Jewish environment for interested military personnel. It also served as the temporary center for the minimal Jewish communal activity that began to emerge after the fighting and burning of Manila by the Japanese was over. By the end of the war there remained in Manila a Jewish civilian population of some one thousand souls. Most were refugees from Nazi Europe, who had been on their way to somewhere else, primarily to the United States, Canada and South America. There was also a small indigenous Spanish-speaking Jewish population which existed somewhat apart from the European Jews. During the war years, the Japanese authorities viewed the Jewish population, most with foreign passports, as white locals. There was little overt anti-Semitism and the existing local Jewish leadership had neither the means nor the strength to maintain community life and activities. Individuals and families had to fend for themselves.

Those local Jews who had an orthodox commitment to Jewish life and practices had a particularly difficult time. Finding appropriate food in keeping with their kashrut needs was not easy. In this connection, my good friend Nathan H. Winter — a fellow serviceman whom I had known from our Teachers Institute days at the Seminary — tremendously assisted this small group of orthodox Jews. He provided them with appropriate army food and involved himself actively in accommodating their religious needs. This group could not be expected to participate in the mainstream Jewish programs we conducted, since they would not ride on the Sabbath and Holidays nor worship as part of a non-orthodox service held temporarily in a church.

The man in charge of the U.S.O.-J.W.B. program was an energetic civilian employed as the J.W.B. representative, Morton I. Netzorg, a long-time resident of Manila and one of the leaders of the Jewish Community there. This building also served as a meeting place for members of the armed forces with some of the local civilian Jewish population. For me, the existence of this U.S.O.-J.W.B.

building and its program became a very welcome place to spend the free time available during these first weeks in Manila. It provided me with the opportunity to meet other Jewish servicemen and to participate in some of the Jewish activity that was beginning to develop among the soldiers and in conjunction with members of the local Jewish community.

As Chaplain's Assistant

After the High Holy Days, those of us who had met at the J.W.B.-U.S.O. house held informal meetings to formulate a plan to assist the Manila Jewish Community. We also sought to erect a fitting memorial to the Jewish soldiers who had fallen in the defense and recapture of the Philippine Islands. It was during this period that I again experienced the unusual and fortunate situation described earlier — being in the right place at the right time. This occurred when soldiers who had served for long periods of time, from the beginning of World War II, were being redeployed and sent home. Chaplain Weinberg's assistant was on the list for return to the United States. Shortly thereafter, Chaplain Weinberg himself was to be redeployed. Upon learning of the pending departure of the Chaplain's assistant, I immediately applied for the position. Happily, I was accepted by Chaplain Weinberg. My Company Commander from the 547th Signal Base Depot Company, Captain Glenn A. Welsch, did not object to the transfer either. And so, by October 1945, I became the Chaplain's Assistant for Base X, the central and general Base for the entire Manila area. Chaplain Weinberg returned to the United States in November, and his replacement was Coleman A. Zwitman, a Reform Rabbi from Florida.

As a Chaplain's Assistant I had various duties to perform. There were the usual clerical duties involved in running an office: army reports to receive and deal with; personal interviews and requests from enlisted men; and general assistance to the work of the Chaplain. The Jewish Chaplaincy was part of the larger Base X Chaplain's office, which included a Protestant Chaplain and a Roman Catholic Chaplain, the ranking officer and a full colonel, who was also responsible for the Chaplaincy. Base X was located near the Manila port, and so there was a lot of action and movement as troops came and went, and many servicemen and women who requested the services of the Chaplaincy.

Base X Army Chaplain Headquarters
Standing right to left: Norman, Chaplain Zwitman, Zvi Schifrin
Kneeling right to left: Leo Laufer, Protestant Chaplain, Fred Katzberg

The most significant part of the Jewish Chaplain's work in Manila was conducted outside the office. In many army and navy installations, the Chaplain's office was housed in a church or synagogue, where most of the religious activities took place. Since the greater Manila area contained a vast complex of army, navy and air force installations, there was need for a central Chaplaincy to deal with all the scattered and smaller units. Consequently, the Jewish Chaplain and his assistant used other facilities in the city for the Jewish activities and programs. The U.S.O.-J.W.B. facility served such a function. We always had transportation available, since every Chaplain had a jeep and, if necessary, other military vehicles at his disposal from the Base X Motor Pool. On Friday evenings we conducted Sabbath services in the Protestant Church in the City mentioned earlier. The Chaplain led the service and I was the Cantor. Afterwards, we conducted an Oneg Shabbat (Sabbath Joy) program which was held at the U.S.O.-J.W.B. clubhouse on 424 Perez Street.

As the Chaplain's Assistant, I had much personal freedom to organize my day and plan those things which I felt needed priority. I was most fortunate in finding Chaplain Zwitman, a warm, jovial and sincere man. We agreed on and shared the work that could or needed to be done. We had a similar perspective of the nature of Jewish life and the meanings of Jewishness. While our first responsibility remained to deal with the needs of the local servicemen and women, we were also cognizant of the unique opportunity available to help the local Manila Jewish Community rebuild and reorganize itself.

The Jewish community, together with the rest of the civilian population, was still suffering from the experiences of war under Japanese occupation and the aftermath of the fierce fighting, as well as the burning of parts of Manila that accompanied the enemy retreat. We thus outlined our immediate priorities for helping the local Jewish community, such as the rebuilding of the local synagogue and the provision of Jewish education for the children and youth. During the Japanese occupation, the local Cantor, Joseph Cysner, gathered children in his home and taught some Hebrew and the meaning of the holidays. Some time after the war ended, he resumed teaching children to read the Hebrew prayer book. In our daily work, Chaplain Zwitman concentrated on working with the military personnel, providing them with lectures and discussion groups, and organizing them in support of the project for rebuilding the synagogue. It was agreed that I was to concentrate on organizing a program for the Jewish education of the children and youth.

Rebuilding the Manila Synagogue

The rebuilding of the Manila Synagogue project began during Chaplain Weinberg's tour of duty as the Base X Jewish Chaplain. On October 24th, 1945, he prepared and distributed a memorandum entitled "Rebuilding of Manila Synagogue." It was intended that all Jewish officers and enlisted men and women in the area would be requested to give financial support. The memorandum was meant to reach other interested military personnel throughout the Philippine Islands, along with their families back home. In the memorandum, he reported on the discussions by a local group of military service personnel, on how best to extend aid to the community. I was a part of this, together with members of the Manila Jewish Community. It was then

Manila Synagogue
before the Japanese
occupation of Manila,
1941

decided to organize a campaign of raising funds to rebuild the Manila Synagogue and Community Center and to designate the project as a permanent memorial to those who gave their lives in the fighting for the Philippine Islands. A "Servicemen's Committee to Aid the Jewish Community of Manila" was formed. Some of my army friends, Fred Katzburg, Leo Laufer, Harold Schiffrin and Leonard Whartman, as well as several former Jewish buddies from the 547th Signal Corps Base Depot Company, were also part of the sponsoring Servicemen's Committee and participated in the program.

A keynote activity in support of the campaign was the service held in the ruins of the synagogue on November 9th, 1945. This date was the anniversary of the infamous burning of the synagogues in Germany on Kristallnacht in 1938. The Board of Directors of the Temple Emil Synagogue met on the day that the above memorandum was drafted. They adopted a resolution to accept the servicemen's commitment to raise funds for the rebuilding the synagogue and to take the necessary legal steps to have the synagogue, the adjacent hall and its land registered under the jurisdiction of the Manila Jewish Community. This latter legal requirement was stipulated as a condition set forth by the Servicemen's Committee. The Temple was formerly managed by the Board of Directors without any Community jurisdiction.

The Memorial Service conducted in the ruins of the Manila Synagogue was a very moving experience. The synagogue overflowed with the hundreds of servicemen and women who stood shoulder to shoulder in the open area between the only remaining walls. The service was led by Rabbi Joseph Schwarz and Cantor Joseph Cysner from the local community, with the participation of leaders from the Servicemen's Committee. Upon the request of the Committee, Morton I. Netzorg, as the American Joint Distribution Committee representative in Manila, negotiated on their behalf with the A.J.D.C. to bank the money raised until it would be made available for rebuilding the synagogue. The sum of $12,500 had been raised by the Servicemen's Committee when the campaign formally terminated. Additional contributions from abroad were still expected.

The Servicemen's Committee invited Lt. General Styer, the commander of the military forces in the area, to present the trust certificate for the sum raised by the Jewish Servicemen's Committee to Aid the Jewish Community of Manila, to the local representatives of the Manila Jewish Community. The presentation was held on December 21st, 1945, at the U.S.O.-J.W.B. building. The Servicemen's Committee found it necessary to formally terminate the campaign, since many of the founding committee members had been or were being redeployed home. There was much instability in the ranks of servicemen in view of the accelerated going and coming and rotation of the troops. Since I was not due to return to the United States until the spring, I became the acting chairman of the Committee, whose main function now was to collect the funds still coming in from abroad, to receive reports of developments within the local community and to bank the funds obtained through the A.J.D.C.

An interesting side note to the campaign that developed abroad was the involvement of my mother. Many of us turned to our families and other groups for assistance in raising funds. Consequently, some of the local New York press picked up the story of the G.I. (popular name for the American soldiers — literally meaning "Government Issue") campaign to raise funds for rebuilding the Manila Synagogue. Articles appearing in the New York Daily News and the New York Post referred to those of us involved who came from the New York area. My mother organized some card parties among her friends which, with their approval, were used for fundraising purposes. Other women's groups responded in a similar fashion.

One of my ideas as Chaplain's Assistant was to print a weekly mimeographed newspaper containing "Topics of Interest to Jewish Men and Women in the Services." With the approval of Chaplain Zwitman, who served as advisor, and with the participation of my friends Fred Katzburg, Leo Laufer and Harold Schiffrin, who worked with me as staff members, we put out a weekly mimeographed newspaper called "Philippinews." Later on Manuel Berlove and Edward L. Weisberg joined the staff when some of the original members were rotated home. Chaplain Bernard H. Lavine, from the 4th General Hospital, became the advisor after Chaplain Zwitman was also sent home. The first issue came out on December 21st, 1945, and we published thirteen issues until March 15, 1946th, when, soon after the Base X Chaplain's section was closed down, I became eligible to be shipped home. I had now completed my duties as Chaplain's Assistant and was ordered to begin the process for redeployment back to the United States. My army days were coming to an end.

The Protest Movement

In the course of the demobilization of military personnel in the Pacific Theater of Operations following the termination of the war with Japan, a series of interesting and perhaps historic events occurred in the Philippine Islands during the winter of 1945/46. A protest effort of officers and enlisted men and women in the Philippine Islands developed. This was due to the confusion and seemingly deliberate slowdown of the redeployment of troops back to the United States, and the demobilization of those eligible to be discharged according to the point system then in effect. It had been reported in the army press that there were some 800,000 military personnel in the Pacific area, and it was estimated that only 375,000 were needed as part of the occupation forces in Japanese home territories. Reports were also being circulated that the President and his military advisors were moving in the direction of adding thousands of soldiers to the occupation forces. They would patrol the liberated areas, in order to destroy the war potential and hostile intentions of anti-American and anti-democratic elements in those territories.

These reports and the official silence of the authorities concerning these questions led to a great deal of confusion and discontent among the military personnel, especially in the Philippine Islands, where more than 100,000 soldiers were stationed, with very little to do. A protest movement began among the 10,000 officers and enlisted personnel in Sub-Base "R" located in Batangas, Luzon, one of the main islands in the Philippine area. They met and circulated an advertisement to be inserted in fifteen leading United States newspapers, requesting a clarification of American policy and urging people to write to Congress and the White House. This protest activity spread to all the other units stationed in the Philippine Islands. Orderly demonstrations were organized in Manila, on January 6th and 7th, 1946, with an estimated 25,000 soldiers participating. Resolutions were adopted and representatives elected to discuss ways to implement those resolutions.

On January 10th, 1946, a meeting was held at which 516 delegates (from 245 army units) representing some 115,000 men and women, participated. The major intention was to request an official hearing before the senate committee investigating war waste. This committee was a sub-committee of the larger Senate Military Affairs Committee. The representatives of the servicemen and women met with the sub-committee which visited the area. What can be added here, at least from my perspective, is that the demobilization process continued as before without any evidence that it was deliberately either being slowed down or accelerated. Perhaps the unusually quiet voice of the servicemen and women, contributed something positive to what was happening with the rotation and redeployment of overseas soldiers who were eligible to go home.

Kvutzat Chaverim

It was a very exhilirating and rewarding experience to be able to recreate and relive the original Kvutza story in such an unusual place as Manila, the Philippine Islands, in the aftermath of World War II. As indicated earlier, one of my major elected tasks as Chaplain's Assistant, was to try and organize some suitable form of Jewish education for the young people we found living in Manila. During and following the Japanese retreat and the burning of Manila, Jewish life in the Philippines came to a standstill. People were desperately trying to survive and rebuild their personal lives and deal with the everyday problems of existence, finding housing, opening businesses or trying to find jobs, just to provide the basic necessities for themselves and their families.

Schools were still not functioning on a regular basis. Jewish education was also nonexistent, since the local civilian and lay leadership was just beginning to reawaken. Only limited funds, primarily those received from the Joint Distribution Committee in the United States, were available. There were no real public facilities that could be used by the emerging Jewish community, since the synagogue building and community center had been destroyed. Many, if not all, of the pre-war transient Jewish population, were anxious to renew their efforts to leave the Islands and find a haven elsewhere in the Western Hemisphere.

This then was the local Jewish situation found by the entering American soldiers and sailors who were stationed in the greater Manila area during 1945 and 1946. Among the many thousands of military personnel that were located in the area, there was, of course, a substantial percentage of Jewish servicemen and women. Those of us who came with any previous Jewish commitments and feelings found it vital to become involved with the remnants of our Jewish brethren there. Those who were interested and concerned found a way of assisting the existing Jewish population. Some joined the organized effort to rebuild the destroyed Manila Synagogue; others befriended local Jews and their families, sharing army and navy food and supplies with them. Others participated in the activities and programs conducted by the Chaplaincy, often together with civilian members of the Jewish community.

In this somewhat chaotic situation, my task of conducting a program of Jewish education was not easy. There were no appropriate reading materials or textbooks available, nor any of the other basic supplies necessary for running an educational program. The U.S.O.-J.W.B. building and its limited facilities were available for small group meetings. As the Chaplain's Assistant, I had access to the small Jewish Welfare Board army storeroom which contained army prayer books, some pamphlets on holidays, a few copies of Margolis and Marx, *A History of the Jewish People* — a very erudite and scholarly volume — kosher wine, Sabbath candles, office supplies, and sundry other items of little use for an educational program. However, a very positive factor was the availability of transportation facilities at my disposal for the program.

I had the use of a personal jeep and, when necessary, a command car for transporting small groups of passengers. When we needed a larger vehicle, a truck and driver were requisitioned for me by the Chaplain. These vehicles were necessary not only for my own use in moving about the city, but also for transporting the young people to meetings, trips and outings. The local public transportation facilities were still not functioning in an orderly manner, and then there was always the question of the personal safety of civilians traveling around.

How and where to begin? I decided to try to organize an educational program with teenagers. At this point in time and place, they were the group most in need of reinforcement, information, basic knowledge and association with other Jews. I turned to Morton Netzorg, the J.W.B. and J.D.C. representative, for advice and information. He gave me a list of names and addresses of young people, who he felt would be responsive to an invitation to join a youth program. I began my work armed with this information and fortified with the strong desire to create a suitable program for young people within the limited framework of my army duties as a Chaplain's Assistant.

One afternoon I appeared unannounced at the doorstep of the Cassel family. They lived in a comfortable house in a compound surrounded by a wall, where there were three other family houses — two of which were Jewish. The Cassel family had a fifteen-year-old daughter, Margot. There was a teenage boy, Manfred, in one of the families and in the other a girl, Gitta. One of the reasons for beginning with this compound was that there were three teenagers eligible for the program and that Sol Cassel was one of the leaders of the local Jewish community.

I was greeted by the Cassel family with some mixed feelings on their part. On the one hand, they were pleasantly surprised to be visited by an American soldier in uniform, a Jewish one no less, who came in an army vehicle. On the

Kvutzat Chaverim: cleaning out our first meeting room, Manila, 1945

other hand, they were curious and unsure about what I was after. They greeted me with much courtesy and hospitality. They were willing to listen to my proposition concerning the organization of a youth group for Jewish educational purposes. I was introduced to Margot and after a while the atmosphere became very relaxed and encouraging. The Cassels had a storeroom on the ground level of their house which they would make available for the use of such a youth group, if it came into being.

Margot proved to be a very energetic and enthusiastic supporter of the idea. In the long run, it developed that I had started my search for young people with the right person. She proved to be a natural leader among her peers, dedicated and committed to her Jewishness, and willing to work seriously in the organization of the program. With her assistance, we began to recruit other teenagers on my list, as well as their friends who were not known to me. We cleaned out the Cassel storeroom, which became our first committee meeting room. When the group expanded, we moved into the U.S.O.-J.W.B. house for meetings and continued to use the storeroom for committee meetings.

The first gathering of the larger, twenty-two candidate membership group was held in October 1945 at the U.S.O.-J.W.B. clubhouse, 424 Perez Street. Three of my fellow servicemen helped me with the group whenever they were free from their regular army duties; they were Leo Laufer, Fred Katzburg, and Sid Meystel. As an advisory committee we had the encouragement and assistance of Cantor Joseph Cysner, Morton J. Netzorg, Rabbi Joseph Schwarz, Mrs. Doris Welisch (the mother of a member, Gitta) and Chaplain Colman A. Zwitman.

Two of the original members, Rosie Hellman and Gitta Welisch, described this opening meeting and the group in these words which appeared in the Purim booklet produced later on by the group:

> What a gathering there was at the U.S.O club Perez, when a group of Manila's Jewish youth came together last October. Old friends met once again for the first time after the great tragedy — the burning of Manila. It was a happy reunion when all gathered together in one large circle to form a Jewish youth group.
>
> We decided after a while to call ourselves, the KVUTZAT

CHAVERIM, Hebrew words which mean a Group of Friends. The decision of the group was to meet together weekly, and have different activities at each meeting. A temporary Executive Committee was organized to prepare the plan for each gathering. The Committee was to meet once a week.

It did not take long before everyone got into the spirit of fellowship. The usual way we conducted our meetings is as follows: First we take up our business, discussing the problems of our group. Next we have the cultural program, which is different each week. We discuss current problems, famous events and persons; we have debates, quizzes, and games. The Kvutza celebrates all Jewish holidays. The most exciting and noisiest part of our meeting is the social part. We sing and dance modern Palestinian Hebrew songs and dances, finishing with some refreshments. We really have a good time at the meetings, and that is one of the reasons why all the members keep coming back and participate in all our activities. In addition to our regular meetings, we have had large community celebrations for Chanukah, and we are now planning one for Purim. Some of the latest activities of the Kvutza are attending the Friday night services that are held by the soldiers in Manila, and contributing money to the Jewish National Fund for work in Palestine.

(Excerpt from a forty-page booklet the group put out for Purim 1946, entitled 'Kvutzat Chaverim,' containing articles, personal experiences and creative writing by members of the group)

In the above booklet the group published its Constitution dated November 1945. In the Preamble there appears a very meaningful and significant statement representing the thinking of the group. It reads as follows:

With the desire to enrich and enjoy our living as Jews, we, the Jewish youth of Manila have constituted ourselves into an organization to be known by the name of Kvutzat Chaverim. We affirm our allegiance to our people, and are eager to take our rightful place in ensuring the future of our people. We join in with Jewish youth throughout the world, in America, in Europe, and in Palestine, to bring about the redemption of our people.

We hereby dedicate ourselves to the task of learning about our people and its heritage, and living in accordance with its ideals and principles. We aim to reconstruct the civilization of our people in accordance with modern traditions and knowledge.

We unite in purpose and action with all youth throughout the world to bring about peace and happiness for all peoples. We will take our stand side by side with them against all evils, intolerance, and injustices.

The regular meetings of the group were held weekly on Sunday afternoons at the U.S.O.-J.W.B. clubhouse. There were five members of an Executive Committee, who met twice weekly on Wednesday and Saturday evenings. These sessions were for the purpose of planning future meetings and activities. They also served as a small study group to prepare the elected executives to assume greater leadership roles in conducting the cultural-learning aspects of the program. Since we knew in advance that, as soldiers, we would only be present on a very temporary basis, every effort was made to prepare the group for continuing with its own better informed leadership. Therefore, every opportunity was utilized at committee meetings and during the major portion of the weekly regular meetings, to impart information and knowledge on a formal and informal basis.

Jewish history was taught with a concentration on outstanding personalities. Instruction in the Hebrew language was attempted even within the limited time available during meetings once or twice a week. Attempts were made to introduce the members to spoken Hebrew by use of terms and simple conversational expressions. The printed Hebrew alphabet was taught with a view to enabling the young people to read the Prayer Book and follow the religious services. The members of the group usually attended Friday evening services together with the military personnel and some local civilians, and then participated in the Oneg Shabbat that followed at the U.S.O.-J.W.B. clubhouse.

During the period of my service in Manila we celebrated the holidays of

Hanukkah and Purim together with the members of Kvutzat Chaverim, some of the younger children and members of the adult Jewish Community. These holiday celebrations became major community events for all involved. The young teenagers in our group were the major participants and planners. They were a great source of inspiration and hope for the future. The holiday celebrations illustrated significantly the rekindled Jewishness of a community that had suffered through the horrors of war, the Japanese occupation and the burning of Manila, the capital city of the Philippines.

The Hanukkah program was held in Santa Mesa, a suburb of Manila, at one of the large mansions in that area called the Casa Blanca (White House). It had extensive outdoor grounds, suitable for the program and party, and its swimming pool was used as a conclusion to a very lovely, meaningful and happy day for all the participants. Since public transportation was quite erratic and inadequate (very few people had private cars), the United States Army, via the Chaplain's office, provided several vehicles. These made the rounds of the city, picking up group members and the many local civilians and military personnel who wanted to attend.

It turned out to be a gala and unusual event for Manila Jewry and their military guests. The program included much Hebrew singing and dancing, taking the oath of allegiance by new members of the Kvutza, candle lighting and a Hanukkah play. It concluded with refreshments, the distribution of Hanukkah gifts to the younger children, and then swimming in the beautiful pool. In the words of Ernst Fuld, one of the members of Kvutzat Chaverim: "All of us will remember this party, as it marked the beginning of a better life for the Jewish youth of Manila." (Page 7 of Purim booklet referred to earlier.)

Another important experience in the lives of the young people in Kvutzat Chaverim was the organization of trips out of the city to recreational areas in the suburbs and countryside. After several years of seclusion, out of fear of the Japanese occupation, such opportunities were welcomed by all. The first trip organized for the group was to the Tagaytay region and beautiful Lake Taal. I was able to arrange for an army truck to transport the group; the young people brought food, athletic equipment and tremendous energy and spirit. Writing in the special Purim booklet, Margot Cassel described the experience in these words:

Sunday morning, December thirtieth [1945], in front of the U.S.O. Club Perez, a bunch of K.C.s were assembled, eagerly awaiting the arrival of the truck which had been placed at our disposal. Soon, above the loud chattering, there could be heard the sound of the horn, and in a flash, everybody piled into the vehicle. A group of noisy and gay youngsters were then off in a cloud of dust. A stamp of the foot then started the singing which did not end till we had actually reached our destination. In Hebrew and English, of all the songs we knew, not one was left out. A spirit of hilarity possessed the entire party.

The day was cloudy and overcast, but we were spared any rain. The wind, however, was strong, and the nearer we came to Tagaytay, the colder the weather became. Acres of harvested rice fields were stretched out before our eyes, and the carabaos [water buffalo] in the mud added all that was necessary for a typical native scene.

Shortly before the end of the trip, we passed through a coconut grove. That was heavenly. Palms were to the right and left, with large clusters of coconuts attached to them. Chickens were scattered all over the highway, reminding us of the fact that we were still in the Philippines. (Purim booklet, pp. 7-8)

Taking other such trips became an important part of the Kvutzat Chaverim program. Even after I returned home, I continued to receive enthusiastic reports from members of the group, usually accompanied by photographs.

One more important event in the lives of the local Jewish civilian population happened on January 6th, 1946, when Kvutzat Chaverim helped organize an additional youth group for the younger children of the Jewish Community of Manila, aged between ten and thirteen. We invited the younger brothers and sisters of the K.C. members and all other younger people interested and available. Some twenty-five children formed this new group which was called the Stars of David. The group met on alternate Sundays and followed the program pattern of their older brother and sister group. The educational emphasis for the group was on Jewish history, largely Jewish historical

Kvutzat Chaverim and Stars of David with Norman, Manila, 1946

personalities, and a heavy Palestine (Zionist) orientation. Some games, as well as lots of Hebrew songs and dances, complimented every program. I was aided in providing leadership for this group by the active participation of members of Kvutzat Chaverim in all the programming and activities that took place.

An interesting change of pace occurred in January 1946 when I became eligible for an eleven-day furlough to an army rest and relaxation recreational site known as Camp John Hay, located in lovely Baguio, about 200 miles north of Manila in the Luzon district. The area was in the mountains, about 5,000 feet above sea level and some thirty degrees cooler than Manila. It had a beautiful nine-hole golf course and some tennis courts. Leo Laufer joined me three days after I arrived, and we spent a very enjoyable and relaxed time, especially on the golf course.

This northern mountain province is inhabited by the Igorot people, who are divided into tribes and sub-tribes. They are shy, short people, whose main occupation is agriculture, native weaving and wood-carving. All are attired similarly, differing only in some details. The men wore loin cloths while the women were dressed in short lengths of cloth, called tapis, reaching to the knees and sarongs tucked in at the waistline. You can distinguish the different tribes by the way they comb their hair and by their use of head, arm and leg ornaments. Although they are relatively primitive in their manner of living, they are intelligent, and some have become doctors, teachers, farmers, and other local professionals.

For me personally, Purim 1946 (on March 17th) was the highlight of my Manila experience of working with these young people in Kvutzat Chaverim and Stars of David. It became the final act in my stay in Manila. A few days later, I received orders to report to the Replacement Depot for redeployment back to the United States and the termination of my military service.

Kvutzat Chaverim and Stars of David decided to hold a large Purim Carnival in the courtyard and garden of the U.S.O.-J.W.B. Clubhouse. I brought to the occasion my years of experience at the East Midwood Jewish Center Religious School where an annual Purim Carnival was held in the gymnasium of the building. We built booths for games, fortune-telling, and for food and drinks. The young people came in all sorts of costumes: Queen Esther, Mordecai, Haman, cooks, maids, clowns and many other original ideas. There was a parade of the young people wearing costumes, and awards were given for the most original and most beautiful. A Queen Esther of the Day was crowned, and the winner of this contest was the Kvutzat Chaverim Secretary, Margot Cassel. There was much singing and folk dancing to the accordion of Manfred Hecht. The younger children in Cantor Cysner's Hebrew class put on a play. The entire area was gaily decorated.

Soldiers and civilians of all ages were invited to the gala event, and a Purim dance concluded the carnival program in the evening. The young people worked very hard and created an exciting Purim Carnival atmosphere with an inspirational program. This was the crowning activity in the short life-span of the youth program. It did wonders for the enthusiasm of the participating members — some of whom I have been in continuous contact with over the years after I returned to the United States and then eventually settled in Israel with my family. Some have also settled in Israel.

My friend, mentor and working partner, Chaplain Zwitman, was transferred from Base X at the beginning of March as the first step to being redeployed for eventual return home. With the transfer of thousands of soldiers back to the United States, and those who left for army occupation duties in Japan, the Base X Headquarters division for the United States Army Forces Western Pacific was disbanded. The Chaplaincy section was broken up and each of the personnel, the Chaplains and their assistants, were reassigned to smaller area units, primarily outside Manila. On March 2nd, 1946, I was reassigned to the 4th General Hospital located outside Manila, along with the new Jewish chaplain, Bernard H. Lavine. I still had a jeep available to continue work with Kvutzat Chaverim and Stars of David, in view of all the hectic and special programs planned for Purim.

On March 20th,1946, three days after Purim, I received notice that I was going home and to report to the 5th Replacement Depot on March 23rd, 1946. There was hardly any time to say good-bye to comrades and friends, especially to the young people, their families and others in the civilian Jewish population. Perhaps it was for the best. I had arrived in Manila unannounced, did what I felt had to be done, and then left, with the work to be continued by those that remained behind and those yet to arrive. This was truly an experience that fulfilled the ideas expressed in the "Ethics of the Fathers" (פִּרְקֵי אָבוֹת II, כא):

"לֹא עָלֶיךָ הַמְּלָאכָה לִגְמֹר, וְלֹא אַתָּה בֶן חוֹרִין לְהִבָּטֵל מִמֶּנָּה"
It is not your duty to complete the work, but neither
are you free to desist from it.

This was a true adage that I have learned to live with in several other situations that I experienced in my career and life in the service of the Jewish people.

Chaplain Lavine only stayed a short while, and he was replaced by Rabbi Abraham Feldbin. Fortunately my replacement as Chaplain's Assistant, now at 4th General Hospital, was Arnulf M. Pins, who shared much of my thinking and had similar pre-army training experience with young people. We never met while both of us were in the Philippine Islands. He stepped in after I left and continued to work with the two youth groups until he was scheduled to be sent home. Incidentally, Margot Cassel and Arnulf Pins married in 1951. Margot had come to the United States to study at a university and her parents eventually took up residence in California. Margot and Arnulf settled in Israel together with their family several years after we had moved here. Throughout the years, we have remained very close and dear friends. Kvutzat Chaverim continued to function with its own leadership until the 1949-1950 activity year, by which time many of its members had already left the Philippines for life elsewhere.

How does one adequately summarize and evaluate an unusual and unforgettable life experience such as I was privileged to have during my short, seven-month stay in Manila? For me, working as a Chaplain's Assistant with the military personnel and the Jewish civilian population, especially with the young people, fulfilled my every desire to be of service to the Jewish people. Consequently, I was able to find much personal fulfillment while in the uniform of the United States Army. In retrospect, those seven months seem to have been an experience of a lifetime, at least as I recall them.

I was very pleased to receive some warm and appreciative words of commendation from Chaplain Zwitman and the leaders of the Manila Jewish Community. On April 4th, 1946, a letter arrived from Morton I. Netzorg, President of the Jewish Community of Manila. It informed me that at its meeting of March 31st, 1946, the Board of Directors of the Community had expressed thanks for my work with Kvutzat Chaverim and adopted a resolution appointing me as an honorary life member of the Manila Jewish Community. Along with all others who contributed to the servicemen's project for the rebuilding of the Synagogue, I was also awarded a certificate naming me a Lifetime Honorary Member of the Manila Synagogue. My work in Manila was completed and I was ready to go home.

My last "Jewish" experience in the army was on the troopship bringing us back to San Francisco. We boarded the U.S.S. General Langfitte on March 28th, 1946. Our destination was the Golden Gate Bridge of San Francisco, the dream site, meaning home, for military personnel serving in the Pacific Theater of Operations. This was a first-class Navy troopship capable of transporting several thousand personnel. Its facilities, though crowded, were generally very good, much better than on the Liberty Ship that took me across the Atlantic and

Pacific Oceans to Manila. The trip back to San Francisco lasted nineteen days. I helped conduct Friday evening Sabbath services, and then we began to prepare for the first night of Passover.

We were scheduled to arrive at our destination on the second day of Passover, and so a group of us prepared for only one Seder. Approximately two dozen enlisted men and officers participated in the Seder. Before leaving Manila, I had asked for some Passover materials to be put aboard: Haggadot, Matzot and wine. Unfortunately the request was not filled. And so we had to make do with what we had. I met with the Italian baker aboard ship in order to describe the nature of the Matzot used during Passover. Our idea was at least to simulate the three Matzot used during the Seder ceremonies. What was produced was really a large cracker-like wafer, but shaped to look like a square Matzah. One of the older officers aboard ship conducted the Seder with our participation, and we had a very meaningful and even enjoyable evening, considering the circumstances and where it took place.

The next day we sailed under the Golden Gate Bridge and arrived in San Francisco. We had assumed that this was the termination of our seagoing journey under military auspices. To our surprise, and with the groans and sweat of carrying our heavy duffel bags during disembarkation, we boarded a ferry boat that took us from this navy port base to an army camp. From there we were to be dispersed throughout the United States to our individual homes. The ferry boat turned about and sailed under the Golden Gate Bridge and continued sailing up the coast for about three hours to a large army camp, probably Fort Bragg. The scenic view sailing up the California coastline was beautiful, but the swaying and undulation of the ferry, compounded by the vibrations and smells of the motor, caused me some problems. During forty-seven days crossing the Atlantic and Pacific Oceans, followed by the nineteen days returning back across the Pacific Ocean, I did not suffer any sea sickness. Yet now I felt that if we didn't land shortly, I would have to heave my last meals overboard. As luck would have it, I managed to hold in everything for a little while longer, until we finally arrived at our destination and went ashore.

After settling in our barracks the men ran to the public telephones, each according to the time frame reflecting where he lived. During the pre-dawn hours of the morning, I telephoned Roslyn and my parents to share the good news of my arrival back on the shores of North America, this time to stay. After many hours and days of being "processed," including physical check-ups to determine if any illness had been contracted during our service in the various islands located in the Pacific Far East, we were ready to be sent to the army camp nearest our homes and then to be demobilized from military service. Incidentally, to my dismay, I learned a few years later that Rabbi Coleman A. Zwitman, the wonderful chaplain I had served with in Manila, had died in the early 1950's, apparently from an illness he had contracted in the Far East. After several days of waiting, I finally boarded a train that was to travel cross-country via northern Texas and St. Louis, Missouri, to New

Demobilization: Sgt. Norman Schanin Fort Dix, New Jersey, 1946

Jersey and Fort Dix, where my final army separation took place on April 24th, 1946.

My military service in the United States Army lasted two years, two months and thirty days. I served for one year and twenty days in the continental United States, and one year, two months and ten days in foreign service. During the course of my service, I had been stationed in the two major military theaters of operation for the United States Army in World War II, the European and the Western Pacific theaters. My army travels took me to three countries in Europe — England, France and Belgium, and two island countries in the Pacific area — New Guinea and the Philippine Islands. In the course of my army travels overseas, I was aboard ships for sixty-eight days and traveled some twenty-one thousand nautical miles, crisscrossing the two major oceans on our planet, the Atlantic and the Pacific. I left my family home and Roslyn on January 25th, 1944, and returned on April 24th, 1946.

When viewed in the total span of time, my army service experience was of relatively short duration. However, it had an everlasting impact on my life. My commitments, my outlook and my personal philosophy were put to a severe test. My search for answers to such questions as to who and what I was brought into focus many important ideas and led to decision-making. Then, too, during this period, I was separated from my home and loved ones, and totally on my own for the first time in unfamiliar and often strange and alien situations.

The differing and often contradictory views of life I experienced left me with much food for thought. The masses of people I was in contact with directly, and indirectly through the media, many suffering and some dying, taught me much about the human endeavor and the harsh realities of contemporary human history. I earnestly believe that I gained a great deal from my army experiences. As a result, I returned home with the determination to go ahead and fulfill my hopes and aspirations as quickly as possible. I was ready to move ahead in the directions that I had begun developing earlier as a teenager and during my university years. My commitments had become a permanent part of my consciousness as a person and as a Jew. I now had developed a strong human and Jewish conscience and identity. I felt ready to go out into the big world and make my way alongside those who were ready to share my dreams.

Chapter 3

Young Judaea

After my army service, I returned to complete a Master's Degree in Education at New York University in 1946. I also resumed my studies at the Teachers Institute of the Jewish Theological Seminary towards the Bachelor of Religious Education Degree (B.R.E.), which I received in 1948. I had, by this time, entered the full-time workaday world and so I could only continue my studies toward an advanced degree on a very limited, part-time basis. After ten years of study and dissertation writing, I received the Doctor of Education (Ed.D.) degree from N.Y.U. in February, 1959. I later enrolled in the Master's Degree program at the Teachers Institute of the Jewish Theological Seminary of America, but never completed it. I was awarded the degree of Doctor of Pedagogy, honoris causa, by the Jewish Theological Seminary of America in March 1977. It was the first time the Seminary had recognized the service of Jewish educators by awarding this honorary degree.

I graduated from New York University Washington Square College with a B.A. degree, in 1943, just before beginning my army service. I was then able to obtain my first full-time position. It had not been easy for my parents economically to see me through college and the Seminary. With such a double load of studies, it was not possible for me to obtain any gainful employment on a regular basis. I served as a part-time teacher on Sunday mornings at the East Midwood Jewish Center Religious School and worked there also as a club leader. During the summer months, I went out into the country where I was employed as a camp counselor in charge of a bunk of six-year-old boys, and I also conducted religious services on Shabbat. These work opportunities provided me only with a very limited income. I even once tried my hand, not very successfully, at working as a busboy at a summer resort hotel. But after returning from the army and having completed my basic academic studies, I was ready to seek Jewish educational work on a full-time and professional basis.

My First Professional Steps

During my early years as a college student, I gained some personal exposure as part of the Zionist movement, particularly Young Judaea. As a teenager I had been a member of this Zionist youth movement and also one of its club leaders. The example of my work with Kvutza was particularly important to those who were in positions of significance as sponsors of youth programs. Consequently, when I was job hunting, I was offered the position of Director of the Brooklyn Zionist Youth Commission. In those days, the American Zionist Youth Commission was a national body established jointly by Hadassah and the Zionist Organization of America. I accepted the position and began to work there during the summer of 1943. It was during that period that I began courting Roslyn, who was also taking a course nearby. My first assignment as Brooklyn Commission Director was as a staff member at the Brandeis Camp Institute in Hancock, New York. This was a Zionist youth leadership program conducted by the American Zionist Youth Commission and directed by Dr. Shlomo Bardin.

During the formative years when I was actively involved with the Religious School of the East Midwood Jewish Center and served as a club leader, I began to formulate a concept of education, with applications for Jewish education. I continued to develop such thinking over the years which helped me formulate a kind of philosophy of Jewish education. In summarizing the developmental and practical applications of this philosophy, one will find a very close relationship between my learning and thinking, and the nature of the professional positions I accepted during more than forty-five years of Jewish public service, until my retirement in August 1988 as Director of the David Yellin Teachers College in Jerusalem, Israel.

During this long period I was engaged in three major assignments: as National Director of Young Judaea; as Educational Director of the Forest Hills Jewish Center; and finally as Director of the David Yellin Teachers College in Jerusalem. Earlier, for shorter periods, I served professionally as Executive Director of the Brooklyn Zionist Youth Commission. (I only did this for a few months in 1943 until I entered the United States Army in January 1944.) Following my separation from military service, I was accepted as the Assistant

Principal and Youth Director of the Park Avenue Synagogue in New York City during the school year 1946-1947. This was when Rabbi Milton Steinberg was the Rabbi of that synagogue, but seriously ailing. Rabbi Morris N. Kertzer served then as his Associate Rabbi and functioned as Principal of the Religious School.

A major aspect of this developing conception of Jewish Education was the blending of informal and formal theories of education, adapting the pedagogics involved, and creating the institutions to formulate and transmit these ideas. My experiences and interests in group work, camping, school organization and classroom innovative teaching styles, fulfilled the need to create and develop programs of leadership training, curriculum development and teacher education. These aspects of my developing theory of Jewish education greatly influenced my choices of employment and the performance direction I was to take. In each of the three major assignments in my career, I served primarily as the head educational administrator with the goal, the opportunity and the responsibility of implementing the philosophy of education I was committed to. This then was the nature of my involvement and the basis for the contributions, if any, that I have made to the educational endeavors I was concerned with professionally.

The Reconstructionist Institute for Jewish Youth Leadership

As indicated earlier, I have been greatly influenced in my Jewish thinking, commitments and religious behaviors by the Jewish Reconstructionist Movement under the leadership of Rabbi Mordecai M. Kaplan. From the beginning, Reconstructionism was a movement within the Conservative ideology of Judaism, with a kind of left-wing religious outlook. The major Jewish religious influences early in my life came from both the Conservative and Reconstructionist movements. The latter, as a movement within the Conservative framework, represented for me an openness, a freedom of expression and thought. It offered an alternative to the traditional halachic Judaism accepted by the orthodox and the more tradition-bound elements within the Conservative religious movement in the United States. Consequently, I defined myself then as a Reconstructionist Conservative Jew.

During the early post World War II era, the Reconstructionist movement began to explore ways of expanding its influences over the Conservative movement and the Jewish community at large. Eventually these efforts, which apparently did not succeed, resulted in the Reconstructionist program severing its affiliation association with the Conservative movement. It became a fourth denomination within American Judaism which, as a result, now consisted of the Orthodox, Conservative, Reform and Reconstructionist movements. At that time I was not in agreement with this development within the Conservative and Reconstructionist movements, and when viewing what has happened to the Reconstructionist and Conservative movements in later years, I still retain my earlier thinking with regard to this matter.

Reconstructionist Youth Leaders Conference, Camp Cejwin, NJ, 1946

The above is included here, since it reflects the development of my thinking and involvement in 1946 and 1947, with the newly formed Institute for Jewish Youth Leadership of the Reconstructionist movement. At a September Labor Day weekend seminar held in 1946 in Cejwin Camp, Port Jervis, New York, the Reconstructionist Institute for Jewish Youth Leadership emerged. I was one of the founding leaders of the group and co-editor of "Tehiyah" (Renaissance), the bulletin published by the Institute. The participants in the seminar and later in the Institute were young people, college students and those of similar age, entering the workforce of America. The main functions of the Institute were planning and conducting regular meetings of a New York chapter that was formed after the Cejwin Seminar experience. It also undertook the publication of the "Tehiyah" bulletin, which served as an informational guide and stimulant to members of the Seminar isolated in their various communities outside the New York area. The Institute only lasted for some two years, for several reasons. Firstly, the membership was a transitional group moving from college and university status to that of working people in their various chosen professions, and secondly the changes within the Reconstructionist movement as it became an independent entity and was no longer a part of the organized Conservative movement.

While encountering these first professional opportunities and undergoing personal involvements, I began to formulate a more operative and functional philosophy of Jewish education. I was now ready for more serious, long-term professional assignments in the American Jewish community and eventually in Israel. The first such major engagement was as National Director of Young Judaea, the oldest Zionist youth program in North America.

Young Judaea National Director

Being National Executive Director of Young Judaea during the period between 1947 and 1952 was a watershed experience for me, both professionally and personally. It was a way to establish life-long friendships with many; some have followed our pattern and settled in Israel. The list of such friends is happily too long for them to be recorded individually in these memoirs. Those I refer to know who they are. I feel they understand my predicament about identifying them individually and the important roles they played in my life. Some unhappily are no longer with us on earth, but their memory remains vivid and alive for me and for many others, who shared the wonderful experience of knowing them and being in their company, even for a short while. (In particular, I dedicate this section on Young Judaea to the memory of Muriel Goldberg Krauss, a dynamic, lovable and vivacious personality who worked as my assistant during all my years with national Young Judaea, and remained a dear friend for many years, until her untimely death.)

I do not intend to record the details of the Young Judaea program development, organizational structure or other factors involved. This I have already done as part of my doctoral dissertation which contained the details of a research study of Young Judaea I conducted during the operational year September 1951 to September 1952.[1] The dissertation is available to those interested in the details in the library of the School of Education of New York University, the Jewish National and University Library in Jerusalem and the Zionist Archives in both New York and Jerusalem. What I hope to be able to do now is share my impressions and feelings in a personal evaluative and reflective sense, some fifty years later. These impressions and feelings in retrospect have been shared with Young Judaean friends over the years and represent more than a nostalgic recollection of days and years long gone by. They have become an integral part of my educational and philosophical thinking and have helped shape much of my professional decision-making in the course of the years that have followed this experience. I still believe passionately in the ideas and ideals they represent.

I became the National Executive Director of Young Judaea at a very crucial time in Jewish history and the Zionist movement. My tenure in this office began the year before Israel was established as an independent state and continued on during its early years. I formally took office on June 1st, 1947, and was introduced to the movement representatives at a Conference of Leaders and Seniors held on May 30th-June 1st, 1947, in Spring Valley, New York.

An analysis of the program of the conference reveals the status of Young

---

1. Schanin, Norman, *Young Judaea: A Survey of a National Jewish Youth Movement in 1951-1952*, submitted in partial fulfillment of the requirements for the degree of Doctor of Education in the School of Education at New York University, 1958.

Roslyn Schanin, 1948   Norman Schanin, 1948

Judaea at that time. It was the conference of an adult-sponsored and directed youth organization, but whose members were primarily young people between the ages of ten and sixteen. The Spring Valley Conference was a milestone in the efforts of the leadership and the adult sponsoring bodies, the National Young Judaea Committee and the American Zionist Youth Commission, to change Young Judaea from a national adult-led youth organization into a youth movement, especially at the teenage level. An organizational structure was created known as Senior Young Judaea or Senior Judaea, and teenagers were to be elected eventually as national officers. This represented a major break in the long Young Judaea tradition of electing national officers who, in the past, were prominent adults in the American Zionist movement, usually from among those who had been Young Judaea members or club leaders during their earlier years. A year later, the first National Convention of teenagers was held at Camp Tevya, Brookline, New Hampshire. At that Convention a national constitution for Senior Judaea was adopted, and plans were approved for an extensive committee system to carry out the developing program.

Senior Young Judaea

The reorganization of the teenagers of Young Judaea into a "Senior" movement was a milestone in its development. All the major efforts and programming were geared to this goal during and after those years. This enabled the teenagers in the Young Judaea movement to respond actively, intellectually and emotionally to the momentous events that were occurring every day in Israel, in the Zionist movement and in the American Jewish community. The "movement" aspect of this new development aided and encouraged a teenage reaction and response to these events.

Coincidentally, it was during this period that I began my studies and research, which led to my receiving a doctoral degree in Education. I specialized in the newly developing field of group dynamics, which I readily accepted as part of a comprehensive educational theory and practice. To this must be added my philosophical involvement with the Jewish thinking (about peoplehood) of Mordecai M. Kaplan, and the loyalty concepts enunciated so well by the philosopher Josiah Royce. I was greatly influenced in my educational thinking by the work on group dynamics of Kurt Lewin and many others who were pioneers in this relatively new field of human understanding, as well as the dynamics of human interpersonal relationships. Kaplan provided me with the Jewish goals and ideas which could be transmitted in the form of ideals and values; Royce offered an outlook on the nature of man's loyalty to a cause or causes, which function as a moral imperative affecting his behavior; while Lewin and others presented me with the instruments by which loyalty to ideals and values can be developed in people so as to affect human behavior.

From the group dynamics theories studied, I understood that the needs and wants of individuals were most often fulfilled by means of their participation in groups; that groups exist in order to satisfy the declared purposes for which they were established. I learned that groups are influenced by the community environment and that group experience can develop and even change the individual's pattern of needs and wants. Kurt Lewin in his book, *Resolving Social*

Conflicts, writes that "...It is not similarity or dissimilarity that decides whether two individuals belong to the same or different groups, but *social interaction or other types of interdependence*. A group is best defined as *a dynamic whole based on interdependence rather than on similarity.*"[1] And finally I learned that groups need to engage in specific task-relevant and maintenance-relevant functions in order to remain united as a group. This, then, could be described as effective group behavior.

The significance of this for Senior Judaea encouraged me to develop an activity-oriented program. This focused on group or movement projects, conventions and elections, policy and decision-making discussions, and study seminars based on the ideology of the sponsoring group, both locally and nationally. From group dynamics, I gleaned the significance of the group and interpersonal relationships which are influenced by the standards of the community, or in Young Judaea terms, by the larger Zionist movement. The immediate group is the environment or the change-agent of the youth movement, which offers a program of individual identification and participation. The question then remained of how to internalize the ideals, values and ideology of the youth movement within the individual member, so as to gain the response of a commitment to that which it stands for.

The key question here is how to develop a strong and meaningful loyalty or loyalties that would influence the behavior and thinking of the individual. The philosopher Royce's answer is that the personal example of leaders loyal to a given cause influence greatly the training and strengthening of one's loyalty. The tendency of loyal followers of a cause is to idealize it. The true cause must be rational; it must have some worth and value, and not be an object of false devotion. However, such a loyalty is developed only as a result of serious effort and devotion in the practical *service* of that cause.

The final consideration in this discussion about the foundations of loyalty to a cause, such as Young Judaea as a Jewish and Zionist youth movement, is a moral issue. How does one's loyalty to a cause become internalized and real in terms of behavior, thought and feeling? The process by which a youth movement accepts and fulfills its goals and ideals, develops loyalty and a

1. Lewin, Kurt, *Resolving Social Conflicts*, Gertrud Weiss Lewin (Editor), Harper, New York, 1948, page 184.

conscience to do and serve, is influenced by effective leadership and good programming over a period of time. The development of loyalties and their internalization, affecting the will of the individual to behave in a specific manner, is a long-term, even lifetime process of acculturation, learning, feeling and thinking in the direction of making commitments.

With the above referred to developing philosophy and thinking, I began my work as National Executive Director of Young Judaea. One of my first tasks was to establish a meaningful balance and relationship between the adult sponsors, supervisors, group leaders and the newly emerging teenagers' Senior Judaea youth movement. The overall sponsoring body and source of financial support was the American Zionist Youth Commission, the joint enterprise of Hadassah and the Zionist Organization of America. The Commission functioned as a national body, with branch offices and staff in several large cities in the United States. Formally, I was engaged as an employee of the Commission and subject to the overall policies of that body under the leadership of its Executive Director, then Dr. Shlomo Bardin.

The Commission during this period consisted of Brandeis Camp Institute and several affiliated youth groups, Young Judaea, Masada and Junior Hadassah. It also sponsored the Intercollegiate Zionist Federation of America and cooperated with the Histadrut Ivrit in sponsoring a Hebrew Arts Committee. Later on, and for a short period, there emerged a second adult body for youth work known as the General Zionist Halutziut Commission, which was also jointly sponsored and funded by Hadassah and the Zionist Organization of America. But more about this later.

When I first became National Executive Director, I was given much freedom in developing the new Senior program and continuing with the Junior Young Judaea program, which was largely a club or local group oriented towards youngsters between the ages of nine and thirteen. In some larger districts, there also existed "intermediate" groups for those young people who were beyond the "junior" level of nine to eleven but not yet ready to enter the "senior" movement. On the Junior level, the adult presence and leadership was more direct and prominent. On the national adult level, the highest internal decision-making body was known as the National Young Judaea Committee. Its chairman and co-chairman were appointed by Hadassah and the Zionist Organization of

America, and approved by the American Zionist Youth Commission. Its constituents consisted of additional adult members of the sponsoring bodies, as well as of representatives elected by the group leaders and the Senior Judaeans.

My first responsibility as new National Director was to establish a working relationship between all these participating bodies involved in the Young Judaea operations. I can honestly state that I succeeded early in developing meaningful relationships with and among these different groups involved in the management and functional operations of Young Judaea. Occasionally, there were differences of opinion and even open conflict among some of the groups and individuals involved, though by and large we were able to work through and reconcile the differing positions.

With the development of the Senior Judaea movement, and later on a formal leadership group, the need arose to redefine the goals of Young Judaea and offer an ideological framework to give direction to the program in its various aspects. In my view, the ideological framework needed two interrelated foci, Zionism and Israel (newly established in 1948 during the first year of my work as National Executive Director), and the American Jewish Community. For me, the unifying components in such an ideology were accepting that Jews were primarily a people (the Kaplan idea of Peoplehood, or Klal Yisrael), and that the Jews who accepted this ideological concept were personally obligated to give service to their people.

During my five-year tenure as National Executive Director, the ideal of service to the Jewish people was stressed as an expression of individual and group behavior. At the National Senior Convention held at Camp Shor, Aurora, Indiana, from August 30th through September 3rd, 1950, the seniors approved a preamble to their Constitution that was adopted at the 1948 Convention. It read as follows:

> We, the members of Senior Young Judaea, in order to perfect our movement, are dedicated to developing in America generations of Jewish Youth rooted in their heritage and devoted to giving personal service to the Jewish people in Israel and America: by fostering group activities; by advancing the ideals and traditions of Judaism in America; by working actively for, and being

educated toward, Zionism and Israel; and by furthering
democracy in America.

During this period, the national program of Young Judaea was identified as "Our
Four-Fold Program: Group Activities; Jewish living; Zionism and Israel;
American Affairs." With the establishment of the new State of Israel in 1948,
the question of the centrality of Zionism and Israel in the program became a key
issue within Senior Young Judaea and its leadership group. Since the movement
spoke of giving service to the Jewish people in Israel as well as in America, the
existence of Israel and its special manpower needs raised serious questions for
both the young people and the adults. How important were Aliyah (going to
settle in Israel) and Halutziut (pioneering work in Israel), to the fulfillment of
the service ideal?

As the harsh War of Independence continued, and Israel struggled with the
absorption of thousands of refugee immigrants who were continuously arriving,
the need for free, strong and skilled young people from the Western countries
was quite apparent. This resulted in an increasing number of Shlichim
(emissaries) from Israel being sent abroad to encourage young people from the
Diaspora to settle in Israel. Garinim (small groups) were organized in many of
the large cities of the United States for the purpose of receiving orientation and
training for Aliyah to Israel. Most of these Shlichim were representatives of
political parties in Israel which wanted to recruit these potential Olim (new
immigrants) for their particular settlements and programs in Israel. Many of
them were charismatic personalities, who could attract, teach and train these
young people.

During these early years of development, the leadership of Senior Young
Judaea, as well as its adult leaders and sponsors, became involved with such
questions as the Young Judaea non-political and educational outlook on
Zionism, Israel and their relationship to the American Jewish community.
Throughout its long history, Young Judaea rejected the idea that was prevalent
in Israel and held by several other Zionist youth groups in America, that there
was no future for Jewish life in the Diaspora. Such was the idea accepted in
Israel, known in Hebrew as Shlilat Ha-Golah (a negation of the Diaspora) which
was called the Galut (Exile). This was the accepted outlook held by most

Shlichim from Israel. Young Judaea's major Israel connection and project was with the Tsofim, Israel's Scout movement, which was identified there as non-political. The Shlichim from the Tsofim who came to work in America with Young Judaea accepted the idea that the Young Judaean approach to Halutziut was based on a positive orientation of giving service to the Jewish people in Israel, and not on a negation of the Diaspora.

These two differing approaches — the ideological and the practical identification with specific groups in Israel — were a natural cause for argumentation, debate and conflict between the adherents of the differing perspectives. The problem was further compounded in Young Judaea by the conflicting attitudes held by the two adult sponsoring bodies of Young Judaea, the Zionist Organization of America and Hadassah. The Zionist Organization of America partner was closely identified with the General Zionist political party in Israel; Hadassah was not.

The General Zionist movement in Israel sponsored its own political youth group there. Hadassah, on the other hand, was dedicated primarily to providing health and youth services in Israel. It did not identify with any particular political movement, so as to be free to deal with any Israeli government and its coalition parties. To the best of my knowledge, at no time was there any open or formal relationship between Hadassah and the General Zionist party in Israel. During 1947 and 1948, in response to the historical events of that period, the General Zionist political party in Israel tried to establish its own youth affiliated program in the United States known as Plugat Aliyah (a group for Aliyah). Other political parties in Israel had already established such youth groups on the American continent.

During the summer of 1948, Plugat Aliyah conducted a small summer tent camp for teenagers. Most of the first dozen or so campers were from Senior Young Judaea. With the emergence of Plugat Aliyah in 1948, which was affiliated with HaNoar HaTzioni (young Zionist youth) of the General Zionist Party in Israel, both the Zionist Organization of America and Hadassah were asked to provide financial support for this new youth program. By 1949, both adult groups agreed to set up a special Commission, the General Zionist Halutziut Commission, to sponsor and supervise working with the other groups supported by the American Zionist Youth Commission. During the two years of its existence, the Halutziut Commission provided a platform for pressure on Young Judaea to change its approach to the idea of Halutziut, and to give up its special relationship with the Tsofim of Israel.

The ideological conflict between Young Judaea and Plugat Aliyah was compounded by some Senior Young Judaeans in the New York and Philadelphia areas, who were members of both groups. There was discussion on the national level about the issues involved. The Young Judaea response was to take a more aggressive attitude towards its own program for Halutziut, and this resulted in the setting up of special Hugei Aliyah (circles for Aliyah) for Senior Judaeans interested in considering aliyah to Israel for themselves. A special Moadon (meeting place) was provided at the national offices for the first group of potential Halutzim who became members of Garin Aleph (first nucleus). A first teenage Summer-In-Israel group of Senior Young Judaeans and leaders left for Israel in July 1951. Following the dissolution of the separate General Zionist Halutziut Commission in 1951, the responsibility for working with all the youth groups involved in Halutziut activities was turned over to a special sub-committee of the American Zionist Youth Commission.

In the February-March 1949 issue of "The Leader," published by Young Judaea, I attempted to clarify the ideological position of that movement in dealing with the question of Halutziut and Aliyah to Israel. I wrote the following in an article entitled, "Whither the Zionist Movement — and Young Judaea?":

> A major function of the Zionist movement today is to develop in the Diaspora a large corps of Jews who will become an equivalent of the Israeli Halutz. A chief attribute, then, of a member of the new Zionist movement in the Diaspora, will be his devotion and personal dedication to the service of his people. The service to be rendered must be in terms of the needs of the people. For some, the service will be in Israel, either on a temporary or on a permanent basis. We need to encourage Halutzim for Israel. This is in keeping with the view that peoplehood transcends boundary lines. With such an approach, Halutziut work, particularly in those countries where Jews live in peace and security, is bound to be crowned with greater success than were previous efforts, since

Halutziut will come as a natural outgrowth of the *service to the people idea*. The majority of Diaspora Jews, however, who may not think in terms of going to Israel, must also be stimulated to serve their people, and provided with the opportunity to do so. Thus they, too, will express through their own lives the new meaning of Zionism, in terms of the totality of Jewishness (Judaism) and the peoplehood of the Jews. The future community workers, teachers, rabbis and other leaders for the Jewish communities will come from such a dedicated corps, which can fire the imagination of our youth.

The above statement, which I wrote in 1949, represented the essence of my personal philosophy concerning Jewish values, Zionism, commitments and loyalties, which has guided my thinking and work with youth groups, in formal Jewish education and in teacher education, both in the United States and in Israel. This was the basis for the decision shared with my family of our taking the next step and opting for Aliyah to Israel in 1968. But more about that later.

Earlier, in January 1948, I proposed the idea of setting up an honor-service society, Hevra (Society), in order to stimulate to serve, and give recognition to, those Seniors who were ready to commit themselves to some form of personal service in the United States and Israel. The idea was approved by the National Young Judaea Committee, but rejected by the Senior leadership, which questioned its validity as a democratic group within Young Judaea. The National Senior Council voted for its abolition in 1951 and the National Senior Convention of that year approved its dissolution.

One of the successful outgrowths of the new Senior Young Judaea movement was the establishment of a national leaders body. Each year, the group leaders in Young Judaea held a National Leaders Conference, sometimes in conjunction with or immediately following the National Senior Convention. At the June 1951 founding Convention held at Tel Noar Lodge, Hampstead, New Hampshire, a new national leaders body was formed which called itself Hever Madrichei Yehudah Hatzair (Young Judaea Leaders Association). The interesting part of this development was the fact that most of the leadership for this new group came from past members of Senior Young Judaea who had grown up and matured in the movement.

Camp Tel Yehudah

During the summer of 1948, Camp Tel Yehudah became the first national teenage camp of Young Judaea. I consider the creation and the establishment of this teenage co-educational camp as the crowning achievement of my work in Young Judaea. I served as its Director, in addition to all my other regular duties as National Executive Director of Young Judaea. Of course, I had the important and capable assistance of many others who served on the camp and the national staff.

The idea of the camp emerged from the realization that there was need to intensify the national Young Judaea program during the summer months, when the teenagers were generally available. Summer camping had long been recognized in America and throughout the Jewish community as a vital educational instrument. For a youth movement, it could serve as a major vehicle for experiencing the true meanings of the program it espoused. A trial program of setting up a two-week Young Judaea Youth House took place successfully during the summer of 1947 at the East Midwood Jewish Center in Brooklyn, New York. The Youth House functioned on the basis of a day camp with a program reflecting Young Judaea's goals. However, the young people who participated in this program were a mixture of pre-teens, together with some teenagers who also assumed roles as counselor assistants. The Camp Tel Yehudah program in 1948 was exclusively for campers between the ages of fourteen and sixteen.

Summer camping was not a new or original idea in Young Judaea. For several years some locally sponsored city and regional area Young Judaea camps had been in operation. All these camps were geared primarily to the level of pre-teenage campers as well as some programs for early teenagers. However, they were organized with separate programs for boys and girls, with some occasional mixed programming. Camp Tel Yehudah pioneered the idea of a co-educational camp for only teenagers; of creating a special community for teenagers to be actively involved in determining the rights and obligations of each camper and staff member; of expecting campers and staff to influence program development. There was a communal dining room for all, where each camper selected where he or she sat and with whom he or she chose to share the meal. All programming — cultural, social and athletic — was organized for co-educational participation. The separated housing for boys and girls was located on one common campus.

As a teenage-staff community, a major aspect of the camp orientation and operation was the central role of the teenagers themselves in the decision-making. This affected camp policy concerning issues of personal and group standards of behavior, and in formulating some of the special and free programming that was not a required part of the daily regimen. A weekly "Town Hall" provided the instrument and setting for discussion and decision-making by the teenagers. The Town Hall meeting was conducted by the teenagers who had elected their own committee and officers. Every effort was made by the camp administration and staff to encourage the decision-making process,

Camp Tel Yehudah: informal discussion group Tel Noar Lodge, NH, 1949

encouraging full freedom of expression for all the campers and staff present. The camp administration and staff served as role models, guides and teachers, while not functioning as the primary authoritative figures in the daily decision-making that affected the functioning of the camp as a joint community of teenagers and adults.

Another important aspect of the camp philosophy and operation was the creation of a camp community in which the Jewish and Zionist components were the essence of the atmosphere that prevailed. This was an experience in living Jewishness in which the camp environment reflected the meaningful expression of Judaism as a religious civilization. The Zionist (Israel) orientation and creative activities, especially in the arts, music and dance, were central in the natural camp environment that was developed and experienced. The earlier Kvutza programs in Brooklyn and Manila, reported on above, provided me with the experience and knowledge that served as the model for the Camp Tel Yehudah community, the Jewish experiences created and the Zionist orientation expounded.

Two difficult incidents in the first Tel Yehudah camp experience in 1948 in Hendersville, North Carolina, are worth recounting. They reveal the problems of great responsibility and the challenge of personal attitudes and beliefs that I encountered as camp director. During that summer, a frightful poliomyelitis epidemic broke out in North Carolina after we arrived at the campsite. The first reports indicated that the outbreak was located in the eastern coastal region of the state. Our camp was situated in the Blue Ridge Mountains, in the western part of that state. Each day the State Board of Health issued reports of the spread of the disease. It became terrible and very draining to plot the spread of the disease daily as it moved westward in our direction.

To minimize the dangers of the disease spreading to our camp community, I decided to declare the camp an isolated area in voluntary quarantine, allowing only food and needed services to be brought in. We notified the parents about the situation, canceled any visitation privileges, and set up a special area in the camp, which contained proper facilities for staff day-off and recreational facilities during off-duty periods. All these decisions concerning the isolation of the camp were taken in conjunction with the local and state medical authorities. The parents, staff and campers responded well to these precautionary steps. By the end of the scheduled four-week camp period, we were able to send home the campers and staff safely, since the epidemic did not reach us, though first cases of the disease were located in White Rock, very close to our site in Hendersville. This was an horrendous baptism of fire for me in my first experience as a camp director.

The second story concerns the kashrut problems we encountered in operating the new camp, which had never before been used by the Brandeis Camp Institute owners. A certified Shochet (ritual slaughterer) had to be brought in from one of the large southern cities to slaughter beef and chickens at a local abattoir. As director of the camp I was invited to observe the work of the Shochet and the local abattoir. I found the experience of witnessing the slaughtering process very difficult and even painful. Consequently, at times I temporarily became a vegetarian.

The most difficult kashrut experience at camp concerned the preparation of chickens for cooking. The large number of chickens used had to have their feathers hand-plucked and seared off over a fire. As was the local custom, a group of Negroes were brought into the campsite to do that work. However, those of us from the North were shocked by the realization that, in accordance with local custom, we were not allowed to bring the workers into the kitchen nor offer them the use of the facilities, because we did not have separate entrances or special facilities for their exclusive use. These two difficult experiences in providing for the kashrut needs of the camp convinced me that we could not accept the local situation for supplying meat and poultry. Instead, we had to spend the extra funds necessary in order to ship to camp, by rail or refrigerated trucks, frozen kosher meat and poultry from Chicago, and later from Philadelphia.

The Camp Program

Throughout the camping season, the program content focused on creating learning situations for the study and experience of Judaism, Jewish history, Hebrew language, Israel and Zionism. Formal and informal classes and discussion groups were held in the morning. The balance of the day was spent in undertaking creative projects of individual choice in arts and crafts, drama,

Synagogue Dedication: Camp Tel Yehudah, Hendersonville, NC, 1948

music and dance, photography and nature study, with time out for sports and swimming. All these individual projects were assisted by specialist counselors, and the level of achievement was generally quite high. The educational environment was very positive, so the staff was generally quite pleased with the program and the responses of the campers.

An important part of the camp program and the environment created was the development of the religious component. The approach to Judaism, in theory and practice, was pluralistic. Those campers who came with a Judaic background were encouraged to continue with what they brought with them to the camp, but were expected to learn about and accept a pluralistic understanding of differences as presented by other campers and staff. For those without an adequate background and understanding, the camp program and Judaic experience was new and different. Many of those campers responded enthusiastically to the Judaic aspect of the camp community. It was exciting and most satisfying to witness the response of the entire camp family, campers and staff, to the common acceptance and participation of all in the Judaic program and in its pluralistic presentation and experience. On July 28th, 1948, I wrote a short summary article in the final issue of "Koleynu" (our voice), the camp newspaper. The article was called "Tel Yehudah — A Dynamic Jewish Community." I wrote:

> From the very beginning, our camping experiment has been based upon the four-fold program of National Young Judaea. This program begins as always with the individual who lives and works in a group setting. We have tried to provide each member of the Tel Yehudah community with opportunities to develop further his interests and abilities. Our program and activities have made use of the best and the most beautiful in Jewish life in order to create a meaningful Judaism. As members of the Jewish Community of Tel Yehudah, we have experienced the reality of a living and creative Judaism. Zionism, an understanding and appreciation of Israel, have been the chief source of our inspiration and enthusiasm. Here at Tel Yehudah, we have recreated the environment and cooperative spirit of Eretz Yisrael. The ideal and practice of American democracy and the American way of life, have been the cornerstones of our Machaneh [camp]. By means of our Vaad [committee] and tsrif [bunk] government, we reached a level of democracy that has made for harmonious and happy relationships among all the citizens of the Tel Yehudah community.

The highlight of the four-week program was its final event. In order to bring the camp program to an original and creative conclusion, we developed a Bikkurim (first fruits) Festival which was a cooperative venture by campers and staff lasting several days and concluding with a final banquet. The campers and staff of each camp season discussed and decided upon a theme. This was then expected to utilize the knowledge and skills acquired through individual participation in classes, the discussion groups and the creative projects which were completed. It was to be a cooperative program involving the entire community, campers and staff. This idea came as an alternative answer to the popular and very competitive "color war" which was usually the culmination of most private summer camp programs. We felt that a cooperative educational venture such as that of a Bikkurim Festival, offered a much more positive value system than that of a highly competitive, group and individual star-studded performance program. At the final banquet, the following pledge, drawn up by the Bikkurim committee, was spoken by all:

> We, the Hevra [members] of Tel Yehudah, dedicate ourselves to a full and active democratic Jewish life in America and in Israel. We pledge ourselves to further the knowledge of Jewish traditions and culture we have learned here, and to convey it to others. We pledge ourselves to live and work for Eretz Israel and through this newly created State, to draw inspiration, pride and love for our people. We pledge to the world our cooperation and our willingness to work and live peacefully with other nations. May we, with the help of God, attain and fulfill these pledges speedily and in our day.

Camp Tel Yehudah: Bikkurim Festival, Tel Noar Lodge, NH, 1951

The Winds of Change

By 1950, the functional, organizational and administrative structure of the American Zionist Youth Commission underwent significant changes. The major change was brought about by the separation of the Brandeis Camp Institute programs from the direct auspices and operational involvement of the Youth Commission. The Brandeis Camp Institute now consisted of three campsites, in New York — Brandeis East, in California — Brandeis West, and in North Carolina — Brandeis South. The latter campsite was never opened and was only used by Young Judaea as the location for Camp Tel Yehudah during the summer of 1948, and again in 1952. During the intervening years of 1949, 1950 and 1951, Camp Tel Yehudah operated on the site of Tel Noar Lodge in Hampstead, New Hampshire, as a joint project between National Young Judaea and the Eli and Bessie Cohen Foundation. Eli and Bessie Cohen were a wonderful, philanthropic, Jewishly committed and Zionist oriented couple, who privately established several non-profit camps in the New England area. Roslyn and I became very fond of Eli and Bessie and developed a fine, warm relationship with them.

As part of the changes taking place within the American Zionist Youth Commission, Dr. Shlomo Bardin Director of the Youth Commission and the founding Director of the Brandeis Camp Institutes, gave up his directorship of the Youth Commission and devoted himself full-time to the Institutes. Rabbi Amram Prero succeeded Bardin, and new lay personalities were brought in by the Zionist Organization of America and Hadassah to constitute the new chairman and co-chairman of the Board of the Youth Commission.

Administering and dealing with the Brandeis Camp Institutes had been the main project of the American Zionist Youth Commission during Bardin's directorship of the Commission. The personnel of the Commission were also actively involved in the functioning of these young adult camps. With the removal of the Brandeis Camp Institutes from the direct involvement and responsibility of the Youth Commission, the latter body began to reorganize and restructure its relationship toward the remaining affiliated youth groups identified with the Commission. The three young adult-sponsored groups, Junior Hadassah, the Intercollegiate Zionist Federation of America and Masada, were basically independent. They received some budgetary allocations and program assistance from the Youth Commission staff. Only Young Judaea remained an active part of the Youth Commission structure with the departure of the Brandeis Camp Institutes.

The Young Judaea Director was an employee of the Youth Commission, and its operational budget was totally dependent on the Commission. Some members of the Young Judaea National Board were appointed by the Commission and also sat as members of the latter Board. Minnie Halpern, formerly Chairperson of the National Young Judaea Committee, followed Dr. Miriam Freund as the Hadassah co-chairman of the Commission. During this period of change, the new Youth Commission Director and the new Commission Board Chairperson, Dr. Morton J. Robbins from New England, tried to become more involved in the internal operations of Young Judaea. I did not welcome this, and it was often a source of tension resulting from differing opinions and attitudes.

The new Commission Director sought ways of filling the void caused by the removal of the Brandeis Institutes from the functioning of the Youth Commission. At the same time, the new Chairperson of the Commission, who was an active leader in the Zionist Organization of America and an advocate of strengthening relationships with the General Zionist political party in Israel, was interested in establishing a relationship between Young Judaea and those General Zionists. Hadassah was not yet ready to do battle with its Zionist Organization of America partner on this and other issues. As it turned out in later years, after I left my position as Director of Young Judaea, Hadassah became the sole sponsor of Young Judaea. This greatly pleased me and it reflected the more significant role in youth work that Hadassah was capable and willing to undertake.

Once again the issue was raised by the Commission about the relationship between Young Judaea and the Tsofim, the scouting youth movement of Israel. The Tsofim were again accused of being part of the labor political youth program in Israel. The leadership of Young Judaea rejected these allegations and insisted on retaining its own non-political identification, together with an on-going relationship with the non-political Tsofim. Dr. Alexander Dushkin, the prominent American Jewish educator who had settled in Israel, was asked by the Youth Commission to investigate the matter of the political affiliation of the Tsofim. He responded to the request and subsequently reported that the Tsofim were indeed a non-political Israeli youth program as we in Young Judaea reiterated. Earlier, my dear friend, Rabbi Jack J. Cohen, who resided for a year in Israel, during 1947 and 1948, had issued a similar report.

Toward the end of the winter of 1950, I planned a visit to Israel to set up a permanent Young Judaea summer-in-Israel program. I was to be the guest of the Ministry of Education and Culture, which sponsored the Tsofim, and the Tsofim youth movement. It was planned that the first group of Senior Young Judaeans and their leaders would spend the summer of 1950 in Israel. The program was to be coordinated by the Jewish Agency for Israel, the Ministry of Education and Culture, and the Tsofim.

When all the arrangements and preparations for the Israel visit were completed, Dr. Robbins called me in to a meeting in which he requested that I postpone my visit to Israel for one year. The reason given was that the new Director of the Youth Commission had not yet visited Israel and that it was, in his opinion, unseemly for his subordinate to make such a visit before him. I felt that I had no choice but to accept the request, unless I was ready to do battle at that point with all those involved in the functioning of the Commission. This incident was but another indication of the difficulties presented for me by the new leadership of the Commission.

During March 1951, the postponed trip to Israel finally took place. I arrived in Jerusalem as the guest of the Ministry of Education and the Tsofim. Mr. Josef Meyouhas, who was also the supervisor-coordinator of the Tsofim for the Ministry, was my gracious host. We became close friends as well as colleagues during the years following this encounter. I concluded arrangements for the first Senior Judaean Summer-in-Israel program which took place during the summer of 1951.

A highlight of my Israel visit was participating in the dedication ceremonies of a training center for the Tsofim, which was to be located in the Hulda Forest, not far from Kibbutz Hulda and the small city of Rehovot. Though Young Judaea continued to raise funds for a while for this Hava (encampment), as it was called, the original plan was subsequently changed by the Tsofim and located elsewhere in Israel. During my visit I met and befriended many of the national and Jerusalem leaders of the Tsofim, with some of whom I remained in contact even after our family moved to Israel.

While in Jerusalem, I was invited to meet with Moshe Kol, one of the world leaders of the General Zionist Party in Israel. He tried to persuade me that the Young Judaea approach of being a non-political youth movement was wrong and that affiliation with the Tsofim was a mistake. I promised to review the situation when I returned to the United States, but I was by no means convinced of the validity of his arguments.

A curious footnote to my visit was the flight to Israel. I flew T.W.A., which was then the primary American airline servicing travel to Israel. The trip, in a four-motor Constellation, took almost thirty hours to complete, with stops at every major city on a route flying over Newfoundland, curving down to Shannon airport in Ireland, and continuing across Europe with stopovers in Paris, Rome and Athens. I had requested kosher food, and while on board, I was served with, as the major kosher products, a jar of gefilte fish and a box of Matzot. Fortunately, in addition there were fruits and vegetables available to fill out my tray.

By the end of 1951 and the beginning of 1952, I had become convinced that my usefulness to the Young Judaean program was coming to an end. My independence was being curtailed and the direction of the Youth Commission, especially in relationship to Young Judaea, was becoming unacceptable. I had little choice but to begin considering leaving Young Judaea and finding employment elsewhere as an American Jewish educator. I regretted this decision, because I felt that there still was so much more I had to offer and to do in furthering the development of Young Judaea as the largest American Zionist youth movement.

While I was contemplating the above, I became aware of the newly competitive threat to Young Judaea posed by the developing synagogue youth movements and that of the Bnai Brith youth program. To combat this development, it was necessary to intensify the Young Judaea efforts to grow and become more involved with the increasing numbers of newly developing synagogue centers which conducted religious schools and youth activity programs. This required greater financial commitment to the budgetary needs of Young Judaea. The sponsoring bodies were not responding sufficiently to the needs of a growing Young Judaea program, especially in this period following the establishment of the State of Israel.

It had become clear to me that the continuing partnership between Hadassah and the Zionist Organization of America was detrimental to the growth of Zionist youth work in America. Hadassah was capable of contributing much more than the allocations limited by the existing principle of financial equality between the two organizations. These and other considerations were documented in my doctoral study of Young Judaea for the operational year 1951-1952, undertaken in 1951, then later completed and approved in 1958.

After much soul-searching and consultation with family, colleagues and friends, I decided that the next turn in my career development was in formal education, with the possibility of also developing an informal youth educational program to complement formal learning in school and classroom. Consequently, I began to investigate, and be interviewed for, positions as an Educational Director of one of the large synagogue centers, which were becoming very prominent on the American Jewish community scene. These afforded opportunities to develop the kind of coordinated formal school and informal youth activity programs I believed in. Once again, my East Midwood Jewish Center experiences described earlier served as the realistic model for the career direction I was now turning to.

I was fortunate to be offered the position of Educational Director of the Forest Hills Jewish Center. This synagogue center, originally located as part of a small institution in the older part of the community, was moving into the new section of Forest Hills and rapidly becoming a major institution in this very desirable location. This had become a much preferred suburb in the borough of Queens, New York City. I was to begin my new career assignment in September 1952, following the end of the fifth Tel Yehudah camp season and the national Senior and Leaders Conventions which followed it. I left the camp in North Carolina on September 1st, 1952, and after driving all night with friends, reported to my new position in Forest Hills on September 2nd, 1952. As Educational Director, I was to serve as school principal and overall head of the youth activities department.

Chapter 4

The Forest Hills Jewish Center
(1952-1968)

Our Forest Hills experience was happy and fulfilling. We completed our family of three sons when Hillel was born during our early years in that community. David was about three years old and Jonathan six months old when we made the move. After a settling in period, we bought our first house and home which served us well and helped immeasurably in providing for the needs of our growing family. For Roslyn and myself, and our respective parents and family, moving away from our roots in Brooklyn to Queens was viewed then as a major change, an adventure in going out into the larger world. Little did any of us know then that, some sixteen years later, we were to move to the other side of the world, to Israel.

During the post World War II years, Forest Hills was a community with two different physical locations, separated by two major thoroughfares, Queens Boulevard and Yellowstone Boulevard. The larger section at that time was a neighborhood of small homes, while the other area consisted of the first high-rise apartment houses. Initially this separation was only a matter of a number of streets located on either side of Queens Boulevard, but it represented two different populations. In what was then known as "old" Forest Hills (whose well-to-do central area was called "The Gardens"), few Jews were accepted into that community as home owners. The Gardens consisted of lovely large and stately homes owned by wealthy people. The feeling among Jews was that they were not particularly welcome as neighbors. The world-famous Forest Hills Tennis Club, located in this area, with its international stadium and an adjacent Hotel, did not accept Jewish membership and guests during this early period.

The situation changed radically after the war, when less expensive homes and apartments were built in the area, and a "new" and enlarged Forest Hills came into being with the construction of many high-rise apartment buildings across the boulevard and several of the sections around "old" Forest Hills. The Jewish population then began to grow substantially as this area became the preferred suburb for Brooklyn, Bronx and Manhattan families seeking to upgrade their lives and status.

This was the community, the old and the new, we accepted as our own. The Forest Hills Jewish Center in 1952 consisted of two buildings, whose separate locations were in the two sections described above. The original building was a small one-story affair with not too large a synagogue for prayer services and several rooms and offices for school, youth and adult programming. When I arrived at the Center to begin my work, the new buildings were already under construction on the primary dividing line between the two communities which was Queens Boulevard. Some of the new classrooms and office facilities were available for use. It was to be a two-building complex of major proportions, with a synagogue that could seat 1,200 or more people, with a small chapel for daily worship, many classrooms, offices, a large auditorium, and in other areas a smaller one and several meeting rooms. It also contained a large gymnasium and indoor swimming pool.

The new facilities were very appropriate for an institution which offered a full program of religious, cultural, social and athletic activities for a growing community. This institution became a prototype of the newly developing "Synagogue Centers" that were beginning to dot the American Jewish community during the post-World War II period. They were quite different from the Jewish "Community Centers" simultaneously developing in some communities during this period. While outwardly they seemed to function as similar institutions, there were basic differences in ideology and program. The synagogue centers had a religious orientation and outlook which influenced their programs; the community centers were community-oriented with a philosophy geared to the idea of providing various services and programs, according to the general wishes and choices of the membership.

I began my work at the Forest Hills Jewish Center as its Educational Director on September 2nd, 1952, and remained in that position for sixteen fruitful and rewarding years. My work concluded at the end of the school term in June 1968 shortly before our leaving for Israel. During the first two years, I traveled back and forth daily by car between the old and the new buildings, since both offered a school and youth activity program. The plan was to eliminate use of the old building once all the facilities in the new building became available. What made my work in Forest Hills particularly effective was the caliber and dedication of the professional and lay leadership I encountered. Many have remained life-long friends, with whom I was able to share my thoughts, hopes and aspirations.

The Schanin family in Forest Hills, N.Y., 1958
Right to left: Norman, Roslyn, David, Hillel, Jonathan

The primary personality was Rabbi Dr. Ben Zion Bokser, who welcomed me as a working partner and friend. Our relationship, during my sixteen years of work in Forest Hills, was rewarding and exemplary. We were each aware of our own strengths and limitations. Both of us enjoyed the comradeship, the stimulation and affection shared by a meeting of mind and spirit. He served as my mentor on many issues. I am grateful to him for what became a very creative, constructive and happy working experience. It was in Forest Hills that I continued to develop the skills, outlook and philosophy of a Jewish educator in search of personal meaning and fulfillment in the service of the Jewish people.

My work with school and youth activities brought me into close association with many of the leaders of the Center. A past president and later Executive Director, Adolph Krauss, became a helpful co-worker and friend. I was fortunate in being able to mold two lay committees, who became deeply involved in the process of policy-making for the school and youth activities program. Solomon Heiferman, and later on Henry Burger, were effective as School Board Chairmen, and Nat Kane led the Youth Activities Committee with dedication during all the years of my work at the Center. These lay leaders, together with many others involved in my work, provided me with extensive assistance and guidance. They and their respective families remained life-long friends to my family and me.

From the very beginning of my professional career, I understood the importance of sharing the work with responsible and responsive lay committees. They provided the checks and balances necessary for the effective work by the professionals. Therefore I spent much time in transmitting to and sharing with these lay leaders the educational and administrative problems and developments requiring their input. Their involvement encouraged them to lend their time, energy and thinking to the problems we were facing. I was quite fortunate in finding such lay leaders and being able to contribute to their growth and understanding, as they did to mine.

The overriding goal of my work in Forest Hills was to offer and provide the leadership with a program of family education. Through the instrumentality of a school and youth activities program, a parents association and an adult education program, I was able to reach out to many families who were responsive to such an approach and philosophy. There were also many families who expressed indifference to this approach, other parents were concerned that our educational direction and effectiveness with their children might interfere with their own lifestyle. Therefore, the major task before me was to encourage the continuity and identification with the program of the many responsive young people without causing family conflict and objection. We did not always succeed in accomplishing this goal. Too many young people eventually dropped out of the program because of parental indifference and some objection.

In order to maximize the success of our efforts and to minimize the number of dropouts, we attempted to create an environment and a program for Jewish living based on free choice and in keeping with an open, conservative and pluralistic philosophy of Jewishness. This Kaplanian philosophy of Jewishness, of Jews being members of the Jewish people, regarded Judaism as a religious civilization, which was compatible with living as an integral part of American democratic society. Consequently, our focus was on the commitment of a family and/or the individual to such an outlook.

The School

Most synagogue schools during this period were based primarily on the development of late afternoon schools (called "Religious Schools" or "Hebrew Schools") for children between the ages of eight-nine and thirteen, who attended local public schools during the morning and early afternoon hours. By and large, the work of the afternoon schools in general was neither effective nor long-term. They hardly influenced the life pattern of most of those who attended such schools. The usual family practice was to register children for the minimum number of years required by the sponsoring congregation for Bar/Bat Mitzvah qualification. The number of weekly hours and years the pupils studied in these schools was therefore very limited. In addition, the motivation was primarily based on the desire to become qualified for the public Bar/Bat Mitzvah ceremony, and then to leave the school and discontinue their institutional synagogue membership shortly after the ceremony. The minority of parents who desired a more intensive Jewish education very often opted for one of the newly developing Day Schools, which offered an alternative to the more orthodox Yeshivot.

When I began my work at the Forest Hills Jewish Center, I found several parts of what could be reorganized into a unified and more intensive school system. The school had a highly rated pre-school department (led then by Shirley Cohen, and later by our dear friend Estelle Feldman), which met daily for youngsters between the ages of three to five. There then followed a primary department (Sunday school classes) for children between ages six and eight.

The largest department was a three-day afternoon school for older children between eight and thirteen, as well as the beginnings of a high school program for teenagers. There was, in addition, a pre-Bar/Bat Mitzvah preparatory program, supplemental to the afternoon school, and also a post Bar/Bat Mitzvah program leading to a Consecration (Confirmation) ceremony held as part of the Shavuot holiday service. The latter program was coordinated with the development of the afternoon and evening high school. It served as an incentive for some young people to continue beyond graduation from the elementary afternoon school and their Bar/Bat Mitzvah ceremony. The possibility of establishing a continuous and interrelated educational program for children and teenagers between the ages of three and sixteen became apparent to me. This concept consequently influenced the organizational and curriculum goals of my work at the Forest Hills Jewish Center.

In addition to the above elements for a more intensive congregational school system, there was a functioning Junior Congregation meeting on Sabbath mornings. This offered all ages a supplemental and less structured religious activity program, compared to that provided by the formal afternoon school. The Junior Congregation served as a major instrument for developing youth leadership roles for young people recruited to lead the services and become officers and active participants in its program. These young leaders and participants became the major candidates for the post Bar/Bat Mitzvah high school and the youth activities programs I was developing on an integrated basis. On the adult levels, there was the program of a Parent Association for which I was responsible, as well as an adult education program that functioned directly under the Rabbi's leadership, with my participation as consultant and lecturer. During the height of the development of the above described Synagogue Center school system, there were some 900 children and youth registered in the various departments of the integrated school programs. In addition, there were several hundred children, youth and young adults who participated in the youth activities program, many in addition to their being part of the above formal school programs. This was one of the largest school and youth activities programs in the city, if not the country.

At a later date, I became actively involved, together with Bokser, in the establishment of the first Solomon Schechter Day School in Queens, as part of the Conservative movement. We encouraged parents who were interested in their children's receiving a more intensive Jewish education to send them to the Day School. We made every effort to maintain an ongoing contact with this group of our children, mainly through the instrumentality of the Junior Congregation and the youth activities program. Children completing our full week pre-school daily morning or afternoon program became a major source for Day School candidates. Our son David became a founding member of the new second grade class when we transferred him from a local orthodox Yeshiva to the new Day School. Several other parents did the same with their children.

The Day School began with two classes, a first and a second grade. During the initial two years, and until a permanent principal was engaged, I served voluntarily as part of the professional team that helped open and supervise the Day School which functioned temporarily on the premises of the neighboring Rego Park Jewish Center.

After my initial years of experience with the above complex of educational programs and vehicles, I managed to merge them into one integrated school system. I then found myself dealing with several crucial questions: how to deal with the differing days and scheduling problems presented by such an organization; how to coordinate and supervise staff involvement; and most important of all, how to design a curriculum that would reflect the various levels, and the needs and interests of the very young, the older children and the young teenagers. There was also a strong need to develop an in-service training program for the teachers and institute an experimental curriculum research program. Personally, I felt that the classroom work had to be evaluated and the validity of our assumptions and directions examined. This, then, became the next stage of my development and on-the-job learning.

After some years of working on my own with this program of educational development on a trial and error basis, I decided to return to the university classroom in order to better prepare myself for the new goals I had set for myself in school organization and supervision, curriculum development and teacher training. I enrolled as a post-doctoral student for independent study and research in the Teachers College of Columbia University. I participated in seminars on curriculum development and social studies. But more of this later on.

My early efforts to strengthen ties between children in the school and their families with Israel included the following experiment. I initiated a plan to have each child open an individual bank account in a local savings bank in order to save toward a visit to Israel during their teenage years. The idea was that the parents and children would fill out a weekly bank deposit statement, enclose it with a check which was then collected by the classroom teacher for a group school deposit with a local bank. Regrettably, the response was minimal. This project was developed in the 1950's, when travel to Israel was still an idea or dream for most Jews, and parents were not yet comfortable with the idea of sending their teenage children overseas. After an extended trial period, the bank program was dropped as an idea too early for its time. I was quite disappointed.

The Youth Activities Program

My primary task in developing an afternoon and evening youth activities program was to work with and supervise the Youth Director in offering an integrated and coordinated program for the school and the youth activities in our building. The latter program was intended to provide supplemental cultural, religious, social and recreational activities for the elementary and high school youth, as well as the young adults. Where there was a response from the children and youth, with the encouragement of their families, the results were outstanding. In such cases, we were to develop a feeling of belonging to the Jewish people and the Synagogue Center. We attempted to build on these feelings to establish Jewish ideas, ideals and a sense of personal commitment.

As it turned out, most of the young people who participated in the youth program were not part of the larger school system. Rather, the older (post Bar/Bat Mitzvah) children of interested Center members and young adults participated as individual members. The Youth Activities program numbered several hundred young people in all the categories described.

Both the school and the youth activities program were a great source of new Center family membership. During the peak period of the 1960's, this numbered some 1,800 families and individual adult members. While at Forest Hills, I worked closely with several very good Youth Directors; Bert Rosenberg, Norman Krasner and Sandy Cohen. They were responsible to me and a Youth Committee of laymen who provided overall direction and supervision.

The major cultural and religious aspects of the youth program were expressed through group affiliation with such national movements as Young Judaea and United Synagogue Youth. In turn, these programs were supplemented by locally organized social and recreational activities, which took place in the building. There was also inter-congregational programming which took place in our Center or in which we participated as visitors elsewhere. We were also able to promote summer camping at Young Judaea's Camp Tel Yehudah and the Ramah Camps of the Conservative Synagogue movement.

The Center was bursting with activities and programs every weekday afternoon and evening. Consequently, my workday schedule was quite full during morning, afternoon and evening hours, and even on the Sabbath with the Junior Congregation. My sons still chide me, with implied gentle, and sometimes not so gentle, criticism that I was not home enough for them during their growing years. They were right. In careers such as mine, it is not easy to find the proper balance between family and work schedules and responsibilities.

Developing a New Curriculum Design

I completed my doctoral dissertation in 1958 at the New York University School of Education. The doctorate, a study of Young Judaea, was based on data obtained from several surveys I conducted in 1951-1952, my final year as National Executive Director of Young Judaea. The volumes of data accumulated were processed, digested and set down in writing during several wonderful summers spent in New Hampshire with the family. We were fortunate to have an apartment in the summer home of the Bokser family located on the river Ammonoosuc in Bethlehem, New Hampshire. The summers were idyllic for the family. In the mornings I worked on the doctorate while the boys kept busy

Norman at New York
University Graduation
Ceremony, receiving the
Doctorate Degree,
June, 1959

building, exploring and playing in the wooded area surrounding the cottage. The memories of those summers remain vivid in the minds of the whole family.

By the time the 1960's arrived, I was ready for new personal projects to stimulate my thinking. I decided to try my hand at creating a new and much needed curriculum design for the integrated school and the supplemental youth activities program I had been developing at the Forest Hills Jewish Center. Included in this creative process was an attempt by me to develop the basis for a philosophy of Jewish education and a related theory of instruction for the Jewish school, suitable in particular for the American Jewish Diaspora.

The time was appropriate for such a task: I had succeeded to some extent in developing a functioning integrated school system within the Synagogue Center for a large number of children and teenagers; I had completed my doctorate; and I was stimulated by the latest developments in curriculum theory published in general education journals and the new materials for classroom use in the public schools that had become available. I attempted to find ways of transferring these new developments and materials for use in the Jewish school.

During this period of research and experimentation, I began to express my thinking and ideas in a series of articles and publications. An early effort in 1958-1959 was preparing a booklet for older school children and teachers on ideas, information and values from the Bible called "The Weekly Torah Portion" (פָּרָשַׁת הַשָּׁבוּעַ). This material was geared to an English reading level of children between the ages of eleven and thirteen. I had prepared the booklet also with the idea of providing teachers with suitable material to guide their teaching of the weekly subject on the five books of Moses (חוּמָשׁ) for younger children who were unable to read it by themselves. The material was concise and limited to one or two pages for each lesson.

A volume on prayers and holidays appeared in 1960. This was a hard-covered textbook for children who had begun to read by themselves in both the English and the Hebrew languages. It is called *An Introduction to Prayers and Holidays for the Student* (תְּפִלָּה וְחַג לַתַּלְמִיד). My wife Roslyn collaborated with me in 1968 in preparing a workbook for children using this textbook. To the best of my knowledge, this book is still being used in some classrooms in American Jewish schools, some thirty-nine years after the text was published by Ktav Publishing House, Inc. of New York.

My interest in research and curriculum development led me to produce the first two Yearbooks published by the Educators Assembly of the United Synagogue of America (today known as the Jewish Educators Assembly). These initiated an annual series of Yearbooks. The first volume in this series was published in 1965, entitled *New Insights into Curriculum Development Part I: Bible Instruction*. I co-edited this Yearbook with Walter Ackerman. The second volume appeared a year later in 1966. It was called *New Insights into Curriculum Development Part II: Jewish Life and Observances,* and I edited this volume by myself. During this period of the 1960's, I wrote several articles on developing new ideas for Jewish education. These reflected my work in researching general and Jewish education, along with the experiences I had in developing an integrated educational program for the Forest Hills Jewish Center. I reviewed ideas on curriculum development and integrating the school with youth activities in a Synagogue Center. These articles were published in the "Reconstructionist" and the "Jewish Education" magazines. The first was the bi-weekly magazine published by the Jewish Reconstructionist Foundation, Inc., and the other a quarterly by The National Council for Jewish Education.

The new curriculum design I worked on led me to consider and struggle with issues dealing with the development of a philosophy of Jewish education and a related theory of instruction for the Jewish school. These issues were also correlative with my work in youth activities at the Center and my collaboration with parents. The central idea which guided me was to develop an integrated program for the school, beginning with pre-school and continuing through high school levels, with implications for supplemental youth activities and parent education programming. I explored the questions of providing for a complete family educational program and the important issue of continuity in educational services.

Central to the new curriculum design were three major themes which supplied an integrative focus. The first dealt with the meaning of Jewishness. The second concerned the teaching-learning act by means of developing a Jewish educational conceptual framework. The third area included some suggested key concepts for building a conceptual framework which would reflect the meaning of Jewishness. The new design I was trying to develop applied specifically to the educational problems experienced in the field of American Jewish education in which Jews live as a minority group in two civilizations, the American and the Jewish.

Later on I tried to apply the above philosophic and pedagogic issues to Israel education, where there is a reversed situation for Jews living as a majority in a Jewish State. In this latter situation, the Jewish civilization is predominant and includes a blend of Western and Eastern cultures comprising the secondary or additional elements which reflect the total Israeli situation.

As expressed in the material prepared for the curriculum project, Jewish education was defined as the process by which the individual experiences and develops an understanding of the meaning of his or her Jewishness. In my thinking and writing, "Jewishness" is viewed as both membership in the Jewish people and sharing the evolving religious civilization, "Judaism," with other Jews living in the Diaspora or Israel. The Jewish school could then be described as a fabricated environment which should function integrally with the home and family, the community and the peer groups. The idea developed here was that the general purposes of the Jewish school ought to be expressed in terms of intended behaviors, as ways to think, feel and act. Such behaviors should reflect the meaning of Jewishness for the individual and the group.

My basic premise is that, to experience and understand the meaning of Jewishness, there is a need to build a conceptual framework from key generative ideas, feelings and experiences. The school curriculum as well as the teaching and learning acts should reflect the development of such a conceptual framework. This, in turn, would explain, order and synthesize the relationships between content, ideas, feelings and experiences. The content details which comprise the conceptual structure are to be *derived* from the teaching-learning act experienced by each individual and group.

The curriculum developed in this project was, of course, prepared for use in the American Jewish school. In the materials prepared, I wrote that some generative ideas about God, the Jewish people, and Torah (as a term which symbolized Jewish culture, religion and relations with Eretz Yisrael) should provide the primary concepts for building a conceptual framework reflecting the meaning of Jewishness. If this material were to be reinterpreted for use in the general (mamlachti) schools in Israel, the word "Jewishness" (yahudiyut) would mean membership in the Jewish people, which has historically produced an evolving civilization. Perhaps for Israel it would be better understood if we substitute the term "Judaism" (yahadut) for civilization as the all-embracing concept describing the culture and religion of the Jewish people. Use of the term Judaism in the Israeli setting should mean the complete culture of the Jewish people. Such a culture would include Jewish history, religion, Hebrew language and literature, the arts and folkways.

Put in other terms, the generative ideas for the Diaspora would constitute a triangle consisting of ideas about God, the Jewish people and Torah. This was a formula expressed in Kabbalistic literature which spoke of God, Israel and Torah as one integrated idea. For the general (non-orthodox) Jewish population in Israel, the triangle would be expressed somewhat differently in generating ideas for the key concepts in a conceptual framework. The apex of this triangle would be the Jewish People (peoplehood) and the two lines emanating from it would be identified as the State of Israel and Jewish culture (Judaism).

The next step in developing this curriculum was to categorize these key concepts into a series of generalizations for each age-level of the overall program, to select the content and recommend the experiences and activities that could translate the theory into practice. To complete the units at each level, materials and resources were suggested for use by the teachers, and when applicable, for the students. In addition to preparing classroom materials, I tried my hand at writing resource units that students and teachers could use. These included: "The World of the Bible" (in an historical context) and background materials on the history of the Forest Hills Jewish community and the Forest Hills Jewish Center.

To implement this project, I conducted many faculty meetings for teachers to react, reflect and respond to the new curriculum, and suggest changes and modifications. Prior to writing down the new material, I had consulted several subject matter specialists and faculty theoreticians associated with the Jewish Theological Seminary in New York. It received their input as researchers and specialists in such fields as Bible, Jewish history and literature, and religious philosophy. My preliminary ideas were shared with several colleagues and the details of the project were also brought before the School Board and Parents Association leadership.

In the December 15th, 1967, issue of "The Message" (the weekly bulletin of The Forest Hills Jewish Center), there appeared 'A Progress Report' on the new curriculum project for members and parents. I wrote as follows:

> Some four months have passed since we began a massive effort to implement the new curriculum ideas developed for our school. We are in the process of creating a new curriculum, which will provide a fourteen-year program of consecutive schooling and related experiences for our children and their parents.
>
> This is in the nature of a progress report. The curriculum

project is now at the stage of development in which pilot classes are experimenting with new ideas, materials and methods. We are concentrating at this time on a group of classes with children between the ages of six and ten. They constitute that group of children who either have completed our nursery and kindergarten classes (the pre-school department) or are late beginners in our educational system. In addition to this specific concentration, we are extending our experimental efforts both into the higher and lower grades, one academic year at a time in each direction.

For most children and teachers this new program has meant an introduction to new materials which have been selected for their value as sources of information about the meaning of Jewishness. Since specially prepared materials are needed for this program, and these are not yet generally available, it has been necessary to utilize a variety of text materials. The children's response has been very encouraging. We have observed some new interest and new meaning in their studies.

A second area of significance in the development of this program is creating new ways of teaching and training teachers to utilize these new methods. At this point, most of our full-time teachers are involved in the program with only one of the three classes which comprise their teaching assignments. The new program requires additional time for preparation and training on the part of all participating teachers.

The third major area of importance for inclusion in this report concerns parent involvement. One of the major components of this new curriculum approach is a significant role for parents which is being built into the total structure. It is part of the underlying philosophy of this program to provide a place for the two important non-school influences which help mold the character and affect the responses of the child, namely, the family and the peer world of friends. Consequently, at the current level of concentration (the six to ten-year-olds) parent involvement is stressed more than that of the peer world. Later, during the adolescent period, involvement of the peer world will be stressed more than the role of parents.

During the first quarter of this school year we have involved parents of these classes in three different ways. They have had an opportunity to attend a monthly seminar which I conduct in order to study on adult levels the underlying generalizations which form the basis of this new program. Secondly, we are now sending home textbooks with the children of six and seven years, which require parent reading to the children. Parents receive homework assignments which they are asked to do with their children. And thirdly, we have invited parents to accompany their children on holidays and during school hours on special class trips (to children's services on Sukkot; to the Masada exhibit at the Jewish Museum in New York and to the local supermarket in order to learn how to distinguish firsthand between kosher and non-kosher products). On these occasions parents are expected to share the meaning of the experience with their children rather than simply attend as teacher-helpers.

The new curriculum program has many rough edges and incomplete aspects which we are working on to correct and improve. What has become clear, however, for all who care to observe is that we are changing the image and content and meaning of Jewish education at The Forest Hills Jewish Center. Ours is now a comprehensive school for children between the ages of three and seventeen. We can say with clarity and full conscience, that only the child who experiences the complete program will receive an adequate and effective Jewish education in our school. All others will at best receive only a fraction of the whole proportionate to the number of years they attend and the degree of interest shown by their parents.

The prospects for the future of this program are bright, especially as an ever-widening circle of interested adults continue

> to extend their enthusiasm, their influence and their understanding into every area of our congregational life.

The new program was put into practice during 1967 and 1968. I can report on modest success during this trial period. Teachers and students indicated some interest and challenge as presented by the new curricular approach and the materials it introduced. However, since my family and I moved to Israel two years after its introduction, there really was not enough time for me to evaluate the effectiveness and the successes or failures of this new project. But for me personally, the creative experience of researching, consulting, developing and preparing the material in its written form was very exciting and invigorating. I had to leave it to others to continue this project or not. In my subjective judgement, the material is still relevant today for further development and implementation. Both Diaspora and Israel Jewish education still lack some new approaches to curriculum development which would reflect the continuing need to seek out the meanings of Jewishness and Judaism for each new generation.

Working with Pre-Service Teachers and Teenagers

During the 1960's I was invited by two departments at the Jewish Theological Seminary of America to teach courses in group work and education, and to serve as a Teacher Trainer. One of my majors for the Master's and Doctoral degrees at New York University was in the field of group work dynamics. As indicated earlier, I became very interested in applying group work theory to my work in informal education, both in Young Judaea and later at the Forest Hills Jewish Center. The field of group work also has much relevancy for the formal educational setting. The idea of dividing a classroom full of learners into small working groups, is the application of group work theory to formal education. I had given occasional one-time lectures to groups on this subject, but my first ongoing teaching experience in this area was at the Seminary School for Jewish Studies during the academic year 1961-1962.

My work with pre-service teachers took place between the years 1965 and 1968. I was asked by the Dean of the Teachers Institute of the Seminary, Sylvia Ettenberg, to teach a course in education. The subjects of the course centered around curriculum development and the pedagogy that were applicable to the Jewish school. In addition to the formal classroom teaching, I functioned as the Teacher Trainer who also visited those students in my course who were doing student teaching in the field. Little did I know at the time that this was an excellent experience which prepared me for work in teacher education. This was to occupy me for the next twenty years after my immigration to Israel.

These teaching experiences were, of course, very much part-time so as not to interfere with my primary work as Educational Director of the Forest Hills Jewish Center. During the 1960's, I also spent several summers at Camps Lown in Maine and Cejwin in Port Jervis, New York. In both camps, I served as head of the Leadership Training program. There, I was able to apply my knowledge and experience in formal and informal education, which was very stimulating and rewarding. The young people I worked with in these special camp programs were older teenagers aged sixteen and seventeen. They were preparing to become counselors for the children at these same summer camps.

During the summer of 1966, Roslyn and I served as group leaders for a United Synagogue teenage pilgrimage to Israel. This was the first opportunity we had, or could afford, to spend the summer months on an extended stay in Israel. It was Roslyn's first visit to Israel, and my second, having been there once before some fifteen years earlier. Our group consisted of teenagers between the ages of fifteen and seventeen. It was not an easy group to work with and chaperone. We were surrogate parents and teachers. Many of the teenagers in the group did not want parent figures and teachers around to supervise their individual activities. During the program we visited many parts of Israel, from Dan to Eilat.

I was overwhelmed and impressed with the developments and even radical changes that had occurred in Israel between 1951 and 1966. For Roslyn especially, much of the excitement of being in Israel was marred by the arduous daily tasks we had to endure with a difficult group of teenagers. The experience left her with some doubts about the question of moving to Israel with our family. However, in retrospect, that summer-in-Israel program contributed much to our development and understanding of how to work as educators with differing groups of young people, especially in unusual situations. It also caused us to realistically consider our aliya options and the implications such a radical lifestyle change would have on our family.

Professional Growth and Development

My early professional experiences, which constituted a continuation of my formative years as club and youth leader, were primarily in the areas of informal education. From club and youth leadership roles, I was promoted to supervisory and administrative positions. During this period, the only deviation from this pattern was working as assistant principal, teacher and youth director at the Park Avenue Synagogue, as described earlier. The principal position I occupied during this early period was that of National Executive Director of Young Judaea.

The move from Young Judaea to the Forest Hills Jewish Center marked a major turn in my professional development. As Educational Director of the Center, I became a formal educator as head of a large school and the supervisor of an extensive informal youth activities program. I was involved with parent education and functioned as an active participant in the adult education program conducted by the Rabbi. In short, I became a full-time Jewish educator involved with formal and informal programs which I attempted to organize and program as two aspects of one whole — Jewish education for the entire family.

After settling into the latter position, I felt the need to have ongoing contacts with other professionals in the field who held similar positions. Over the years I was able to maintain contact with many such educators and to develop a lifetime friendship with some of my colleagues. Periodic local meetings were held with such educators in the larger area of Queens where I lived and worked. These meetings were usually attended by the professional advisor-supervisor from the Jewish Education Committee of New York, the overall community agency for Jewish education in the greater New York city area. However, for a broader influence and involvement with other educators, I joined the Educators Assembly of the Conservative movement and the National Council for Jewish Education, whose members were from Bureaus of Jewish Education and the larger educational institutions located throughout the United States and Canada.

After several years as an active participant in the activities of these two professional organizations, I was invited to join the Executive Committees of both groups. My major interests in these groups was to enter and share in an environment which would concern itself with the larger issues in Jewish education. In both groups I looked for sources of information, guidance and a discussion of shared experiences in my desire to find or develop a meaningful philosophy of Jewish education. Such a philosophy would provide directions developing a new curriculum, enabling the establishment of a supportive school administration and organization, and, of course, for teacher education. I was often impatient with these groups, especially with the Educators Assembly, due to the inordinate amount of time and energy spent on questions involving the status of the Jewish educator, his conditions of employment and the problems of educator-rabbi or community leadership relationships that existed in many institutions and areas.

My major organizational involvement was with the Educators Assembly, whose membership consisted primarily of educators who held congregational positions similar to mine. My growing interest in educational research was related to the work of the synagogue school and youth activities. I therefore advocated the establishment of a research committee as a major program for the Educators Assembly.

For the February 5th, 1960, meeting of the Educators Assembly Executive Committee, I prepared a memorandum entitled, "Rethinking the Role and Operation of the Educators Assembly." In it, I recommended the establishment of a permanent research committee to engage in action-research. Such a program would influence the content of the annual conventions of the Educators Assembly, and provide the opportunity to publish a research yearbook. I was asked to serve as the chairman of the new research committee that was to be set up during the school year 1960-1961. Regional research committees were also established as an extension of the work of the national research committee.

As a major part of its work and direction, the national committee conducted two research seminars each year, one in the form of a mid-winter seminar and the other as a Labor Day weekend program. The committee developed an ongoing relationship with the newly established Melton Research Center at the

Teachers Institute of the Jewish Theological Seminary, and during the period between 1962 and 1964, joint seminars were held. The first major research area shared by both groups was the subject of Bible instruction in the congregational school. The 1964 annual convention program of the Educators Assembly focused on this subject within the framework of the title, "New Insights into Curriculum Development," and subsequently a yearbook was produced to summarize the findings of the research committee and the deliberations of the 1964 annual convention on the subject. A similar process of research-oriented development took place during the 1964-1965 school year on the subject of Jewish life and instruction. The 1965 yearbook published material on this latter subject.

At the 1965 convention of the Educators Assembly, I was elected president

Schanin awarded Honorary Degree Doctor of Pedagogy, honoris causa, presented by Chancellor Gerson Cohen of the Jewish Theological Seminary of America, in 1977, assisted by Dr. Sylvia Ettenberg and Rabbi David Kogen

of the organization, having served as committee chairman and vice-president. The work of the Research Committee and the publication of an annual yearbook were turned over to others on the Executive Committee. I served for two years as president during 1967 and 1968. I was also elected secretary of the National Council for Jewish Education. I held this position for two years, until we emigrated to Israel during the summer of 1968. Later on, in March 1977, the Educators Assembly invited me back from Israel to receive one of the first honorary doctorate degrees awarded to Jewish Educators by The Jewish Theological Seminary of America. At a special Academic Convocation, held at the annual convention of the Educators Assembly, I was awarded the degree, Doctor of Pedagogy, Honoris Causa.

Our Hearts are in the East

During the initial years of our life in Israel, visiting friends and relatives often asked questions about our decision to emigrate to Israel as new Olim. In our own family circle we had not really discussed this question directly or with the intent for decision-making for the short or long-term future. There was no doubt as to the central place Israel occupied in our thinking and feelings as Jews. We were firm in our conviction that Israel was the homeland of the Jewish people and by its very existence would contribute profoundly to the reconstitution of the Jewish people as a people. We were committed Zionists, who were prepared to ensure that Israel fulfill its historic role of reestablishing an independent and democratic Jewish entity on its ancient soil. Therefore, we were able to say with ease, together with our prophets and thinkers throughout the ages, that our hearts were always in the East.

As described earlier, I was privileged to visit Israel twice before we decided to come and settle here; Roslyn had only visited once under difficult circumstances as a U.S.Y. group leader. The sudden outbreak of the Six-Day War on June 6, 1967, came as an electric shock to us. We feared for the continued existence of Israel. I remember that when the war broke out, I was working at the Center in the capacity of Educational Director. We were stunned by the news of the fighting and remained glued to the radio, and later on to the television, as the first conflicting reports were announced. The master controls for the school public address system were located in my office. The radio remained on throughout the afternoon and evening, and people were constantly coming in and out of my office to listen to the news and express their shock and concern. I broadcasted news reports throughout the building between the sessions of the school.

We felt helpless, fearful and had the very strong need to respond to the difficult situation confronting Israel, as Jews who were devoted to Israel and committed to the Zionist movement. A first response for individual and community action was to answer the call received from the United Israel Appeal section of the United Jewish Appeal to immediately organize and raise emergency funds for Israel. The office staff of the Center, augmented by many volunteers who began to arrive, proceeded to organize a telephone campaign for immediate response. This effort continued throughout the war and for a while after the cease-fire went into effect.

Upon arriving home that night, I was very troubled and shaken by the turn of events in Israel. Roslyn and the boys were likewise concerned and confused by the developments. I remember that Roslyn and I expressed our feelings, wanting to do more than raise funds during this period of crisis. For the first time we expressed our sense of guilt at not being in Israel at this difficult time, when Israel's continued existence seemed to be in jeopardy. We felt that our place during such a trying period was Israel.

In the stress of the moment, we did not give adequate thought to our boys. What about their feelings and then their responsibilities living in a country which suffers from unpredictable situations of war and peace? Our sons could shortly be faced with this major question. The obligation to perform military service in Israel had not yet become part of our thinking or understanding.

Fortunately for Israel and the rest of the Jewish world, the Six-Day War was short and resulted in a stunning victory for Israel. We shared the naive thought, along with many others, that after this great victory, wars in Israel would be a thing of the past. We believed that Israel would be free to develop without fear and filled with hope and expectation for the future. It was at this point that we began to realize that if we were to fulfill our dream of living in Israel, then now was the time to make the decision to immigrate. I was forty-five years of age, and if I expected to be employed in Israel in my field, then realistically now was the time to make this move. The alternative option was to wait until retirement age and settle in Israel as retirees. With the latter option, the question of our sons, who would have reached adulthood, would have to remain an open subject based on their individual decision-making. We wanted very much to settle in Israel as a family. Therefore, Roslyn and I concluded that we should begin investigating employment and housing options available to us. Our hearts and minds drew us to Jerusalem, which represented for us the ideal and the reality of being in Israel.

During the period following the Six-Day War, the issue of Aliyah was dealt with in the United States by the Israel Aliyah Center at 515 Park Avenue, New York City. Attached to this Center, and to other branches located throughout the United States, was a cadre of staff known as Shlichim — agents or representatives of the Immigration Department of the World Zionist Organization, whose headquarters were in Jerusalem. These Shlichim had to assist individuals considering Aliya, providing them with all the necessary guidance and information. They were also available to work with groups of potential Olim, to address larger audiences, and to coordinate the work between the local Aliyah offices and headquarters in Jerusalem. It was to such Shlichim that Roslyn and I turned, as we began the process of working out the details for our eventual aliyah.

The two major questions posed by most Olim from the West, especially those from the United States, were employment and housing. These questions were particularly critical for family units. While these questions were not new to the Aliyah authorities, they continued to present problems for them. By and large, Israel had experience in dealing with the overwhelming majority of Olim who came from lands of distress. It was easier to deal with Jews who were being pushed to go on Aliyah because of the problematic situations where they lived. They had to leave. Upon arriving in Israel, they were usually given temporary housing, where the absorption process began for them. They attended an ulpan to learn Hebrew, then they sought employment and more permanent housing. For potential Olim from the West, who were being pulled to Israel for reasons of religious belief and/or idealistic and nationalistic reasons as Zionists, the need arose to change this orientation and the absorption process.

Most potential Olim from the West, especially family units with children, who were voluntarily giving up jobs and homes to settle in Israel, wanted to know where they were going to work and live. Some individuals requested and were granted support and assistance to visit Israel on a pilot trip to find employment and housing before going on Aliyah. Most prospective immigrants from the United States encountered difficulties with regard to these two vital questions. The attitude in Israel was understandable but not practical when dealing with potential Olim from the West. It was felt in Israel that the new immigrant should move to Israel, and upon arrival he or she would be offered temporary housing in special Absorption Centers. After settling in physically, the new immigrant could then be interviewed and find employment. At that point, he or she could seek permanent housing in the vicinity of the employment. This approach was neither effective nor pragmatic.

Most mature Olim from the West were seemingly not prepared to give up an existing job and dismantle their homes or apartments before knowing with some assurance what they would find in Israel. The Aliyah record from countries such as the United States was not too encouraging. The numbers emigrating were small to start with and the percentage of those who returned to America from Israel after a year or two was quite high. This was the reality of the situation in 1968, when my family began assessing its Aliya prospects.

If we were to make Aliyah in the summer of 1968 as we hoped to, I would have to give notice to my employers of our plan to leave Forest Hills and the Forest Hills Jewish Center. The people at the Center were like an extended family to us, and I was not going to put them in any difficulty by a last minute decision to leave. We were now in our sixteenth year in that community and we wanted to leave under conditions that would be acceptable to them and us.

Since my employment was based on the school year, this meant giving proper notification in March. Then, too, we would have the problem of time required to sell our home in Forest Hills. We had decided to go to Israel and, come what may, give it some three to five years to make the adjustment permanent. We reasoned that to keep our home, renting it to others while we were in Israel, would make it too easy for us to return if things were difficult. We felt we had to cut our immediate ties and make a real effort to remain in Israel as we hoped to. In hindsight one of our errors was not to give our children more input into these early deliberations.

After our basic decision was made, I began the normal process of registering with the Israel Aliyah Center in New York. The Shlichim I dealt with were helpful within the limits of their abilities and function. Their basic task was establishing links with Israel, first through the immigration offices of the World Zionist Organization, and then with potential employers. They also had to provide information about life in Israel and our adjustment needs. Matters progressed slowly, and the weeks seemed to fly by rapidly. As an educator, I was interested in education-related employment opportunities, preferably in the Jerusalem area.

The education field in Israel also functioned on an academic year basis. This meant that looking for an educational position in the fall of 1967 for the school year beginning in September 1968 was not realistic. Few positions were immediately available or would be known about before the end of the school year. Then, too, those responsible for engaging school personnel and informal youth program staff were not prepared to engage the services of an educator from abroad, sight unseen. This was understandable. Hence prospective employers would have to come to the United States to conduct interviews, or the candidate would have to travel to Israel for such an interview.

While I was beginning to deal with the problems of employment and housing, I gradually became aware of others. Some colleagues from the American Jewish education scene were quietly also making similar plans for Aliyah. In casual conversations it became obvious to most of us that finding employment in advance from the United States was quite unlikely. Both the potential employer and the employee needed to be brought together somewhere, preferably in Israel, in order to work out the specific details for each situation. Because of the delay in organizing such a meeting of both parties, the tensions surrounding each candidate and his family began to rise. Deadlines had to be met if Aliyah to was to become a real possibility during 1968. It had become increasingly clear that something drastic had to happen in order to unlock the problems that had become evident.

Shortly after making the decision to settle in Israel, I revealed privately to my assistant principal the possibility of our moving to Israel for the 1968-1969 school year. I intended to recommend that he succeed me as Educational Director of the Forest Hills Jewish Center. I was surprised to learn that he, too, was planning to go on Aliyah next year and therefore would not be available for the position. This assistant, Barry Chazan, had been dating Naomi Harman, the daughter of the Israeli ambassador to the United States, and they were married in the spring of 1967. Barry, too, was experiencing a similar difficulty in finding employment for the next school year. He was completing his doctorate and was interested in obtaining academic employment in a university setting in Israel. He, of course, shared some of his thinking with the ambassador and indicated that there were other American Jewish educators interested in Aliyah but encountering difficulties in finding employment. Harman was very interested in the general problem of Aliyah from the West and indicated he would try to be of help in dealing with the Israeli bureaucracy.

I was asked to prepare a list of names of potential educators interested in finding jobs in order to make Aliyah to Israel. The list drawn up consisted of eighteen American Jewish educators with differing qualifications and experiences. It was circulated to Ambassador Harman in Washington, then to Avraham Frank, director of the Israel Aliyah Center in New York, and finally to Moshe Yakir, director of the immigration department of the World Zionist Organization in Jerusalem. All three were very interested and helpful in working with us and other candidates in fulfilling our desire for Aliyah.

While the list was being circulated, most of the people in that group held informal discussions and meetings in order to share experiences and information. It became quite apparent to most of us that there was need for some coordinated action on our part in order to overcome some of the problems encountered. Gradually, we developed the concept of self-help and the need for some organizational structure to enable the group to function as a lobby for potential Olim that would be independent of the existing Aliyah establishment and solely represent collectively the interests of individual members of the group. Eventually, we established an informal "Committee to Promote Western Aliyah" for this purpose.

After much discussion with the three above leaders of the Aliyah and Zionist movement establishment, some of the candidates went to Israel as an organized delegation. They consulted with the educational authorities in Israel for themselves and for the other names appearing on the list of educators seriously interested in Aliyah for the school year 1968-1969. Joseph Bruckenstein from

Washington D.C., Barry Chazan and myself, comprised the delegation to Israel on behalf of this group of educators, and for ourselves. This pilot visit took place during the period between December 24th, 1967, and January 2nd, 1968. Ambassador Harman took it upon himself to contact the Minister of Education, Zalman Arranne, who in turn alerted the Director General of the Ministry, Yaakov Sarid, about the scheduled delegation. He was asked to set up meetings with other department heads of the Ministry of Education and Culture.

The program and schedule of our visit were well planned. We met several of the key department heads of the Ministry of Education and Culture collectively and individually. We also had time to contact other individuals and institutional representatives who expressed interest in meeting with us as potential employment candidates. We met and consulted with other veteran American Jewish educators who had emigrated earlier and held important educational positions. Some were encouraging, others were not.

On a more personal level, I presented myself as an educator interested in teacher education, curriculum development and the administration of an educational institution. By chance, during our meeting with the several Ministry of Education and Culture officials, one of the department heads, Yehoshua Yadlin, turned to Emanuel Yafeh, the Director of the Department for Teacher Education, and asked him about the Bet Hakerem Hebrew Teachers Seminary. He knew that the Department was then looking for a principal-director.

After the meeting, Yafeh invited me for some private discussions to explore the possibility of presenting me as a candidate for the Bet Hakerem vacancy. He explained the process by which the ministry would issue a tender for the position in February inviting local educators to apply. He agreed to submit my name as one of the candidates eligible to meet the requirements of the tender. Since I had not been guaranteed the position, I continued to meet with other potential employers on my list. This list had been prepared by Moshe Yakir. Meanwhile, Barry and Joseph met with other representatives from the universities and community centers in Israel.

Upon returning home, and after discussing the visit with our families, we were asked to meet with some of the other leaders involved in the Aliyah program from America. We reported that our pilot trip had been successful, but with too little time for all the meetings. Our recommendations stressed the importance of such pilot trips for professionals seeking employment in Israel and the need to extend the length of such visits from one to two weeks.

The Association of Americans and Canadians for Aliyah

Following our positive report to the Committee to Promote Western Aliyah, and in consultation with officials and staff involved with the Israel Aliyah Center in New York, it was decided to call a conference on Aliyah on January 21st, 1968, in New York. Potential Olim were invited to attend from throughout the United States and Canada, some representing themselves and others as delegates from hugei aliyah (Aliyah groups) that existed throughout the country. The conference, which was sponsored by the Committee to Promote Western Aliyah, was conducted in conjunction with the Israeli Embassy in Washington D.C., the Israeli Consulate in New York, and the Israel Aliyah Center of the Jewish Agency in New York.

Throughout our consultations and involvement with the Zionist establishment and its Aliyah offices, the committee was very specific about functioning as a separate and independent entity representing potential Olim and not part of any other existing establishment. This was important, since the committee, and any other formal organization to be established later on, would serve as the ombudsman for the individual or family groups needing assistance in dealing with all the established agencies and institutions.

The conference took place as scheduled. I served as the chairman for the program and also gave one of the reports presented by the three of us who comprised the delegation sent to Israel at the end of December. Ambassador Avraham Harman was the major speaker on the program. The formulating committee presented a proposal for establishing a permanent Aliyah organization that was to be independent of any of the existing agencies, movements and organizations. It was envisioned by the leadership to be a self-help group of potential Olim needing assistance in their important and personal decision to go on Aliyah. Membership was to "be restricted to those individuals in the United States and Canada who seriously plan to go on Aliyah within a period of three years maximum." The organizational plan was to be modeled after the Israeli organization known as the Association of Americans and

Canadians in Israel. The local group expected to develop special ties with that Israeli organization and to function as a kind of sister group in North America.

An Executive Committee was elected at that conference and I became its chairman. At our first meeting (held one week later on January 28th, 1968), the name recommended for the new organization was the Association of Americans and Canadians *for* Aliyah [italics mine]. During the months that followed, much effort was expended to recruit members, set up a well-organized and functioning office to help the membership and begin negotiations with the existing Zionist and American Jewish community establishments for recognition and financial assistance.

In a letter (dated March 25th, 1968) to Avraham Harman, who was then back in Israel, I reported on the progress we had made during the past two months. I was also pleased to inform him that I had been accepted as Director of the David Yellin Hebrew Teachers Seminary in Bet Hakerem. Emanuel Yafeh had cabled me the good news at the end of February. In the letter I reported that we had approximately 100 paid up members and a mailing list of about 600 people. We planned to publish a newsletter and to call for a first annual membership meeting-conference on aliyah to be held on May 19th, 1968, in New York City. We had received some financial assistance from the Rabbinical Assembly and a group called the American Friends of Israel.

There were lengthy and often difficult meetings held with the Zionist organizations and the representatives of the Jewish Agency in the United States. We wanted organizational recognition and assistance, but without any restricting conditions or official ties. We were convinced that this was necessary in advancing and protecting the interests of potential immigrants to Israel. In the meantime, the American Zionist Council (an official umbrella organization of the various Zionist groups in America) had been trying to organize an American Aliyah program of its own. The A.Z.C. had been goaded into taking some action as a result of the Jewish Agency meetings held in Jerusalem in December 1967. The pressure now was to change the image of the American Zionist movement and make Aliyah to Israel a major element in its program. They spoke of organizing a T'nuat HaMagshimim (self-realization for Aliyah) movement. They were not too satisfied with the new Association of Americans and Canadians for Aliyah (A.A.C.A.) program that we were developing, especially regarding the issue of independence.

In the minutes of the February 6th, 1968, meeting of the A.Z.C., it was reported as follows: "The efforts of this group [the A.A.C.A.], said Rabbi Kirshblum, created a dilemma for the Movement. On the one hand, it is recognized that as Zionists we must give all help to potential Olim, but that support for a Magshimim group outside the framework of the Movement would not enhance the image or status of the Movement." The issue of image or status for the "movement" and the American Zionist organizations seemed to have been more important to the leadership of these groups than encouraging a self-help group of potential Olim to provide more effective assistance in planning their Aliyah. Meanwhile, the A.A.C.A. retained its independent status and began working out of the home of the part-time director of the association, which served as its temporary office.

As things finally worked out, the First Annual T'nuat Aliyah Conference held on May 19th, 1968, was sponsored by the A.A.C.A. in conjunction with the American Zionist Council and the Jewish Agency's American Section. These latter groups were pacified somewhat by our use of the Hebrew name T'nuat Aliyah to indicate the nature of the group and its sponsors. More than 300 delegates from thirty-two communities attended the conference. By the end of the conference, some 426 people (which included husbands and wives) had become members of the A.A.C.A.

The program focused on problems of employment and housing and provided potential Olim with the opportunity to meet with invited consultants and resource people who could provide some answers to their many questions. The closing session, attended by more than 400 people, featured an address by Yitzhak Rabin, who was then serving as Israel's ambassador to the United States.

We had made a very promising beginning. However, since several of us who were prominent in organizing the A.A.C.A. were leaving shortly to settle in Israel, a problem of leadership continuity emerged. Bruckenstein, Chazan and Schanin, the founders of the group, turned over the leadership to new people with different experiences and perhaps other needs. Then, too, the problem of relationships with the Zionist establishment remained. We had continued to resist their involvement and controlling influences, despite the pressing need for adequate financial and other material support, such as office space and clerical services.

After several months of limping along and with the continuing problem of leaders making Aliyah, the new replacement leadership gradually succumbed to the pressures and became part of the establishment. Eventually, the A.A.C.A. lost its own identity and was absorbed by the Aliyah program offered by the Jewish Agency and the individual Zionist organizations. It then disbanded, while, at the same time, the number of Olim from the United States and Canada dwindled.

For me and my family, the A.A.C.A. experience and the efforts that preceded its organization, contributed a great deal to the realization of our dream to settle in Israel. I expect that many others who shared these experiences with me can say the same. We left for Israel on July 9th, 1968, sailing on the Queen Anna Maria, a Greek flag ship, and arrived in Haifa, Israel, on July 22nd, 1968. Our sons Jonathan and Hillel shared with Roslyn and myself a very delightful thirteen days of Atlantic Ocean and Mediterranean Sea travel. We stopped at the ports of Lisbon, Portugal; Milano, Italy; and Piraeus, Greece, en route to Haifa, Israel. David was to join us at the end of the summer after completing his work commitments at Camp Ramah.

There were some 160 new Olim to Israel aboard the ship, adults and children. This was the largest group of Western Olim to arrive together at the same time in Israel. The A.A.C.A. received much publicity and credit for this event and the Israeli welcome and press coverage were outstanding. My family and I were interviewed by the Jerusalem Post newspaper soon after our arrival in Jerusalem.

Our choice of ocean travel was a very wise and practical one. We had two weeks to recuperate from the excitement and pressures of leaving Forest Hills and the United States, and we were also provided with 200 cubic feet of free shipping space aboard the ship. The latter meant a considerable financial saving in transporting our many household possessions and library to Israel.

Our leaving for Israel was not a simple act for my parents to accept. Roslyn's father and mother had died earlier. As we waved goodbye from the ship to my parents, friends and relatives, I understood the heartache and feelings of

As new Olim in Jerusalem, Israel, 1968

sadness, and even guilt, that my parents experienced when they left Europe to emigrate to America some fifty years earlier. My father, in particular, left a mother and siblings behind. It was a strange feeling for us to pass the Statue of Liberty in the opposite direction from our one-time immigrant parents and sailing under the Verrazano Bridge linking Brooklyn with Staten Island, in order to leave the United States for settling in another land across the ocean.

One of my last written expressions about leaving Forest Hills for Israel appeared in the June 21st, 1968, issue of "The Message," the weekly bulletin of the Forest Hills Jewish Center. It was a short farewell statement entitled, 'We Came With a Vision — We Leave With A Vision.' It stated as follows:

> Sixteen years ago, my wife Roslyn and I crossed over from Brooklyn to Queens, together with our then two sons, David and Jonathan. We had come in search of fulfillment. Years before, in a similar Synagogue Center in Brooklyn, a vision was crystallized for us. We began to understand the meaning of our Jewishness. With understanding and maturity came commitment which transformed this vision into a cause to be served. We wanted to

share with others, especially young people, our happiness and our self-discovery in the meaningfulness of being Jewish.

Ours is a large and busy institution. We stand for many things and we witness much activity within the walls of our building. And often we discover that there is the problem of containing this great activity and relating it to the larger cause we serve. The synagogue and the school which helps young people discover its meaning, are the heart and kernel of our institution. For after all, this building of beautiful brick and stone is more than a monument to our ideas and affluence. It is the means toward the achievement of our larger goals. It serves us well in our efforts to pursue the cause of meaningful Jewish living and fulfillment. For me, the greatest challenge presented by my assignment in Forest Hills has been my need and desire to keep the vision which brought me here clear, bright and purposeful, for myself and for all those who were ready to accept my leadership.

I am grateful for these past sixteen years during which time I have been very happy in Forest Hills. We have been blessed with good health and with many friends. We have worked with wonderful, loyal and devoted colleagues. We have found understanding, response and support from many of you who were willing to share our vision and the commitment to fulfill it. We have grown as a family with the welcome addition of our son Hillel, whose Bar Mitzvah we recently celebrated. I am grateful beyond words for all of this.

Sixteen years ago we came here to serve a cause. Our experiences in Forest Hills have been rewarding and the vision has remained bright and become clearer. We are now ready to move on in search of greater fulfillment and service to the cause of our Jewishness, which we love and cherish. We join the return to the sources of our being and heritage, in the land of Israel. May God bless all of you with health, happiness and the fulfillment of your own good wishes.

Chapter 5

The David Yellin Teachers College (1968-1988)

We arrived in Israel on July 22nd, 1968. Our friends had already found us a rented apartment. It was sparsely furnished, enabling us to add our own belongings gradually to complement and supplement our living accommodations. The large lift we had shipped as part of our accompanying baggage did not arrive with us. It had been left behind on the dock because of lack of room aboard the Queen Anna Maria. It did arrive on a subsequent voyage of that ship. By then, we were sufficiently settled so as to be able to unload the lift and bring most of our possessions into the apartment. An outside balcony provided us with the needed storage space for the many items for which we could temporarily not find space.

Our pre-arrival decision was that Roslyn would be in charge of our absorption into our new society. She was not to work during the first year, so that she could concentrate on the many details involved in settling in. Her primary concern was dealing with those issues relating to our three sons' adjustments to living in Israel. There were many such things to deal with. I had to devote most of my time to settling into my new employment. I reported for work at the College (then called "Hebrew Teachers Seminary") toward the middle of August. My formal employment as Director or Dean began on September 1st, 1968 — the beginning of the new academic year.

First Steps

Since all the preparations at the Seminary for the new school year had been completed before my arrival, I accepted the earlier decisions and planning. I had much to learn about the institution, the field of teacher education and the educational system in Israel. My first task was to understand the way the existing administrative staff worked, as well as the faculty and the student body, and enable all of them to get to know me. In addition, I had to familiarize myself with the details involved in providing leadership for a school that was part of a governmental educational system. The Ministry of Education and Culture was closely involved in the functioning of the Seminary, administratively, financially and programmatically. It influenced and even controlled some aspects of institutional policy concerning the employment of personnel and teaching staff, the admission of new students, formulating the financial base of operations and providing operational funds and salaries.

By and large, I was well received by most of my new colleagues. Yet there were some who found it difficult to adjust to the fact that the new head of the institution was an outsider with ideas and experiences from America, and not a polished and proficient Hebrew speaker. This latter fact had significance for some of the veterans, especially since this Seminary in particular had a very distinguished history in the grand story of the early struggle to make Hebrew the main language of communication, culture and education of the Jewish State yet to be born. My American-accented Hebrew no doubt grated on the ears of some of the language purists.

The Ministry staff was particularly accepting, especially since the Director of the Department of Teacher Education, Emanuel Yafeh, had been personally involved in engaging me for the position. He was extremely helpful and supportive throughout the long period that he was head of teacher education at the Ministry. We shared a common commitment to academizing teacher education in Israel. It can truly be said that Emanuel Yafeh was the real architect of the development for turning teacher education in the country into an academic program with standards appropriate to awarding graduates a first academic degree. He was not only a colleague and supervisor; he was a real friend. We shared many common ideas and values concerning education, the Jewish people and the meaning of Jewishness. Our two families gradually became part of one extended family.

A Two-Year Seminary

As I began my work, I found the internal functional and operational structure of the Seminary difficult and problematic. The institution offered a two-year teacher education program leading to teacher certification. In the meantime, the few more advanced and developed seminaries in other parts of Israel had begun to offer a more prestigious three-year program which awarded a Senior Teacher Certificate to its graduates. The David Yellin school was still struggling with the Ministry for permission to offer such an advanced program.

The Teacher Education Department of the Ministry felt that the David Yellin program, the level of the student body, and the generally low academic status of the faculty did not warrant permission to offer such an advanced program. Then, too, the physical facilities of the school were very inadequate and below standard for a post-high school institution. The science laboratories and the library — two primary facilities needed in any institution of higher learning — were totally inadequate. In general, the maintenance level of the physical facilities and amenities were below even elementary school standards.

The building had open corridors with inadequate protection against rain and the cold winds of winter, no central heating facilities (kerosene stoves were in use), and totally inadequate toilet facilities. The main building had been constructed in 1927-1928. Some ten years later, two dormitory buildings had been completed and a second floor was added to the main building. Few physical improvements had been added to the facilities during the twenty years after the establishment of Israel. The property and its facilities were owned and managed by a public non-governmental body known as the Building Association, which had at its disposal a limited budget for maintenance and physical improvements. The existence of this Association was to provide me, later on, with the important opportunity to begin a process of campus reconstruction that was to go on for many years, and continue beyond my retirement.

I had to endure much physical discomfort from the cold winters and the hot summers during the first two years of my tenure. Consequently, my first initiative was to concentrate on improving the quality of life at the Seminary, not only out of personal considerations but also as part of my philosophy that the environment of a school greatly influences the attitudes, standards and values of the personnel and students. I am convinced that the surroundings offered by an institution affect the educational process and its results. I believe that it is the function of the teacher training institution to present the best in education. This includes the environmental setting in which the training takes place.

A first task I decided upon was completion of the installation of a central heating system which had been approved in principle by the Ministry even before my arrival. However, for the usual bureaucratic reasons, no budget had been allocated and no orders had been given at the Ministry to complete the job. I also began to concentrate on improving the sanitary conditions and facilities, largely with monies allocated by the Building Association of the Seminary, which was responsible for the physical upkeep of the buildings and campus.

The school continually suffered from an inadequate budget for maintenance and the lack of additional support from the Ministry or outside sources for major campus improvement and reconstruction. One of the problems in maintaining the facilities and attempting to improve them was putting an end to renting out facilities to the Jewish Agency during the summer months for use as dormitories and classrooms for teenagers who were brought to Israel from abroad. This practice, while a source of needed income, was one of the major causes for the continuing deterioration of the facilities, due to the lack of time needed to improve and repair them during the summer period when Seminary classes were not in session. The administration and the lay board of the Seminary — the Building Association — had justified this practice and accepted the situation because of the revenue produced.

The Mechina Pedagogic High School

Upon settling into the work as Director of the Seminary, I was confronted with a very strange and anomalous situation. It was completely unknown to me when I began work and certainly not described in the terms of my responsibilities. By virtue of my new position, I found myself as the sole head and responsible person in charge of a private four-year high school which had more students and faculty than the Seminary itself. During the 1968-1969 academic year, the Mechina High School had registered some 250 students, while the Seminary itself had a student body of only 176!

During this period, most high schools in Israel were considered to be private, non-governmental schools, supported by local municipal, national and international public bodies. The Ministry of Education provided supervision and required these schools to use an approved basic curriculum. But in this specific situation at the Seminary, I was expected to accept and receive the faculty and student body as recommended by the internal high school administration. The high school functioned as a self-contained school within the Seminary with its own administration. I was expected to be involved in overall issues and to approve policy recommendations. I was also the sole signatory of the salary checks for all employees of the high school, including the faculty. I found this latter situation strange and disconcerting. The budget was largely provided by the tuition of students, a Ministry allocation for instructional purposes, and whatever budgetary allowances the Building Association could provide.

Physically, the high school occupied more than half the classroom and office facilities available for use by the Seminary. A public elementary school belonging to the city and the Ministry, but located on Seminary property, also occupied a large section of the main building. This latter arrangement had been in effect since the early days when the Jewish National Fund, in the 1920's, allocated the land for the Seminary. This allocation had two requirements: (1) to provide the local community with space for an elementary school; and (2) to provide space for the community to organize a local synagogue on the premises. The Israeli army also continued to occupy some basement facilities that it had been using for assembly and storage purposes since the days before and during the War of Independence in 1948.

When I became aware of the implications of this situation with regard to my personal responsibilities and liabilities as the so-called "owner" of this private high school and other facilities, I sought legal advice. I was given to understand that the situation, as I feared, was neither acceptable nor advisable for me, since I would be personally and legally responsible for any and all eventualities that might develop. Fortunately, during this period when I sought this clarification, the attitude throughout the country concerning the continued existence of private high schools was in the process of change. The private schools were becoming public schools, sponsored and supported by the local municipal authorities, and were receiving financial assistance and supervision from the Ministry of Education and Culture.

After prolonged and sometimes difficult negotiations with the Jerusalem city authorities and the existing high school staff, who were rightly concerned with protecting and advancing their rights as employees of the Seminary, it was finally agreed to transfer the jurisdiction of the Mechina High School to the municipality and to relocate it elsewhere. The Mechina was to provide the foundation classes for a new high school being organized in the Katamon area, a bus ride away from the Bet Hakerem location. During the 1970-1971 school year, the negotiations were completed. The jurisdiction and responsibility were transferred to the Jerusalem municipality.

Historically, the original idea had been to provide a "Mechina" (preparatory class) for those Seminary candidates deemed suitable as future teachers but who lacked the full matriculation certificate usually required for admission. Gradually, the program became more than a high school completion program, and developed into a full four-year high school. The original assumption was that those students who successfully completed their eligibility for a matriculation certificate would enter a special army deferment program. This was available for promising students who could delay their military service until after completing the teacher education program. Upon graduation, they were expected to serve as teachers in border area schools which had difficulty in obtaining trained teachers.

In practice this theory did not work. An overwhelming number of the Mechina High School graduates preferred to begin their military service together with their classmates immediately upon completing high school and reaching eighteen years of age. Consequently, when I became aware of the realities of the situation, it became obvious to me that the existing full Mechina program had no justification to continue, particularly since it was occupying a large portion of available classroom space required for additional Seminary growth and development. Hence my positive response to the opportunity to transfer the Mechina Preparatory High School from my responsibility and to free space for the new programs I wanted to offer.

I was very pleased with this development, not only from the point of view of protecting me from personal legal responsibility and liability, but also since it coincided with my conception of the Seminary as a post-high school and an independent institution of higher academic learning. As an academic college, it would be able to provide a limited Mechina or pre-academic program for those promising post-high school students potentially eligible for admission, but who needed to complete certain educational requirements for acceptance.

The Early Childhood Center

The transfer of the Mechina High School out of the Seminary facilities provided the unusual and wonderful opportunity to develop an idea that had intrigued me for a long while. During all my years of educational preparation and my developing ideology and experience, I have been convinced of the significance of the early childhood years, pre-school, kindergarten and the early grades of the elementary school for the young child and his development into adulthood.

My work with the Forest Hills Jewish Center school reinforced my commitment to early childhood education. The work of the pre-school department there was outstanding, fruitful and rewarding. I continue to be convinced of the importance of continuity in education as children move from one developmental stage to another. In my experience, children who enter an early childhood facility are most often those who remain constant and interested in the larger educational program as it develops from one department (and level) to another. The learning and social skills acquired are impressive.

In the David Yellin Seminary setting, I set two important goals for myself. The first was to upgrade and establish the primacy of early childhood teacher training at the Seminary as a major, advanced and experimental teacher education program. In Israeli teacher education in the 1970's, and even into the 1980's, early childhood programs were considered to be secondary and the least significant of all teacher education programs offered. Most early childhood teachers in the field were not adequately prepared in subject matter background and training. During earlier years, the pre-school and kindergarten teachers were not even required to be high school graduates and holders of bagrut (matriculation) certificates. Their educational achievements were minimal.

Such professionals were at the lower end of the salary scale and had little status. That was in contradiction to my entire educational commitments and understanding. While early childhood professional training in Israel was considered of little import, subject matter teacher education programs — especially for the older child and adolescent — were considered crucial. They were the prestige programs for future teachers. This emphasis on subject matter reflected the elitist concepts put forward by the universities in Israel. They considered programs for doctoral candidates as the focus of academic achievement and those of the lower levels at the bottom of the ladder.

Coming as I did from a background of American university academic study and teacher education, theory and practice, such attitudes and ideas about early childhood education were strange and unacceptable to me. My basic concept of what constituted a properly prepared and trained teacher, whatever the level of the teaching specialization, has been that of a well-rounded cultural and academically trained teacher who is knowledgeable in educational theory and practice. Consequently, I took the position from the very beginning of my work at the David Yellin Seminary that early childhood teacher education had to be no less important than any other academic program.

My convictions remained that, as we turned the Seminary into an academic college, the early childhood program would have equal academic status. This was an attitude that was not easy to communicate to other educators, to the Ministry of Education teacher education department, and especially to subject matter teachers and specialists. However, it was readily approved, understood and actively supported by the Seminary faculty involved with the early childhood program.

The second goal I set was to establish some experimental model teaching programs on the premises for the various age levels of teacher education offered by the school. I wanted especially to develop an early childhood center which could achieve this goal. My institutional model was the renowned Bank Street College in New York City, which developed such a center as part of its teacher education program. Then, too, during this period of the late 1960's and early 1970's, the "Open School" concept pioneered in England began to filter into American and Israeli education. In this new educational development, the pre-school and the kindergarten groups became an integral part of the elementary school programs, often even in the same building or adjacent to it. This program attracted my attention and created a desire within me to try to provide opportunities to conduct a similar experiment.

The transfer in 1970-1971 of the Mechina Pedagogic High School to a new area, under the responsibility and supervision of the municipal educational authorities, enabled me to establish an Early Childhood Center. This consisted of four groups of children between the ages of four and seven who were assigned the space vacated by the Mechina. The Jerusalem municipal educational authorities approved and supported this idea. This was the first such center for early childhood education established in Israel as part of a teachers seminary. It was considered to be an innovative and model program in teacher education by many. Others viewed it with skepticism. The Center quickly became a desired place to visit for educators from all over the country. I was fortunate to find a good and responsive staff for the program.

A major personality then at the Seminary, Miriam Eden, understood the

The open classrooms in the College Early Childhood Center

importance of early childhood education and was an outstanding Teacher Trainer. She became a willing partner in this endeavor and shared with me the vision of upgrading the level of early childhood teacher education and establishing a model Center. We worked well together to improve the level of students and found additional faculty members who shared our ideas. All of this development in early childhood teacher education was coordinated with the establishment of the Early Childhood Center on the campus. The fulfillment of this vision was a highlight of my first accomplishments as Director of the Seminary. I am also pleased to acknowledge that the Center has continued to flourish at the College after my retirement.

The Early Childhood Center consisted of four classroom groups, a pre-school class for four-year-olds, a five-year-olds kindergarten, and the first and second grades of elementary school. These four groups functioned as one integrated unit, often with multi-age grouping, and later on with handicapped children in a mainstreaming program. The Center served as an observation area and a place for student teaching, and as an experimental and model demonstration program for visitors by appointment. Educators from all parts of Israel, teachers, principals and supervisors, came to observe. During the extensive period of campus reconstruction and new building, the primitive facilities available were gradually rebuilt and upgraded. We were then able to provide high-level, appropriate facilities for open classroom education and model programming.

The Board of Directors

During this period of legal consultations, change and internal development, I questioned the function and purposes of the Building Association. It became clear that a Board of Directors or Overseers needed to be developed, which would work alongside the administration. Such a body would govern the institution in non-academic matters and expand its responsibilities in areas of budget and finance. It seemed to me that this was the logical role for the future of the Building Association. Such an enlarged body would continue to be responsible for the land and property of the Seminary, but would also become involved in the functional operations of the school, especially in areas of budget.

Therefore, I proposed a program of greater involvement for the Association in the work of the Seminary. This would enable it to function as a Board of Directors for the four-year College to be developed out of the existing Seminary.

This program was accepted, and the Building Association became legally reorganized as the Board of Directors with wider duties and powers in the functional operations of the school. It was then able to play a major role in planning for the future. I was fortunate to have some excellent chairmen of this body with whom I was able to work well. During the years of my service with the Seminary-College I was privileged to work with four outstanding chairmen of the Board: Professor Ben Zion Dinur, Dr. Israel Mehlmann, Judge Elazar Halevi and Rehavam Amir. We were colleagues in every sense of the word and good friends, too.

70th Anniversary Celebration at the Knesset
Right to left: Dr. Schanin, Judge Halevi, Varda Halevi, Rehavam Amir

Presenting a Long-Range Plan

After a year of adjustment, study and reflection, I was ready to submit a first draft of a long-range plan which would project the Seminary into the 1970's and focus on the goal of having the school become a four-year academic institution, a full teachers college. This practice of preparing a written plan or program for the future was one that I adopted consistently throughout my professional career in the United States and Israel. I prepared written documents for staff and faculty, lay boards and all those involved in the institutions and programs for which I was responsible. I was thus able to formulate more clearly proposals for the future and have an approved written record to substantiate and clarify issues. The recipients were able to react and help me improve the quality and details of what was being recommended. I found from experience that this approach was effective and satisfactory to my colleagues, lay people and professionals alike.

On December 10th, 1969, I distributed the first statement of a long-range plan and program for turning the Seminary into an academic College of Education. It was quite comprehensive and detailed and appeared in Hebrew, as well as in English for friends of the Seminary living abroad. The basic premise was that the Seminary could not remain a two-year non-academic school; it had to become a four-year academic college of education in order to grow and to improve substantially the quality of the teacher preparation that these students aimed to achieve. This was the direction in which teacher education was heading in Israel. However, before going into some detail about the long-range plan and program that I presented, it is important to understand the role of the Hebrew University of Jerusalem in all past and future developments affecting the David Yellin school.

The Seminary is located in close proximity to the Hebrew University, an institution of national and international repute, where students receive a first academic degree after three years of study, and teacher certification generally after a fourth year. The new college to be developed would have to offer an equivalent four-year academic program in order to attract higher caliber students and faculty members with greater academic status. It had become clear to me that the status quo situation could not be maintained. To do so would cause further deterioration brought about by lack of status, vision and an

appropriate support system. The latter had to be provided by the Ministry of
Education, the Board of Directors and friends of the Seminary, both in Israel and
abroad.

Historically the Seminary had a long-standing relationship with the Hebrew
University, albeit tenuous in nature. During the pre-state period there was no
formal relationship between the two institutions. The primary contact was on a
faculty level. The Seminary absorbed many fine teachers and scholars who
arrived from the distressed European Jewish communities during the pre-World
War II period. For many of these outstanding personalities, the teaching
positions at the Seminary were a stepping-stone toward eventually becoming
part of the University faculty.

David Yellin, and especially his associate Ben Zion Dinur, had personal
relationships with faculty members of the University. Dinur eventually became
a renowned University professor. He conducted many discussions with officials
in the administration concerning the possibilities of developing some type of
working relationship between the two institutions. In 1935, the project of
organizing a University-sponsored high school was made jointly between the
two, with the projected new high school to be located on the campus of the
Seminary.

The problematic relationship existing between the Seminary and its
neighbor, the Hebrew University, continued to play an important part in the
Seminary's struggle to become a recognized academic teachers college. The
Hebrew University was founded and continues to function to this date primarily
as a research oriented institution staffed by scholars. The role of teaching
remains secondary for most of the senior members of the faculty.

During its early years, the University at first offered only a doctorate degree
and post-doctoral studies to qualified graduates, and research facilities for
others. It was only later on, in the 1930's, that the University accepted students
for a five-year program of subject matter specialization leading to the Master of
Arts degree. During the post-World War II years, the demand developed for a
variety of public officials with an academic degree. The University responded to
this need and organized, for the first time, in 1949, a program for undergraduate
studies leading to a Bachelor of Arts degree.

My very good friend and mentor, Dr. Alexander M. Dushkin, was invited to come to Israel to head this program. The first B.A. degrees were awarded in 1952. This development opened the way for establishing a School of Education at the University which offered a program of teacher education, primarily for high school teachers. The graduates were awarded a B.A. degree signifying specialization in subject matter, along with their teaching certification.

During this period of change in the University's direction, Prof. Ben Zion Dinur became the Minister of Education in Ben Gurion's government in 1951. Dinur continued his very close relationship with the Bet Hakerem Hebrew Teachers Seminary while maintaining a role in the University. He was committed to the idea of turning the Seminary into an academic institution as part of the University, or at least in conjunction with it. One of his first undertakings as Minister of Education was to follow through with this idea. After much deliberation and many objections from both sides, a program was adopted whereby the David Yellin Teachers Seminary became part of the University's new School of Education as its department for training elementary school teachers.[1] This joint program was conducted between 1952 and 1956.

From the very beginning, this venture was plagued with many problems resulting from inadequate preparation, the inability of representatives of both institutions to agree on the academic degree to be awarded the graduates (B.A. or B.Ed.), personality clashes and the senior university faculty's generally negative attitude to the idea of expanding the scope of academic degrees in the field of teacher education. In general, the University professional personnel looked down upon the Seminary since it was not a recognized academic institution. To compound the problems, there was a lack of significant response by student candidates at the University to study for a first academic degree in elementary school teaching, especially since the degree was not required then for teaching certification in Israel. Students interested in elementary school teaching could complete a two-year seminary program anywhere in the country and still receive certification and employment.

This experimental program was discontinued in 1956. The Seminary

---

1. For a more detailed report and analysis about this development in the history of the Seminary and the University, read chapters two and three in my book written in collaboration with Hillel Agranat, *The Academic Development of Teacher Education in Israel*, The Magnes Press, Jerusalem, 1996.

returned to its former status as a two-year teacher training school and continued to be part of the Ministry of Education's teacher education system. From a long-term point of view, this unsuccessful experience in establishing working relationships between the David Yellin Hebrew Teachers Seminary and the Hebrew University negatively influenced the interest of the University in participating in the process of raising the level of the Seminary to that of a teachers college.

The Drive Toward Academization — From Seminary to College

It became clear to me, after my initial adjustment and integration into the life and program of the Seminary, that a plan for the future was needed. There would have to be a major reorganization, change and rejuvenation of the existing situation. Such a plan would have to include the physical reconstruction of the Bet Hakerem campus as well. I was prepared to dedicate myself to and provide the necessary leadership for whatever had to be done. I had to convince my co-workers, on all levels, professional and lay, that my suggested direction was correct and very much needed. I knew from what I had learnt from previous experiences of the dynamics of organized groups (of organizations in general and educational institutions in particular), that they had to progress on a continuous growth basis, or face decline and disintegration. These thoughts have been an integral part of my personal and professional approach in working with educational and other public institutions.

In the 1969 long-range projection for transforming the David Yellin school from a two-year Seminary into a four-year College, I proposed major changes in the balance between academic studies, educational theory and practice, and skill training. I understood the need for a teacher education and training program that would be developmental and sequential in nature. Then, too, I advocated changing the emphasis from frontal class teaching of subject matter, to focusing on the student as an individual learner. This shift in approach and emphasis resulted from the challenges presented by the information explosion currently available to all those who were motivated and prepared to deal with it.

I envisioned the Seminary and the College as the center of an educational complex in Bet Hakerem. It would function as a Jerusalem center for teacher education, pre-service and in-service, for a united Jerusalem. The complex concept meant making available in one physical area (Bet Hakerem) all the educational teaching levels and specializations necessary for observation, demonstration, experimentation and practice teaching. It called for developing learning-teaching centers at the various school levels, such as early childhood, elementary and junior high school, and the inter-relationships between them. The plan aimed to focus on specialized areas such as special education, subject matter concentration (in the Hebrew language, social studies, Judaica, mathematics, science, foreign languages, English and Arabic), and the teaching of the arts. Educationally it included working with the complete family of the learner, involving the parents, the various siblings and any others in the nuclear family.

The concept of serving as a Jerusalem center necessitated including the needs of the Arab population of Jerusalem. It also called for dealing with the special problems of integration presented by the various ethnic Jewish communities of Jerusalem. In the post-Yom Kippur War period, this concept of offering teacher education programs for the Arab communities in and around Jerusalem met a real need, as expressed by the Jerusalem municipal authorities and the Ministry of Education and Culture. It suddenly became clear that most Arab teachers in Israel had received their teacher education in countries and institutions which were markedly anti-Israel or non-receptive to the idea of the Jewish state.

All of these ideas, concepts and programs required a major change in the selection of personnel and called for a reclassification of existing personnel, faculty and administration. This was a tall order but one that I felt was essential to ensure the Seminary's becaming a four-year academic College of Education. This was the long-term program I projected for the 1970's (and which extended into the 1980's). It formed the basis of all my work and direction as head of the institution. I was most fortunate to receive full support for this program from the Ministry, and internally from the Board of Directors, a goodly portion of the existing faculty and the administrative personnel. But it remained a long and arduous task to get things moving in the directions I recommended.

Happily, most of my hopes and aspirations for the new direction and program, were, in the main, implemented. It took me twenty years to accomplish many of the goals I set for myself and the College. I retired in 1988 with a sense of fulfillment, contentment and satisfaction. In presenting these thoughts, and words, I have had the pleasure of reliving a major period in my personal and professional life.

As indicated above, a first important step was the effort to turn the Seminary from a two-year into a three-year school. This required upgrading the selection of students and strengthening the academic credentials of the teaching faculty. My determination to include kindergarten and early childhood education in a three-year training program was initially thwarted by the different departmental representatives of the Ministry of Education, who still felt kindergartners did not need the same level of education as elementary school teachers. This policy of the Ministry was also influenced by the shortage of teachers available for kindergartens and the early grades. The Ministry functions to this day with separate departments for kindergarten and the early grades of the elementary school. There still exists the practice of providing kindergarten facilities away from the physical proximity to the elementary school.

In the early 1970's, we succeeded in exacting permission from the Ministry to offer the option of a two-year kindergarten teacher education program and a three-year early childhood program that would include training for kindergartners and teachers of first and second grades. When we were able to prove later on that the numbers of students for the combined early childhood program was greater and of a higher level than those applying for the two-year option, the Ministry finally authorized our eliminating the two-year option in favor of only a three-year program. We were one of the first teacher education institutions in Israel to offer only a three-year program for kindergarten and early childhood teachers. This innovation eventually became the norm for all teacher education schools in Israel associated with the Ministry of Education and Culture.

Upon completing the process of instituting a three-year Seminary in 1973, I embarked on the major task of turning the institution into a four-year academic College of Education. As an important first step in this direction, I invited a committee of outstanding subject matter professors from the Hebrew

University and Bar Ilan University to function as a voluntary advisory committee to help us reconstruct and reorganize the contents of the teaching program. It was obvious to all that the problem of the academization of teacher education in Israel centered around convincing the Council for Higher Education (the body responsible for granting accreditation for institutions requesting academic status) to approve the academic level of subject matter teaching in the institution requesting accreditation. Since membership in that Council consisted mainly of senior university faculty representatives, it was clear that the basis for evaluating academic qualifications would be that of university standards. Hence the need for the internal committee that I assembled.

Most of the members of this internal committee were outstanding university faculty personalities. They were also intrigued by the challenge of helping this historically prestigious Seminary to become a recognized academic College. The original members of this committee of professors were Binyamin Frankel (Physics), Moshe Greenberg (Bible), Abraham Halkin (History), Uzi Ornan (Hebrew language), and Alice Shalvi (English literature). I am much indebted to them for their pioneering efforts on behalf of the academic development of the College that emerged.

As a result of the work of the Internal Academic Committee of University Professors, we were able to receive valuable assistance in creating a new academic model. Gradually, we began the process of changing the program and organizational structure of the Seminary. During the many years that preceded these academic developments, the Seminary had functioned on a post-high school basis.

Many of the students complained that the environment in the school was not very different from that experienced in high school. Individual students were organized into classes that were limited only to those who chose a specific level of teacher education, such as kindergarten, early childhood, elementary school and junior high school. Students in each specialization followed a self-contained pre-arranged program as a group. There was no interaction with other students majoring in different levels of school teaching. Each level had its own subject matter classes in Bible, language, history, Judaism, mathematics, science, etc. The earlier theory was that subject matter should be taught while keeping in mind the content and methodology to be used in teaching a specific subject to a given age level. This practice led to the justifiable criticism that the level of subject matter teaching in the seminaries was far below the level of acceptable academic learning. Consequently we decided to reorganize radically the structure and curriculum.

The concept of pre-arranged classes for students was eliminated and, instead, each student organized his or her own program within the limitations of the teaching level selected. Each program level had its foundational requirements, but the study of subject matter was raised to a more uniform academic level. For example, students could now gain a more fundamental academic knowledge of the subject matter, rather than being limited to the level of the teaching required within the framework of the curriculum to be taught. The subject matter areas were organized into departments, each with an academic head of some distinction, who was expected to plan and supervise the development of the subject area to be presented. The methodology of subject matter teaching was of course separate, specific, and geared to the needs of teachers of specific levels of children.

This revolutionary change in the organization and structure of the curriculum of the Seminary required a massive effort for change and implementation. I was very fortunate to have the able assistance of one of the teacher-trainers, Esther Mishael, who accepted and met the challenge of reorganizing our curriculum structure and schedule so as to enable the above program to come to fruition. After one or two years of trial and error, we arrived at a very satisfactory organizational structure, justifying our claims for becoming an academic college. Esther Mishael remained at my side as Assistant Director during the many years of our institutional struggle to become an accredited academic college with the right to award a first degree and teaching certification to our graduates.

The Yom Kippur War

The Yom Kippur War of 1973 broke out on a Shabbat. From the next day, schools were closed for a period of time. Few persons knew the extent of the invasions by Egypt and Syria. There was no news about the welfare of husbands, sons and daughters in the army, or friends who were called up as reservists. Roslyn and I did not know the whereabouts of our sons, Jonathan and Hillel. At that time David was completing his university studies in the United States and beginning to develop his career plans. Jonathan had been on his first tour of reserve duty in the army when the war erupted, and Hillel, who had been home on leave for Yom Kippur, had returned to his base an hour after the fighting began. Hillel was then in the midst of completing his basic training as a recent recruit. He had been scheduled to read the Torah for the Maariv service, but left earlier, trying to hitch a ride back to his base near Hadera. I read the Torah in his place; I could hardly hold back the tears as I did so. It was a fearful and terrible moment for me personally and for all those brave souls who returned to the synagogue for Minhah and Neilah.

The next day, Sunday, normally a regular work day, was incredibly difficult for all in Israel as we waited for some words about our loved ones and the news of events on the various fighting fronts. I returned to the College to see what had to be done there, and to try to occupy my time during the difficult waiting period. The shock and confusion felt by all in Israel were of course shared by the few staff members and workers who had the courage and the need to report for duty. Most of our students were young women, and only a few of them in essential reserve duty assignments were called up. The younger male staff members were immediately drafted by the army; others waited for the call-up signals broadcast repeatedly on the radio. The College dormitories were largely deserted, as most students either went home or were in the army.

Schools gradually reopened when the physical safety of the children, students and teachers was assured. We at the College began to reassemble many of the faculty, staff and students whom we had sent out to the local elementary and junior high schools, where they could serve as teacher replacements and helpers when needed. The College faculty and students contributed greatly to the morale of the children and functioning teachers. By the end of November, following the cease-fire agreements, the faculty, staff and students were able to regroup, reorganize and create a functioning program at the College.

The war itself, and the part played by faculty, staff and students in this and other colleges and universities in maintaining some sense of sanity and morale for others in the school system is a tale that has yet to be fully told. During the war, some of our College facilities were conscripted for army use as an assembly point for much of the Jerusalem area. The contributions made by the College faculty, staff and students during the Yom Kippur War, and later on in the Lebanon War, provide additional chapters in the rich history of the David Yellin Teachers College which has continuously served Israel in pre-State days and then an independent Israel during times of peace and war.

The Hebrew University

I will now continue the report of the drive toward academization and the required changes which took place in the Seminary organization and structure. While all these changes at the College were occurring, the Ministry of Education and Culture played an important role largely through the efforts of Emanuel Yafeh, the Director of the Teacher Education Department in the Ministry. Yafeh, together with the several former Ministers of Education who served as chairmen of the Council for Higher Education during this period, Yigal Alon, Aharon Yadlin and Zevulun Hammer, provided much of the national leadership needed to advance the academization of teacher education in Israel. It remained clear to all, that in Jerusalem, the academization of our Seminary could not occur without the active involvement and subsequent approval of the Hebrew University of Jerusalem. Due to Ministry pressures, the University decided to become more actively involved in the academic development of the Seminary. During the 1970's and 1980's, the University appointed more than a half-dozen committees to deal with the larger questions and the specific problems of implementation at the David Yellin Teachers Seminary/College. These questions had been defined by the Council for Higher Education and then interpreted by the University.

The first three University committees to deal with the academization of the Seminary were known by the name of its chairman, the Lam Committees. Prof. Lam was a graduate of the Seminary, in the early 1960's became its acting head for a short period, and then joined the faculty of the School of Education of the Hebrew University. Throughout all the years, he remained an active friend and participant in the academic development of the Seminary, later the College. The first Lam Committee met in 1969 to discuss the nature of the pending relationships between the University and the Seminary, but without any conclusion. The second Lam Committee began in 1973 and worked closely with the administration and faculty. By 1975 it was prepared to recommend through the University to the Council for Higher Education, that the Seminary be granted temporary permission to call itself a College and register students for a first academic degree. However, this recommendation was limited then to only the Seminary junior high school teacher education program.

The Council accepted this recommendation and on November 11, 1975, the Seminary received approval to call itself a College. It was permitted to announce a program leading to a Bachelor of Education (B.Ed.) degree only for students majoring in junior high school teacher education. Shortly thereafter, the Seminary received approval from the Ministry of Education and Culture to change its name formally from the David Yellin Hebrew Teachers Seminary to that of the David Yellin Teachers College. This College, together with an orthodox religious seminary in Bayit V'gan which only offered a junior high school teacher education program, became the first two teacher seminaries to be recognized as academic institutions by the Council for Higher Education.

I must admit that I hardly expected our work to advance so quickly toward even such a partial academic recognition. For me, this was a personal victory in the long battle that still remained ahead in our drive to receive full academic recognition for all our teacher education programs. Upon our receiving Council approval, a third Lam Committee was appointed on May 5th, 1976. Its function was to serve as an accompanying supervisory committee until the time when the Council was expected to grant full academic recognition to this junior high school program.

From the beginning of this stage, it became apparent that the Hebrew University would have to continue to remain active in the academic development of the College. Such involvement was expected to assist the College in achieving higher academic standards. It would also grant the University the right of approval in all areas that affected it, so that it would be able to protect its own interests. Consequently, when on June 27th, 1979, the Council granted full academic recognition to the junior high school teacher education program, it added the proviso that this recognition was granted under the auspices of the Hebrew University. Though I was somewhat disappointed by

Minister of Education Zevulun Hammer presents certificate
of academic recognition, 1979

this condition, this final academic recognition was greeted with great enthusiasm as a first step toward full academic recognition for all the programs offered by the College.

The complicated and difficult process of completing the academization of the David Yellin Teachers College took another nine years, beginning June 27th, 1979. The College finally received permission to award the B.Ed. degree to graduates of its early childhood and elementary teacher education programs (including special education) on May 27th, 1987. To say that the process was difficult is almost an understatement; it was also very tiring and at times discouraging. But we persisted. In the end, we were able to close the circle of development from a two-year Seminary to a four-year academic College. It was a glorious feeling of satisfaction for me, that finally the dream of so many who had labored hard in the course of the seventy-five years since its establishment by David Yellin, had come to fruition.

After the College received this first recognition in 1979 as an academic institution of higher learning under the auspices of the Hebrew University, a new accompanying or supervisory committee was appointed by the University. The committee was to be identified by the name of its chairman — the Yaakov Zussman Committee. It functioned as an advisory body and followed up on all developments in the College junior high school education program. This committee also worked with the College administration in developing an academic model that could be presented to the Council for Higher Education for the early childhood, elementary school and special education programs offered by the College.

By 1982, the new academic models were ready to be presented to the Permanent Committee for Academic Programs in the Teachers Colleges (the Dan Committee), as a sub-committee of the Council for Higher Education, for approval and recommendation to the Council. Meanwhile, the Zussman Committee was preparing to recommend also the removal of the "under the auspices" provision required of the University to grant recognition status to the College for its junior high school program.

By way of explanation, it should be pointed out here that the cumbersome process of receiving academic recognition from the Council for Higher Education, was indeed a very slow one. It usually required one to four years for an institution or program to receive final approval. The process included three major steps: Firstly, applications to the Council were examined by a special investigating sub-committee of the Permanent Committee. This dealt with matters pertaining to the teacher colleges. If the examination was favorable, it was then recommended for temporary approval by the Council. Next, an Accompanying Committee was appointed to serve as an advisory and supervisory body to monitor developments toward final approval. Finally, upon recommendations from the Accompanying Committee, the full Council considered the matter and voted for extending full academic recognition, or not.

The Accompanying Committee usually consisted of several members from the Council who were key faculty members of the university located in the area in which the college was situated. All the universities in Israel were well represented on the Council by senior faculty members. If the application pertained to specific academic specialties, then a senior university faculty member, working in the field of such specialization, could be invited to serve as a member of that committee, together with a representative from the Teacher Education Department of the Ministry of Education and Culture.

The new general academic model developed by the College for early childhood education, elementary school and special education, was submitted to the Permanent Committee in 1982. Subsequently, the Leah Adar Investigating Sub-Committee was established to determine its worthiness for academic recognition. Within a year, the Adar Sub-Committee submitted a positive recommendation to the Council and requested temporary academic approval for the above programs of the College. This was another major step forward in achieving the full academization of the College. The Council approved and established an Accompanying Committee to be chaired by one of the members of the Investigating Sub-Committee, Professor Itamar Greenwald. At the same meeting, the Council approved the recommendation of the Zussman Committee to remove the Hebrew University auspices provision from the academic recognition extended to the College for its junior high school teacher education program. These two decisions were essential to completing the process whereby the College could offer its own academic degree to all its four-year graduates.

The Greenwald Accompanying Committee proved to be the most difficult of all the several committees that the College administration had to deal with following its first steps toward academization in the 1970's. There were different attitudes that often needed accommodation and reconciliation. This last Committee expressed many ideas that, in the opinion of the College leadership, were more suitable for a university setting than a teachers college program. Then, too, there were some personality clashes which unfortunately marred the smooth flow of communication and developments. However, by the winter of 1987, some four years after the Committee began to function, the last rocky hurdle was overcome and the Accompanying Committee made a positive recommendation to the Council for Higher Education. It advised awarding final academic recognition to the early childhood, elementary school and special education programs offered by the College. The approval was issued on May 27, 1987.

We had come full circle. The academization process of becoming a full four-year academic College was now complete. The long-term program I had first presented to the faculty, the Board of Directors and the Ministry of Education and Culture in 1969, came to fruition on that spring day in 1987. The elation shared by so many colleagues, friends and generations of graduates of the Seminary/College was an experience which will always be remembered by them. It was shared with those involved in the successful completion of the academization process. Emotionally and physically, I was now ready to accept the fact of retirement in 1988, as required by the Ministry after reaching the age of sixty-five.

Innovative Programs

During the twenty years that I served as Director of the David Yellin Teachers College, there were several innovative programs introduced which reflected my educational theories and commitments. From the very beginning of my tenure, there was never any wavering from the basic conviction that teacher education has to be an academic process and must include a methodological approach to working with people. Therefore, it was unacceptable to me that a teacher education institution could be anything less than an academic institution. Similarly, I had ideas and strong convictions about the nature of early childhood education which differed from the locally accepted concepts.

I remain firm in my belief that the period of early childhood, from pre-natal to the beginning of the formal school years, is very crucial to the child's intellectual and social development. Everyone is in general agreement about the significance of this period for the child's motor development, for his character and moral behavioral formation. In Israel there existed an artificial — and to my way of thinking — erroneous conception about the role and subsequent training of nursery and kindergarten personnel. They were not considered "teachers" and consequently were not required to have any formal educational background beyond secondary school levels. They were most often required to complete only one or two years of seminary training in order to receive an appropriate certificate. In some areas of the country even less training and no certificate were required.

Nursery and kindergarten training during this period emphasized the role of personnel working with the very young as caregivers and practitioners. They were expected to possess a warm and motherly type personality. They were taught how to create a standard stimulating and motivational environment for young children, but not to engage in "teaching" of any specific subject matter. Nursery and pre-nursery seminary training were less structured, but did emphasize early childhood development and appropriate methodology.

As a result of my past experience and training, I was committed to the concept that the pre-school period is crucial to the cognitive, emotional, and motor development of the young child. This is the period when the child becomes a thinking, feeling and behaving personality, with learned controls, skills and values. These were expected to guide him throughout life, first as a child, and then, later on, as he or she becomes a teenager and adult. Consequently, the intellectual and educational training of the person who is to teach children, teenagers and adults needs to be on an academic level to promote understanding, knowledge and appropriate methodological training.

Fortunately, the College faculty in the Early Education Department had similar convictions. They readily responded, with much enthusiasm, to the leadership I was prepared to offer in this field. For most, the fact that I was a male, the head of the institution, and committed to ideas they shared about early childhood teacher education, came as a surprise and welcome revelation. This led to the development of very positive working relationships and the mutual encouragement to fight for the fulfillment of these ideas. The general educational system, including the Ministry of Education departments and the officials involved, accepted and even formalized the difference between "teachers," "kindergartners" and "pre-school personnel." The Ministry sources involved were not immediately responsive, and sometimes even antagonistic to the position we stated.

It was interesting to note that even the Teachers Union accepted the difference between "teachers" and "kindergartners," who consequently received less pay. The Teachers Union did not offer any program at this point in time, while acknowledging the need for improving the working rights of pre-school personnel as teachers. It even supported the Ministry position. These workers by and large, unfortunately accepted their status as secondary personnel with a lower salary scale.

Developing New Models

One of our major tasks during the many years of struggling to gain academic recognition, was the need to develop teacher education models, especially for early childhood and elementary school programs. These, of course, would have to meet the requirements of the academic world as represented by the Council for Higher Education. Our College education program was geared specifically to educating and training teachers for the general school system of Israel. The academic models developed would thus have to reflect the needs and wants of the teachers in the field. We developed a basic model, incorporating many innovative and original ideas, and served as sources of information for other teacher education seminaries seeking academic status. Over the years, the model was adjusted in accordance with our growing experience while working with it.

There were four interrelated elements to the model. These are to be viewed as a whole. The first consisted of foundation courses in mathematics, Hebrew language, English, science and geography. These were offered to all the students as a general cultural basis for functioning as a teacher educator. The second was a series of basic introductory courses in Judaic studies and the required courses offered by the various subject-matter majors. Students were free to choose these as part of their specialization. The third element was the individual choice of one or more subject-matter areas for specialization, such as Bible, Hebrew language and literature, history, science and mathematics.

The number of areas of specialization, as well as of related courses to be chosen by students, was determined by the school level the student was preparing to serve as a teacher (junior high school, or elementary school, or early childhood as a teacher of kindergarten and/or first and second grades of the elementary school). The fourth and final element in the model dealt with educational courses in psychology, pedagogy and methodology, and actual practice-teaching under supervision within the school system.

Special Education is a popular field of specialization in Israel, chosen by many students with high motivation and ability to work with children with learning disabilities of various kinds. Over the years, this field of teacher education became a major one offered by the College. In fact, the high level of specialization was acknowledged by the Psychology Department of the Hebrew University, which turned to the College for assistance in training its special education teachers. Then, too, many university graduates who studied psychology, sociology and related areas of specialization, turned to the College for retraining as teachers in special education. Such students were awarded teaching certification, usually upon completion of a two-year program.

The College opened a very unusual and unique program in special education during the academic year of 1970-1971. This was initially known as the Institute for Remedial Education for children with cognitive limitations. The Institute was established with the encouragement and assistance of the President of Israel, Zalman Shazar, and his wife Rachel. They had a personal family interest

Meeting with President Zalman Shazar about the Institute for Remedial Education, 1972
Left to right: Rina Biran, President Shazar, Dr. Schanin, Dr. Sue Zohar Desheh, Sybil Kaufman

in, and relationship to, the subject of remedial education. In 1973 the Institute was named in memory of Rachel Shazar.

As the program for special education continued to develop at the College, it received national recognition. The Institute grew into a kind of post B.A.-B.Ed. graduate program dealing with a wide spectrum of learning disabilities. Meanwhile, the College continued to offer several different specializations in the field of special education on an undergraduate level. The Department of Special Education and the Rachel Shazar Institute became jewels in the crown of achievements and development at the College during this period of academization. A very capable and highly dedicated staff was assembled and led by Miriam Dayan, an unusually gifted special education expert.

One of the results of the Yom Kippur War in 1973 was a review by the Ministry of Education of the situation within the Arab school system in Israel. It had become apparent that there was a great need to prepare, train and offer in-service programs for Arab teachers for the schools in the Arab sectors of Israel. Most Arab teachers in the field were trained in Arab colleges and universities not friendly to Israel. Consequently, the children and students in the government-sponsored Arab school system were often being educated by teachers with negative attitudes about the country. They lacked both accurate knowledge and positive information about Israel and the Jewish people. This situation was especially true for Jerusalem, which had become a united city after the Six-Day War.

The Mayor of Jerusalem, Teddy Kollek, together with officials in the Ministry of Education, began to seek solutions for the problem as it existed in 1973. In the long-term program I presented in December 1969 for the planned College, projecting a program of development and growth for the decade of the seventies, I wrote of the College becoming a Jerusalem center of education and teacher training for all of the residents of the city, including specifically those in the Arab sectors. Thus I expressed to Mayor Kollek and the Department of Teacher Education of the Ministry our readiness at the College to offer a training program for Arab students and Arab teachers. It would be available for those prepared and ready to study at a Jewish institution for teacher education and retraining.

Our offer was accepted, and we became one of the first specifically *Jewish*

Arab students are part of the College teacher education programs

institution of higher learning in Israel to organize such a program. Over the years, the difficult issues of offering such a program in a mixed environment, which was subject to political pressures from both sides, were gradually overcome. I am happy to report that eventually many of the Arab students were able to join their Jewish counterparts in studying some courses offered in Hebrew. However, the basic and foundation courses dealing with Arab culture, religion and traditions were studied in Arabic — the primary language of the schools they would teach in. During more recent years, qualified Arab students have been able to enter the regular academic degree program offered by the College.

Jewish Identity and Judaic Studies

It was some time before I began to understand the tensions and lack of knowledge and understanding on the issue of Jewish identity. This was a period when most students and teachers viewed themselves primarily as "Israelis." The few Judaic courses taught at the College were very basic, usually a repeat of what students had studied during their elementary, junior high and high school years. They were often received without any interest, enthusiasm or success. The faculty members who taught these courses were usually Orthodox in religious orientation, and there was little real communication between them and the students on issues involving the Jewish identity of the Sabra generation.

Obviously, from my past experience and continuing personal ideology, this was an area of the College program which was of great concern to me, and so I felt a strong need to deal with it. It became clear to me that my religious background and specifically Jewish commitments found little enthusiastic expression at the College. This was a situation which I had strong desires to change. As a first step, I tried to suggest the introduction of a broader range of courses in Judaica. I also understood the need to find new and additional staff with a more open Judaic orientation to join the faculty.

During the seventies, increasing numbers of Conservative and Reform rabbis arrived in Israel as new Olim or as temporary residents for one or two years. There were also those who arrived on Sabbatical leave from Jewish teaching institutions abroad. I turned to this group when I was seeking part-time faculty. For a while, I suddenly found myself the object of contact for many new Olim seeking employment, especially Conservative and Reform rabbis. I was able to employ those most qualified as teachers, and they were an important source of upgrading the level and successes of the newly expanded Judaic program. From a long-term viewpoint, I hoped to develop a department which would offer a major in Judaic studies, including Jewish history. However, over the years, the obstacle remained of being unable to attract sufficient numbers of interested students for such a track.

To create a vehicle for intensifying the Jewish and Judaic studies and environment at the College, I discussed the issues with the faculty and Board of Directors. I succeeded in convincing them of the need for a special supplementary project to be known as the Institute for Judaic Studies. This was to deal with the issues involved in establishing and strengthening the Jewish identity of the Jewish students and to deepen their knowledge and understanding of Judaic sources. As a first step, an ongoing longitudinal research project was developed to evaluate the meaning and strength of the Jewish identity of entering freshmen students. The results were then measured to note the changes in their identity, if any, after three or four years of study at the College. The early results were not too encouraging, with some exceptions. Unfortunately, this project was not continued after my retirement.

One of the themes later developed as part of the overall project of the Institute was how to strengthen Arab-Jewish relationships. This was related to the question of clarifying the meaning of an Israeli identity with regard to the co-existence in a State which defined itself as being Jewish, of Jews and Arabs. As well as the above programs, the Institute conducted lectures, study days and conferences, tours and trips to places with Judaic, historical and Zionist significance. There was also a one-time attempt to organize a Sabbath Retreat away from the city. The latter was an interesting experience but enjoyed limited success. The logistics were difficult, the financial costs high, and there was a general lack of enthusiasm for the subject, particularly in view of the fact that it was a Sabbath activity taking place in the free time of students and faculty. Consequently, the Shabbat Retreat was not repeated.

To my great disappointment, I can only report limited accomplishments for future teachers in the areas of Jewish identity and Judaic studies. I was unable to give enough time and energy to dealing with these problems. Other faculty members did not take on these challenges in the way I would have hoped. The general attitude in Israel on these issues was, and continues to be, not very positive and often even negative. The problems of Jewish religious pluralism and the meanings of the Jewish identity, especially for Jewish teachers and students in Israel, are very real. They have become more charged as national and political issues as the years go by. Despite many attempts on the part of the Ministry of Education and Culture to deal with the questions involved, no real progress can yet be measured. The political divisions of the country and the conflict over religion and state issues in Israel, especially in those areas of the controls exercised by the Orthodox establishment on personal, religious and social issues, have yet to be resolved.

Campus Development

As indicated earlier, the physical condition of the campus and its facilities in 1968 was unacceptable to me as the proper environment for a teacher education institution. I thus made this the place where I chose to begin my work as head of the school. Curriculum issues, faculty relationships and recruitment, and student selection, were matters requiring long-term change and development.

The new image of the Seminary, which was to become a College in the future, required a supportive and facilitating environment. In the long-term plan I presented in December 1969, the first blueprint for change and development was submitted. The emphasis was on upgrading the facilities and equipment necessary for the functioning of an institution of higher learning. In the plan prepared for the Ministry and the internal Board of Directors, the focus was on the modernization of all existing facilities and on the construction of new laboratories for science and foreign language instruction. The need to improve the library to the extent that it would become the major knowledge source of materials for the academic institution being developed was emphasized.

Aerial view of the David Yellin Teachers College campus

In the short-term plan, new facilities were projected for housing the future Early Childhood Center to open in September 1970. Finally, construction of additional student dormitory facilities was also set forth in the long-term building program presented. However, this latter recommendation was dropped from the program several years later, in 1976, when it was decided to close the two small dormitory buildings and reconstruct them for use as needed classroom and faculty facilities. Out-of-town students requiring living quarters were then able to share available rented apartments in the private sector.

Throughout the 1970's and the 1980's, there was a continuing program for erecting additional buildings as well as the reconstruction of the old facilities. After a short period of respite, the building program was reinstated in the 1990's by the new administration that followed after my retirement. During all these years, the face of the College has changed considerably and grown physically in a substantial manner. The number of faculty and students increased more than tenfold over the last three decades of the twentieth century. A very spacious library and new cultural auditorium building are outstanding achievements as a major part of fulfilling the vision for the future of the Seminary/College that was projected in 1969. The original Seminary facilities, built by David Yellin and Ben Zion Dinur, are hardly recognizable today except for the entrance facade of the original building. This will remain, since that building has been designated as an historic site to be preserved in perpetuity.

Friends of the College

From the beginning of my tenure in office, it became clear that depending primarily on the Ministry of Education and Culture for development and building funds was problematic. There were many times when the Ministry was quite responsive and even generous. At other times, it became difficult to receive even minimal financial aid for basic purposes such as internal program development and building maintenance. During the late 1970's, while in the midst of the construction and rebuilding of the main building with funds from the Ministry, notice was received that a continuation of funds might not be forthcoming for completion of that specific program then in progress. In other areas of the College program, such as faculty recruitment, student scholarships, and supporting special projects originated by the administration and faculty, it became obvious that there was a need for outside supplementary funding in order to advance and proceed on an orderly and systematic basis. It thus became necessary to raise funds for such purposes, privately from the public at large and friends of the College, wherever they were to be found.

Fortunately, the historical origins of the Seminary as a private institution enabled me to develop an independent apparatus for providing supplementary support for the school operational and developmental budgets. The property and buildings never belonged to the government or Ministry of Education and Culture. They were owned and managed by an independent but public body called the Building Association. The original plot of land was owned by the Jewish National Fund and then deeded to the Building Association for the agreed purposes of establishing a teachers seminary, providing space for an elementary school and a community synagogue. The Association viewed its role as primarily custodial and maintenance.

After much legal consultation, internal discussion and planning, it was decided, as indicated earlier, to expand the function of the Association and enlarge its role and responsibilities as a Board of Directors or Overseers, especially in areas of budget and finance. Then, too, due to my earlier experiences as an American Jewish educator, I was able to suggest a program for organizing a Friends of the College program to be established in the United States and Canada. This was the pattern developed by most educational institutions in Israel

With the able assistance of two very close and long-time friends, Henry Burger of Forest Hills, New York, and, later, Sanford Batkin of New Rochelle, New York, we were successful in organizing a Friends of the David Yellin College for fundraising and project support programs. Henry and Lottie Burger had become firm family friends after our working together with the school and youth programs at the Forest Hills Jewish Center. Henry was the chairman of my School Board in Forest Hills. Sandy Batkin was a childhood friend going back to the days when we were students at the East Midwood Jewish Center Religious School, when we both became involved with the Junior Congregation of the Center. Following our reunion in Israel in the aftermath of the Yom Kippur War,

Ceremony presenting Honorary Fellowship Citations 1983
Seated right to left: Judge Elazar Halevi, Henry Burger, Yitzhak Navon (Minister of Education),
Sanford Batkin, Mordechai Ish-Shalom

some thirty-five years later, Sandy and his wonderful late wife Ruth, became major forces in the functioning of the Friends program in the United States.

Much of the supplemental funding for the major construction and reconstruction of the College, as well as support for scholarships and innovative projects, continues to come from the work of the Friends program abroad. It was a marvelous and happy experience for me personally to be able to bring these two close friends together, who previously did not know each other, as partners on behalf of the David Yellin Teachers College.

Retirement and Continuity

On my sixty-fifth birthday, in November 1987, I was notified by the Ministry of Education and Culture that it was time to retire. It came as no surprise, since I was aware that this was the Ministry's policy. Since the school year extended from September through August, I, of course, felt it necessary and proper to request an extension of time until the end of that school year. The request was granted, and so I planned to formally retire at the end of August 1988. There was much to be done in preparation for the completion of my twenty years of service, the selection of my replacement and the orderly transfer of leadership.

I accepted the fact of retirement with mixed feelings. On the one hand I felt that there was so much more that I wanted to do for the College, and there were many things that I had begun but had not completed. On the other hand, I was also aware that time and responsibilities had taken their toll on my continued ability to function, as compared to when I was younger and in more robust health. However, as that final year progressed toward a rewarding conclusion, I was again mindful of the admonitions of Rabbi Tarfon in the "Ethics of the Fathers" (II, 20-21):

הַיּוֹם קָצֵר, וְהַמְּלָאכָה מְרֻבָּה... לֹא עָלֶיךָ הַמְּלָאכָה לִגְמֹר, וְלֹא אַתָּה בֶן חוֹרִין לְהִבָּטֵל מִמֶּנָּה.

The day is short; the task is great; ...It is not your duty to finish
the work, but neither are you free to desist from it.

Members of my administration and the faculty at large were very helpful and understanding as the time for separation approached. I was truly blessed with many friends and colleagues who were responsive to my needs and desires. They made the transition to the leadership of the new Director, Dr. Etai Zimran, easy and comfortable. My major concern lay with the period of transition for the Board of Directors of the College. This was a body that I had created and developed, and its membership comprised dedicated and responsive laymen, who had become my personal friends. I prepared them for the change in leadership orally and in a final written report which not only summed up my work with them but also suggested a blueprint for continuity.

Judge Elazar Halevi, the chairman of the Board, was a most competent leader, dear friend and colleague. At his request, I agreed to work with the Board during the period of professional leadership transition and to continue to working part-time in the areas of College development and public relations. I was to concentrate especially on continuity and working with the Friends abroad program that I had initiated and organized. I served as vice-chairman of the Board for a period of two years. At the end of that period I requested to be relieved of the responsibility since the period of transition to the new Director had been completed. I continued afterward, by invitation, for a period of time as a member of the Executive Committee of the Board of Directors.

After Twenty Years of Service

This is neither the time nor the place to write a concluding evaluation and summation of my twenty years of service as Director of the David Yellin Teachers College. No doubt, elements of self-evaluation and summation appear above. Others will have to conclude the evaluation. Happily, a sequence of events led to my completing a history called *The Academic Development of Teacher Education in Israel*, published by The Magnes Press of The Hebrew University in 1996. Since our experiences at the Seminary/College, and those who had preceded me as its head, were seminal and pioneering in beginning the process of academization and seeing it through to fulfillment, the story needed to be documented and presented for posterity. No such volume had been produced previously in Israel. The publication of the book received very favorable comments and reviews by those interested in the subject of teacher education in Israel.

It is an interesting story how the preparations for the writing of the book developed. During the early 1980's, the shortage of classroom, workroom and storage facilities became acute. We then embarked on the task of renovating basement areas that served as storage facilities for old furniture, equipment, printed materials, and to our surprise, old records of importance. Much of the paper-based materials and files were in a terrible condition due to the dampness and water leakage that had seeped into the rooms. Incidentally, much of this area had been used during the period preceding the War of Independence and during the war itself as training areas for the Palmach and as storage areas for military supplies.

We removed valuable printed materials and files, after which began the slow and laborious process of restoring and preserving the vital materials and files for the archives we then developed. I engaged the services of Hillel Agranat for the job of preparing the materials and files for the archives. This was a slow, complicated and painstaking process involving use of the National Library facilities which had the necessary equipment for drying out and restoring documents, often page by page. Later on, after my retirement, when I was ready to work on writing the history of the academic development of teacher education in Israel, I invited Hillel Agranat to join me as a collaborator in doing the research and preparing the book for publication.

In my final report as Director of the College, dated August 1st, 1988, entitled "Looking to the Future — After Twenty Years of Service," I briefly reviewed the developments that had occurred during the years of my tenure. I described the critical significance of the growth and quality of the student body, the achievement of academic recognition and the nature of the pluralistic society of faculty and students that had come into being. I stressed the significance of completing the master building plan for campus development that had been submitted over the years. In my final remarks, I emphasized the important accomplishment of transforming the College into a national as well as a regional Jerusalem academic center for teacher education.

I concluded my final report with a description of some suggested future goals for the College. I stressed the uniqueness of the institution as the only general teachers college in the Jerusalem area that functions as a microcosm of Israel as a pluralistic society. Within our classrooms, and as part of the variety of programs offered, there were differing and occasionally opposing points of view and lifestyles which met together on one campus. There were the religious and non-religious, Ashkenazim and Sephardim, Arabs and Jews.

The report proposed a program that could continue to promote the College as an educational center. It would include on its campus several demonstration and model programs important for educational innovation. It called for providing opportunities for basic and applied educational research. Though full academic recognition has been achieved, there is still the need and opportunity to add more programs for graduates and others. Then, too, it is important to expand into new subject matter areas requiring academic recognition. In this connection I stressed the need for additional special efforts to recruit qualified faculty and to provide special scholarship assistance for outstanding students capable of excellent performances as future teachers. Such students need the financial incentives to attract them to careers in education.

I retired from my position as Director of the College with a sense of fulfillment that many of my aspirations and commitments had been realized. I ended my final report with the words: "The David Yellin Teachers College has regained its historic significance as one of the first and the best of Israeli teachers colleges."

• Part II

Reflections on
What I Believe

Chapter 6

The Meanings of Jewishness

What I have accomplished and the way I have lived my life, both privately and professionally, is based on an evolving educational philosophy built upon the meanings of Jewishness that I have discovered for myself. What follows is an attempt to share this with the reader.

The twentieth century has seen great cultural, social and technological achievements. As men and women continue to conquer space, control and influence nature, we are witnessing the rise of civilization levels to heights unknown since the beginnings of recorded history. Perhaps no other century can sing in greater praise of the magnificent human performance in search of enlightenment, freedom, knowledge, truth and understanding. Yet it has been this same century which has encountered the horrible depths of depravity, cruelty, and destruction that people are capable of reaching in their relationships with one another. No century has been witness to human suffering, deprivation and the destruction of natural resources on such a scale as the twentieth century, when measured in terms of the millions of people involved. World Wars, the Holocaust, genocide and ethnic cleansing, have become words that are not theoretical expressions, but real in all their horrible manifestations.

All the great achievements accomplished have occurred alongside the ignoble deeds that have been observed and recorded for future generations. The fantastic technological advances in mass communication have made it possible to record the information for posterity. We have all experienced or witnessed the striking depths of good and evil that have been the products of human endeavor during the twentieth century. And what can be our expectations for the next one?

A small, but nevertheless very significant, accomplishment during the twentieth century was the establishment of Israel as an independent, Jewish and democratic state — the homeland of the Jewish people. The creation of Israel was the result of the interplay of all the forces described. These have been coupled with the strong individual and collective will of the Jewish people to survive and improve the quality of its collective life and the lives of all those who share with it a sense of kinship. It would appear that it is sometimes possible to right the wrongs of history, at least with regard to the existence of the Jewish people.

The establishment of the State of Israel has provided world Jewry with both the feeling of justice achieved, and the unprecedented opportunity for the reconstruction of the Jewish people. The emergence of the State of Israel and the continuing evolving nature of Judaism have served as major new sources for contemporary Jewish culture and religion. The uniqueness of Judaism continues to be a comprehensive blend of culture and religion. It remains a primary source of Jewish culture even for the secularist, who may have rejected traditional religious beliefs and practices.

There are new meanings of Jewishness today. These have evolved out of a process that began with the period of Jewish emancipation during the eighteenth and nineteenth centuries. The new freedoms achieved by Jews living in the West European and American domains created unusual opportunities for cultural interaction and opened the door to a new world of ideas in such areas of thought as philosophy, democracy, religion and nationalism. This has resulted in a change in the status of Jews and created new meanings of Jewishness. It has led to new beginnings in the reconstruction of the Jews as a people.

During the long period of exile from the original homeland and the resulting changes in the Jewish status as a people, the religious element became primary. With its growing behavioral demands of Mitzvot (commandments) sanctioned by God, this has protected the continuing existence of Jews as Jews by setting them off in a self-made isolation, which in some places later provided some local authorities with the opportunity to create physical ghettoes. The non-Jewish world sought to convert, isolate, and in some places forcibly destroy Jews and what they stood for. The inner pressure of Jews to survive and the external attempts to destroy them in one way or another resulted in the rabbinic leadership building a wall of Halachic (Jewish religious law) controls to protect Jews and provide some meaning for their continued existence. The wall of separation between Jews and non-Jews began to crumble for many Jews as a result of the process of emancipation and enlightenment.

Zionism is a product of that process, influenced further by new generations of Jewish thinkers, writers and leaders, who recreated the meanings of Jewishness. They espoused the old-new idea that Jews were first and foremost a people. Zionism then became a movement dedicated to the reconstruction of the Jewish people with its center in the ancient pre-exilic Jewish homeland. This focus on the Jews as a people has led to a redress of the balance between religion and Jewish peoplehood for many Jews. The process of reconstruction of the Jewish people and changing meanings of Jewishness are today the central forces at work in the ingathering of Jews to Israel and for the continuity of Jews living elsewhere.

It should be noted that in defining Jews as a people, particularly in democratic societies, there is no one unified image or model which crystallizes the meaning of one's Jewishness. There are broad parameters, including some Halachic ones, which allow for different meanings and expressions of this Jewishness. The common denominator, however, is that which unites all Jews as members of one Jewish people. This belonging as a member requires a binding loyalty by the individual who accepts his Jewishness, however interpreted.

Jewish Identity

The multiplicity of unusual and often extreme experiences, as well as the explosion of ideas, knowledge and understanding, has become the heritage of men and women living in the space age. These factors have often produced chaos and misdirection in the process of assimilating and understanding the meaning of all that has already taken place and is currently happening. Concomitantly, this has often resulted in confusion and even turmoil in man's search for meaning and understanding. This has been the case with regard to the changing lifestyles, patterns and thinking of Jews living in the twentieth century. The educational significance of this situation has resulted in an enormous challenge to all those involved. They have to cope with the process of dealing with the issues, in transmitting knowledge and creating understanding in experiencing the meanings and realities of these developments.

The basic problem facing most Jews today concerns the matter and meaning of one's identity as a Jew. This primary question has arisen because of the great achievements of most Jews — particularly those living in the western world — in having the freedom to choose and define one's self-image and the nature and extent of belonging to different groups. For many Jews, the freedom exists today to decide whether or not to be a Jew, and how to define and express their Jewishness. These quandaries have become particularly relevant for Jews living in Diaspora Jewish communities.

Even in Israel, where Jews live as a majority in a Jewish State and Judaism functions as the national culture and religion, there are issues of Jewish identity and meanings. In many instances, these issues have become the source of political conflict, ethnic and national confusion. These questions in Israel have the added dimension of understanding the differences and the sameness between the meanings of Israeliness, which emerge from Israeli citizenship, and Jewishness; and the relationship between these two identities. The identity problem is not that of belonging to more than one group; it is this uncertainty of belongingness. An individual can be loyal to many groups at the same time without having a conflict of loyalties. It is this element of uncertainty and the search for meaning that is at the core of the problem. For the secularist, the question exists of how to identify with Judaism as a culture and not as a religion.

The term identity as used here has been defined by social psychologists, such as Kurt Lewin and others, as being the individual's identity as influenced by the nature of his social interaction with others. Simon Herman has defined Jewish identity as "(1) the pattern of attributes characterizing the Jewish group; or (2) the relationship of the individual to the Jewish group and the reflection in him of its attributes."[1]

The nature of Jewish identity can be expressed best in terms of the Jewishness of the individual who identifies himself as a Jew. These terms and questions have great relevancy when we try to define the meanings of Jewishness for the individual and the group. When dealing with the problems of Jewish education, these issues are crucial to finding answers to questions of selecting the content and influencing the direction of the educational process at

---

1. Herman, Simon N., *Jewish Identity*, Herzl Press, New York, 1977, page 30.

work with families and the schools children attend. They affect the relationships of the individual child and adult to the many groups and activities which make up and influence their feelings, thinking and lifestyle, all of which express their identity.

Let us here consider some ideas about the problems of Jewish identity as experienced by several models of belongingness and meaning. These characterize the existence of the Jewish people in different parts of the world, yesterday and today. Kelman describes Herman's conceptual framework of Jewish identity as follows: "The historically unique features of the case... [are]: ...the inextricable blending of religious and national elements in Jewish identity; the role of Jews' self-definition as a people in exile in shaping their identity; the central place of the Holocaust and of the creation of Israel in contemporary Jewish consciousness...."[1] This description helps shape the different models I am presenting.

The uniqueness of Jewish identity, brought about by the particular interweaving of the national and religious elements in its formulation, is both different from many other peoples' identities as well as problematic for Jews living freely in a mixed, open and democratic society. "Judaism is not just a religious creed analogous to Christianity. It is the religious civilization of one particular nation; it resides in the Jewish people and reflects its history."[2] Judaism has to be understood therefore not only in religious terms, but as the specific culture of one people. An individual may reject the religious component, but Judaism remains the culture of the Jewish people. This definition of Judaism in its fullest sense also includes a particular language and literature, Hebrew (and in some periods of history it included additionally more than one particular language and literature, as for example Aramaic, Ladino and Yiddish), folkways and customs, and the arts.

The problematics of Jewish identity definitions can be demonstrated by three examples in the post-Emancipation eras (from the eighteenth to the first half of the twentieth centuries). The first were the early efforts of Jews in France and Germany to consider themselves Jews in only a creed or religious sense. The second was the policy of the Soviet Union to view formally its Jewish citizens as

---

1. ibid., page 10.
2. ibid., page 20.

members of a national group. In an internal policy and ideological sense, religion in the Soviet Union was not considered part of one's national identity. The third example was to be found in pre-World War I Poland and Russia, and to a lesser extent in some sections of pre-World War II Poland, and possibly still in the former Soviet Union. In some of these areas there were Jews living somewhat isolated in a Shtetl (a kind of independent, ghetto-like town or village). In such communities, Jews lived among themselves in a full religion-centered life. They had limited exchange with the outside non-Jewish world, except for the necessary contact with official government bodies and control agents.

The twentieth century American model attempts to define itself in a somewhat vague blend of religious and national identities, with the religious element gradually becoming more dominant, in keeping with other minority ethnic models of American identities that already existed. This became more evident as Jews ceased to speak in languages other than English; when they began to move out of largely Jewish neighborhoods to upgraded and often mixed neighborhoods, and to seek better employment opportunities in a more open society.

In some local American communal areas, there continued to exist ultra-orthodox and Hassidic groups, which still attempted to recreate something of the European Shtetl model. This necessitated a particular dress and lifestyle, as well as isolation from the mainstream. In all these models, the religious component became the major force and obstacle to an individual's becoming assimilated into other models and out of any Jewish one. However, the freedom to opt out is available to all. The process of assimilation remains the primary concern of those dedicated to maintaining and advancing a Jewish identity and continuity in the American Jewish community.

The Israel experience is different and problematic in its newness. Profound environmental and social changes continue to develop in Israel, where Jews live together as the majority group. As the majority, they are continually absorbing and integrating into their midst additional Jews who immigrate from other countries where they formerly lived as members of a minority group. The nature and dimensions of this evolving model of Jews living as a majority in their own sovereign state is changing almost daily, with the arrival of new groups. Each group of immigrants brings to Israel different experiences, as well as cultural and religious baggage of its own.

The evolving Israeli model has effected significant changes in the balance between the Jewish religious and national components and their respective developments. The concepts of nationhood and peoplehood have become dominant and primary for most Jews living in Israel. The religious component on the other hand, has become part of the general national culture and milieu, but in detail remaining the private choice of its citizens. In a larger sense then, Judaism has become the national source of Jewishness for the State of Israel.

However, this definition is not acceptable to a growing minority of Jews, especially in Israel, who have accepted a Haredi (ultra-orthodox) view of their Jewishness. In their model of Jewishness the Halacha determines their way of life. They have rejected the idea of Judaism being the national culture of the Jewish State, since they do not recognize the State as being Jewish. Such a religious Jewish State, in their thinking, will only come into being when the heavenly-sent Messiah arrives on earth and proclaims such a happening. The halachic-dominated Haredi groups have constantly challenged, and pushed to the more extreme right of the religious spectrum, the more moderate orthodox Zionist groups in Israel. They have succeeded in silencing the opposition of moderate orthodoxy to the extremism and rejectionism of the Haredi groups. The latter situation has become aggravated and more complicated by the political decisions of the various Israeli coalition governments since the establishment of the State, which have been forced to invite Haredi groups to participate in the formation of such governments.

These coalition governments have granted special status and authority to the orthodox and ultra-orthodox Haredi religious trends. This situation often creates problems of religious coercion for the secularists, limiting the rights of non-orthodox religious Jews growing up in Israel and of those living or coming from abroad. The orthodox and ultra-orthodox have created their own specific political parties. When they succeed in becoming part of coalition governments, they gain access to the instruments and institutions of governmental power and financing. In this way, they are able to fortify and support their extreme religious positions at the expense of the majority of Israeli Jews, secular and religious.

The Israeli Zionist model has stressed the centrality of the Jewish people. It is based on the Zionist ideal of an independent Jewish State, Israel, as a fulfillment of the need and the means for the survival of the Jewish people. It is still in a developing stage. The Israel model seeks to find new meaning and balance between the religious and national components, between Judaism as a culture and as a religion. In developing this model, tensions have been created between what can be described as the evolving nature of the Israeliness and the Jewishness of the State.

In Israel there has been a conflict between the existing status of the non-orthodox religious and secular majority, and the authority granted to the orthodox and Haredi religious establishments. For many Jews, these conflicts have increasingly resulted in their adopting an ideological position stressing the Israeliness of the Jewish State. In my view, this position is often formulated at the expense of accepting the full meaning of the Jewish components. Hence, Jewishness is frequently viewed, inaccurately, as being the religious component. Such a view usually comes at the expense of the idea of Jews being *one* people, especially for those who consider themselves as non-orthodox or non-religious. This kind of thinking leads to a sense of confusion in which many Jews consider themselves primarily to be Israelis, citizens of the Jewish State, in a rather limited Jewish peoplehood sense.

The danger in such a development is weakening and even destroying the existing unity of the Jewish people living throughout the world in Diaspora Jewish communities and those in Israel. It also leads to an alienation or loss of much of the rich religio-cultural heritage from the historical past. It creates an anomalous and even dangerous situation for the non-Jewish minorities living as equal citizens in a democratic Israel. Are they not also Israelis in a national sense of identification, with rights and responsibilities? Israeliness, in this sense, should be viewed as the national citizenship identity of all peoples living in the sovereign State of Israel — Jews, Arab Moslems and Christians, and other minority groups. They all share a common language, some folkways, mores and the arts.

So long as Jews continue to be the majority in Israel, then it will be known as a Jewish State with the religio-cultural heritage of the Jewish people being dominant. The Jewish Sabbath — the Shabbat — will be observed nationally on Saturday as the seventh day, rather than Friday for Moslems or Sunday for

Christians. In a democratic state, the latter two minority groups will be entitled to observe the Sabbath on the day of their choice in accordance with their traditions, and not be obligated to accept the Jewish one. The Jewish religio-cultural heritage will form the national character of Israel.

It is quite evident that the experiences of modern Jewish history during the twentieth century require clarification of their meanings, and in many instances, a rethinking of the issues concerning Jewish identity and Jewish consciousness. Is there still a common denominator that can continue to bind together all Jews scattered throughout the world, especially in view of the weakening or rejection of the religious component by many? In the past, as we have stressed, this component was the key to Jewish group survival and creative internal development. Another major question to be asked is, how will the sovereign State of Israel continue to influence the fulfillment of the Zionist dream and its ideology of reconstituting the Jewish people?

In Pursuit of Meaning

Since the beginnings of recorded time, men and women have been asking themselves and others questions about the meanings of human existence and the nature of an individual's humanity. Primitive peoples sought and found answers by assigning various aspects of life to the many gods they created. Later generations sought and found other answers. The Jewish people, at its inception, discovered and developed an evolving monotheistic concept of God that became the foundation of the three major religious faiths, the Jewish, Christian and Islamic. This concept has enabled the believing and thinking Jew to put into meaningful contexts some answers to life's puzzling questions.

The eternal character of such questions about the meaning of human existence and the nature of one's humanity is expressed wisely in the words of the Psalmist (8:5; 90:5-6; 90:12):

> Lord what is man, that Thou hast regard for him?
> Or the son of man, that Thou takest account of him...?
> Man is like unto a breath;
> His days as a fleeting shadow.
> In the morning he flourishes,

In the evening he fades and withers away...
O' do Thou teach us to number our days,
That we may attain a heart of wisdom.[1]

The act of living is being aware, conscious and experiencing what is happening around us. This often requires our response and involvement. Human beings have the innate ability to find or discover meaning or meanings in that which they are experiencing. This power is a distinctly human quality that can be cultivated and creatively developed. All individuals establish for themselves a pattern of meanings which constitute their *Weltanschauung*, their character and personality.

Viktor E. Frankl, in his profound presentation of an introduction to Logotherapy, in the volume *Man's Search for Meaning*, explains these thoughts in the following way:

> Man's search for meaning is a primary force in his life and not a secondary 'rationalization' of instinctual drives. This meaning is unique and specific in that it must and can be fulfilled by him alone; only then does it achieve a significance that will satisfy his own will to meaning.[2]

Frankl further emphasizes that understanding the very meaning of our existence is a discovery each human being makes for him or herself, rather than its being something self-invented. Every individual can only discover answers to life's questions by self-evaluation and then being responsible for one's own life. Like Frankl, I believe such an act of responsibility is the very essence of human existence.

Being responsible requires a commitment to fulfilling the meanings of life that the individual has to discover for him or herself from moment to moment. The process of discovery is a lifetime effort shaped by experiences that have been realized or acquired by learning. In accordance with this thinking, a human being can become self-determining. What the individual actually becomes is largely dependent on one's own decisions within the context of surrounding

1. Bokser, Ben Zion, *The High Holiday Prayer Book*, Hebrew Publishing Company, New York, 1959, page 375.
2. Frankl, Viktor E., *Man's Search for Meaning*, Washington Square Press, New York, page 154.

conditions. A major quality of being human, therefore, is the ability to determine the direction one wants to go. In moral behavioral terms, this is the capacity to choose between good and evil.

The ever-present threat to a life of meaning is the meaninglessness of so many experiences brought about by the trials and tribulations of living in a period of doubt, criticism and skepticism. The threat of meaninglessness is accentuated by the conditions of experiencing life in a modern industrial and technological society. Such factors as living in an age of great scientific achievements and the explosion of knowledge available to contemporary men and women, have often led to conditions of depersonalization, fragmentation, overabundance and impermanence. These can all confuse and even destroy meaning.

Another major source of meaninglessness and the resulting apathy in life is the loss of values and ideals brought about by conflicts, frustrations and doubt. The antidote to such a situation is to find a pattern of meanings for the individual, that would enable each person to function creatively and achieve individual happiness and self-fulfillment. Such a pattern is based on a hierarchical value system that needs to be discovered and understood by the individual seeking meaning in life.

As a social being, a human often finds that belonging to one or more groups serves as the source for developing a pattern of personal meaning. This is what transpires when one feels a sense of belonging with a given family, peers, and career associates. The process of belonging to a religious community, an ethnic group, and a nation, provides a pattern of meanings for each of the constituents who identify with them.

Values and Ideals as "Pacemakers"

In the open and free society of abundance in which we live, commitment to values and ideals is not an easy position to uphold. The freedom to choose, and the options available for personal choice of all kinds, are virtually unlimited. Therefore, making and keeping a commitment is not a simple task, especially since there are no absolutes, unless one chooses to accept a given value or ideal as an absolute. The commitment serves as a behavioral control upon the individual. An individual who is truly committed to specific ideals and values wants to actually live them, and even die for them in very extreme situations. This is the real meaning of commitment to values and ideals.

Values do not drive or push an individual; they pull. To be pulled toward something implies the freedom to accept or reject that which is available or offered. It was the writings of Frankl which introduced me to the concept of goals, values and ideals serving as "pacemakers"; something which gives us the courage to reach for that goal, ideal or value. Such pacemakers are usually established first for the young person by parents in a family setting, and then reinforced by the efforts of teachers and youth leaders. The individuals who represent these goals, ideals and values often place them in some sense of a hierarchy.

In later years, the peer group, close friends, business and professional associates, teachers and group leaders, and one's choice of spouse, supplement and sometimes replace these earlier sources of pacemakers. They may even change them. The freedom to change the hierarchy of such commitments is inherent in the democratic process. It defines the rights of the individual to influence the choice of pacemakers he or she finds acceptable or preferable. For the religious person, God may serve as the "Eternal Pacemaker." The seriousness and the strength of one's belief in God influences to what extent the believer is committed to specific goals, ideals and values.

In developing a hierarchy of values and ideals, there is the need to avoid or deal with a collision of values and ideals. We are constantly making value judgements by preferring one value to another. This process is continuous and changing, as the individual must decide about the ranking of conflicting, or seemingly conflicting, values. This decision-making process is influenced by the individual's inner "still small voice of conscience," which is an exclusive human quality; for some it is the voice, the spirit or will of God, or some combination of both the human and the divine. For others, it may be a group orientation as a source of conscience.

This quality of influence is not absolute, and since it is human, it has the ability to err. Therefore, though the human conscience is part of reality, it should be considered as something that will guide, not control the free individual. Such a person must still evaluate and review the situation in which one finds oneself, so that the individual can make personal value judgements of how to act or understand its meaning. Such an evaluation and review can lead to a new awareness, or the rediscovery, of truths and values one holds dear. These truths and values form the basis of what we can define as the character of the individual involved.

The Still Small Voice of Conscience

A person's conscience exists as a distinctive human quality known only to each individual. It contains a hierarchy of ideals and values, and basic thoughts and feelings about one's self and others. It is an integral part of an individual's awareness and consciousness. It acts as an effective guide to behavior. The ideals and values one accepts have become internalized as the principles considered and tested by the individual as part of the maturing process. Conscience becomes the essence of a person's moral character.

In his guide to the theory and application of Viktor E. Frankl's Logotherapy, Joseph B. Fabry presents Frankl's teaching about man's conscience in these words: "Conscience is reality. True conscience is not just what father, or religion, or society tells us. All these forces are indeed real, but at the core of ourselves we still have this strange little device. It plays a central part in our lives: how we listen and how we act upon what we have heard, can make our life either meaningful or empty; it can cause happiness and fulfillment, or tension, conflicts, frustration, and mental disease."[1]

An individual hears the voice of his or her conscience. The condition of being truly human is the act of listening, hearing and thinking. An individual living in a democratic society has the opportunity to freely respond, or not, to what one's conscience tells him or her. Such an individual chooses one's actions because one has decided to do so in keeping with the beliefs one thinks and feels. Hopefully, the individual can do so voluntarily and not out of fear of punishment. The hierarchy of values and ideals accepted serves as a pacemaker pulling the individual in a given direction, usually of one's own choice. The individual and societal implications of these concepts for educational theory and

---

1. Fabry, Joseph B. *The Pursuit of Meaning*, Beacon Press, Boston, 1968, page 69.

practice, especially in working with the very young, are profound and need further exploration and development.

The human conscience functions as a kind of listening post. It relates to the ideals and values one holds, and creates the challenge to willingly make a decision or commitment in one direction or another. Since an individual's conscience is a genuinely human quality, it has the ability to err. It can guide and also, on occasion, mislead us. This possibility of error does not eliminate the need to try to make the correct decision in accordance with the hierarchy of values and ideals we hold dear. The voice of our conscience speaks to us, but we are free to say *No*; this is our choice. To do otherwise, means to surrender the freedom to govern and control one's personal actions and private thoughts. In other words, actions are not necessarily determined by conscience, rather they are directed by it.

Since conscience serves as a guide for human behavior, there is a need to discover anew what one believes in, and what values to hold high. For the person with some form of religious outlook on life, the "voice of God" speaks out from one's conscience. For the believer, this is the essence of reaching out to the highest meaning or value. Frankl describes true behavioral morality as the decision to act not for one's own sake but rather as a commitment to a cause, a human relationship or a deity. Loyalty to a cause or to someone else reflects the efforts of an individual to reach out to something beyond oneself. This sense of morality can serve as a positive and strong force to educate and offer direction to the individual who searches for meaning in life.

For the religious person, whatever the basis and content of one's belief, Godliness is a kind of divine presence within human consciousness. Such a presence is only real when it is reflected in human behavior. For the truly religious person, one would expect that behavioral choices be made in relation to the extent and nature of the belief in God which may become one's conscience. This, then, is the essence of what may be identified as the human "soul."

There is an intimate relationship between conscience and will. This manifests itself in the willingness to express loyalty to a cause, to a human relationship, or to a deity. In reality, the cause then becomes the individual's conscience, or the object upon which conscience is fixed. These are the moral issues of right and wrong. They may originate from outside the individual or from within, as one is called upon to choose which commitment or right takes precedence over others.

An individual is born neither with a conscience nor an awareness to act in a specific way. These are acquired and developed through imitation, learning and experience. The desired plans of life eventually determine will and conscience. We often develop such plans by becoming aware of those of others. Our social existence as imitative beings is what acquaints us with such plans of life. The child begins to become aware and understand the nature of his or her own conscience by first learning from the surrounding environment, particularly in the setting of the family unit. This process of imitation over a period of time is replaced and often changed, by social conformity and social training, until such time as the individual learns to have and exhibit a will and a conscience of one's own. The implications for any theory of education should be eminently clear.

Loyalty

Concepts such as conscience and loyalty have been particularly difficult for men and women to live with in these times. For most people in Western cultures, there exists an almost unlimited freedom to choose their behavioral actions and thoughts. This has created a cornucopia of opportunities for individual development. Simultaneously, this freedom has caused confusion, despair and often serious conflict and even illness for many. This confusion results from the inability of some people to cope with the freedom available, and yet suffer the restraints often encountered from contact with the others in one's life, with family, friends, colleagues and other associates.

The desire for freedom and the need for social contact with others often creates conflict among people. Freedom and conflict are basic to human endeavor and history. Consequently, when considering such concepts as conscience and loyalty, it is necessary to redefine their meanings in the light of contemporary thinking and options. In my search for the truer meaning of these concepts, as expressed earlier, I have found that the philosophy of Josiah Royce offers some understanding and ideas which seem to answer my quest for the meaning of such terms as conscience, will and loyalty.

During my undergraduate years at New York University, I took a course in philosophy, which introduced me to the thinking of Josiah Royce on the subject of loyalty and loyalty to a cause. I wrote a term paper entitled, "The Concept of Loyalty and its Application to the Problems of the Jewish People." The paper was well received by the course instructor, and its contents remain indelibly a part of my thinking and educational philosophy. In it, I wrote that loyalty is a natural phenomenon which is part of the individual as a social being "...who represents in his makeup a heterogeneous group of loyalties, the interplay of which makes him what he is." I also pointed out that "...Every aspect of a man's nature which desires some expression and identification with other individuals or institutions involves some form of loyalty. Therefore it becomes apparent that to have a loyalty means to identify one's interests with that of a group which also shares these same interests. The devotion of an individual to his group and its activities is an expression of loyalty. No one can truly be a social being if he does not subscribe to some code or group."

In all my work as an educator, I have been influenced by Royce's thinking that there is a direct relationship between forming and having a conscience and a will, with that of loyalty to a cause or causes. In reality, what is being said here is that one's cause *is* his or her conscience or the object upon which one's conscience is fixed. As indicated earlier, we are not born with a conscience or will; we learn and develop them by interaction with others, parents, siblings, the extended family, peers, teachers, group leaders and the larger community.

The subject of loyalty has become an integral part of my Jewish philosophy and central to much of my thinking about educational theory and practice. I have become committed to the idea that it is only the individual with a viable conscience who can demonstrate loyalty to something or someone. Every aspect of human nature which desires some means of expression and identification with other individuals or institutions involves some form of contiguous loyalty.

Concepts of loyalty relevant for today need clarification. Generations of conflict between peoples, caused by centuries of ignorance, the absence of real freedom for many, wars and the subjugation by force of external powers, have distorted and perverted its truer meanings. As Royce puts it: "The loyalties of the past have lost their meaning for many people, simply because people have confounded loyalty with mere bondage to tradition, or with mere surrender of individual rights and preferences."[1]

Loyalty is an ethical principle as well as a social phenomenon involving others. Loyalties involve the whole process of social living. A man or woman who is a wholesome and an integrated social being has many loyalties. Every aspect of an individual's nature which desires some expression and identification with other people or institutions involves some form of loyalty. To have a loyalty means to identify one's interests with that of another or a group which also shares these same interests. The devotion and love of one individual for another, to a cause or a group, is the true expression and meaning of a loyalty.

No one can be truly a social being and experience the full meaning of one's humanity if the individual does not identify with another person, group of people or some cause. When the happy union takes place between the outer world of associations, ideas and behavioral patterns, with the inner natural self of the individual as a social being, then loyalty results. The loyal individual is the person who has found a partner and/or social cause whose will he or she can share as his or her own. Since an individual does not possess just one loyalty, but rather many loyalties, or an entire system of loyalties, one is often faced with the need to choose between what may become conflicting loyalties. The challenge of life is to resolve such conflicts, thereby creating human happiness and meaningfulness.

Some Educational Implications

A major objective of Jewish education should be the strengthening of Jewish identity, the Jewishness of the individual learner of all ages. As indicated, the Diaspora model and the Israel model are similar but different, reflecting matters of curriculum content, direction and emphasis. At the heart of both models is the centrality of the Jewish people as a people with a rich history that encompasses a common past, a developing present and aspirations for the future. Israel, as the central home of the Jewish people, should be the major force for the continuity and enrichment of the Jewishness of the individual Jew,

---

1. Royce, Josiah, *The Philosophy of Loyalty*, Macmillan, New York, reprinted 1936, page 223.

wherever he or she may live. To achieve such an objective it is necessary to reexamine seriously the educational strengths and weaknesses of both models and develop an educational philosophy and program reflecting the meanings of such a goal.

The transmission of information and knowledge cannot replace or serve as a substitute for the achievement of meaning in the learning process and the experience of Jewishness, in an identity sense. Then, too, there is often a striking difference between the Jewish identity of the teacher, as a model, especially in the Diaspora, and that of the learner and family members. Similarly, in the Israeli educational system, the confusion and ambiguities as to the meanings of Jewishness as different from that of the Israeliness of the learner, are conditions that must be dealt with by the curriculum, the experiences provided by the educational establishment, and the perceived personalities and commitments of the educational personnel who serve as models for the learner. The Israeli teacher needs to have clearly formed his or her own Jewish identity which inevitably will be communicated to students, directly or indirectly.

Mordecai M. Kaplan, in 1916, wrote one of his earliest articles on Jewish education which appeared in the magazine, "Jewish Teacher" (vol. 1, no. 1). Extracts from the article appear in the Kaplan biography written by Mel Scult. He writes about this article, including quotations from it: "A group such as the Jews should use its educational agencies and institutions to foster Jewish consciousness. By Jewish consciousness, Kaplan meant 'becoming so integrated with the House of Israel that he conceives for it a loyalty which gives meaning to his life and value to his personality.' Such loyalty should not be construed as in any way being in conflict with the loyalty of the Jew toward the society at large in which he lives. Jewish consciousness will not endure, Kaplan insisted 'unless by means of it, our children will make better citizens of the state, unless it will fit them spiritually for the larger world in which they must live [and] unless it will give them worth and character.' The goal of Jewish education is thus particularistic and universal at the same time. It should foster 'adjustment to environment and not to abstract principles.' It should create 'in the child a sense of warm intimacy with the Jewish people... and a sense of exaltation in those experiences of his people which have constituted for the human race the very footprints of God.'"[1]

In the Jewish education process envisioned here, developing a commitment by establishing a viable Jewish identity and transmitting values and ideals are of paramount importance. In the long term, these are the measuring rods to determine the success or failure of the educational program. The awareness of these values and ideals, when understood and accepted by the individual learner, are the elements which constitute the person's conscience. In turn, this awareness becomes the source of the loyalties one develops, which ultimately form the basis of commitments. This is the way character is formed, and the wholeness of one's personality is determined. Over the years I have persistently tried to emphasize the development of an educational model for Jewish education "which is based upon the idea of the centrality of Jewish peoplehood and the primacy of Israel in the life of the Jew..." This educational model was presented and stressed in an article I wrote for the magazine "Jewish Education."[2] Such a model provides direction for establishing a Jewish identity and transmitting related values and ideals.

The Meanings of Jewishness

Implicit in these reflections about the nature and problematics of Jewish identity is the central idea that Jews constitute a people. During the pre-Emancipation periods, Jews were spurned as a disgraced and disinherited people, living on the mercies of the local authorities and of their neighbors. With the granting of emancipation in many parts of the Western world during the nineteenth and twentieth centuries, the status of Jews began to change. The idea that Jews constituted a religious group similar to other religious groups in a given society, replaced for many that of Jews constituting a people with a specific national identity. The changes in status that took place as a result of this ideational replacement considerably weakened the idea that Jews constituted an identifiable people. This weakening, the ambiguities and subsequent confusion of status for many Jews, still exist today; it is a process that began some 200

1. Scult, Mel, *Judaism Faces the Twentieth Century: A Biography of Mordecai M. Kaplan.* Wayne State University Press, Detroit, 1994, page 126.
2. "Jewish Education" Volume 47, Spring 1979, page 13.

years ago. The Zionist dream, the Holocaust and the founding of the State of Israel have brought about major changes in the course of contemporary Jewish history. The reborn idea of Jews being a people and the reconstitution of this historic people in its ancient land have become a reality due to the establishment of the sovereign State of Israel.

I remember during my youth and formative period the many discussions and arguments on the subject of whether we Jews in America constituted a race, religion or nationality. Much material was produced, especially by the various agencies of the Zionist movement, to emphasize that we Jews constituted a nationality and that Palestine-Israel was the old-new home of the Jewish people.

It was the Reconstructionist movement in Judaism and the philosophy of Mordecai M. Kaplan which helped me understand and gradually formulate an ideology in which the concept of Jews constituting a people became the central tenet and contained a religious affirmation. Kaplan coined the word and idea of Jewish *peoplehood* as being the common basis uniting all Jews throughout the world. Judaism for me then became the cultural and religious civilization of the Jewish people.

It has been the religious component and strong feelings of commonality which have kept the Jewish people alive during the many centuries of exile and dispersion. The idea of peoplehood was an integral and key part of Jewish religious beliefs and practices, even though it was not always understood as such in this connection. A child, and any individual becoming part of the Jewish people, first became aware and conscious of his or her Jewishness by means of the roots of family orientation, reinforced by a religious consciousness and experience. This historical record of experiencing living dispersed throughout the world, with a fusion of the religious and national components, provided the basis for the continued existence of the Jewish people, finally culminating in the reestablishment of the Jewish national home in Israel. This is the ultimate fulfillment of the concept of Jewish peoplehood.

In my view, religion, all religions, are a cultural phenomenon discovered by men. For some it may be considered as the revelation by God; for others it may be an attempt to deal with the fears and mysteries of life and human experience. Religious thoughts and experiences, and resulting practices, are at the heart of cultural Judaism. It follows from this that Judaism should be viewed as the cultural content of the religious civilization created and developed uniquely by the Jewish people. For some who define themselves as secularists, this concept of Judaism can be expressed somewhat alternatively in a more limiting fashion as the cultural civilization of the Jewish people. For others who can accept the basic belief of the existence of God, religion (monotheism) serves as the unique and coordinating component of Judaism as the religious civilization of the Jewish people.

The Challenge of Zionism

During the last century of Jewish history, the existence of the Zionist movement has brought about a profound change in the balances between the various meanings of Judaism and Jewish peoplehood. The major change for many was the shift of emphasis in understanding that Judaism is the cultural component at the heart of the religious civilization of the Jewish people. For "Zionists," the return to Zion became an ideological commitment and not only a philosophical idea. For many it meant picking oneself up and going to settle in Palestine. And so the Zionist movement began with the different Aliyot to Palestine and Israel during the last century. The dream of Zion became an act of commitment and fulfillment for those Jews who returned and began the full settlement of the country, the historic home of the Jewish people.

The question remaining for Jews who continue to live in the Diaspora is whether they can still be identified as Zionists. This question continues to be argued within and without by the Jews of Israel and the Diaspora. My view is based on the primary commitment to the survival of Jews as members of the Jewish people, wherever they may live. It was in fulfillment of this commitment that I became a Jewish educator in the Diaspora and then opted with my family in 1968 to emigrate and settle in Israel. Therefore, for me, a Zionist is anyone, wherever he or she may live, who accepts the idea of Jewish peoplehood with the center in Israel. The Zionist is also the one who sees his responsibilty to work for the continued existence of the Jewish people wherever Jews may live. It should remain a primary goal of Jewish education, then, to stress the centrality of Israel as the Jewish national home and the importance of Jews to return to it, as well as a commitment to Jewish continuity in the Diaspora.

The Holocaust which decimated European Jewry has become the ultimate experience which brought home to the Jewish people the strong need for providing a definitive Jewish answer to its continued existence. Israel is that answer which has been accepted by the greater majority of Jews the world over and endorsed by almost all the democratic countries in the world. Israel is a recognized member state in the United Nations organization of the world community. In dealing with the meanings of Jewishness for contemporary Jews, the Zionist movement has successfully reaffirmed the idea that Jews are a people, with their national homeland in Israel. Judaism remains the content and the cultural-religious expression of Jewishness. The only really dissenting voices to these meanings of Jewishness are to be found in the Haredi group and the so-called Canaanites. The former rejects the State of Israel and the larger meanings of Jewishness. They live enshrined within their narrow religious ghettos, awaiting the appearance of the Messiah sent by their God. The latter small group of Canaanites in Israel rejects the idea of Jews as a people with a specific Jewish civilization, qua Judaism, that it has developed.

Jewish Commitment, Loyalty and Service

The primary task of the Jewish educational process, transmitted by either the home or the school, is to develop a commitment to the meanings of Jewishness that are presented. Commitment refers to behavioral action or actions; one must do something about a commitment in order for it to become real and meaningful.

Commitment implies an awareness or a consciousness of that something which becomes the object of the action. The realm of human consciousness is involved in the process whereby a thought or an idea becomes a material reality. A conscious decision is based upon one's conscience. When beliefs and values are internalized, they become part of an individual's conscience and help form one's character, which can then lead to conscious actions. True morality reflects one's motives and responses.

Parents and teachers are the primary sources of such early awareness and consciousness in young people; youth leaders and peer associations contribute significantly later on to this development among teenagers and young adults.

Colleagues, family and friends help adults form new or reinforce old norms and values. In developing a commitment to aspects of Jewishness, the home and school should seek to present meaningful experiences which will reinforce the commitment by developing a loyalty to that which it represents. Loyalty becomes part of one's character when it becomes attached to someone or something which represents the meaning or meanings of that commitment. A commitment without the element of loyalty remains an intellectual exercise rather than the practical application or action which expresses its true meaning or meanings.

Once a commitment is transformed into a loyalty, it becomes a real part of one's conscience. At this point in one's development, an individual's conscience becomes the internal bell which calls to mind the commitment, but also allows for a decision whether one is to behave in this way or that; whether he or she is loyal to a specific commitment or not. This ability to choose is inherent in human nature and an integral part of democratic education. Therefore, in the educational process, the parent, teacher and group leader needs to be aware of the forces at work in creating commitment and loyalty, which in the last analysis indicate the success or failure of the process.

In this discussion of commitments and loyalties, I should like to suggest that giving of oneself in service to the Jewish people as a cause and an ideal can be considered as one of the most significant active components of Jewish commitment and loyalty. This for me, personally, has become one of my highest aspirations, and one that affects greatly the response of my conscience to life's experiences as a Jew. The cause and ideal of giving service is something that can be presented in an educational framework. It can be observed and demonstrated by the personal example of parent, teacher, group leader, colleague and friend, who serve as role models. As indicated above, loyalty to a cause becomes a reality when it becomes part of one's conscience, which calls for the individual to arrive at a moral decision in making a judgement as to how to behave in a given situation. The educational implications for such a process at work should be clear and decisive.

The choices involved in making a commitment to one's Jewishness and the decision to give service to the Jewish people, remain very personal ones, based on the options available to the individual at any given time and place. These are individual decisions, whether they be in the voluntary or the professional realm. In my view, the issue of Aliyah from a free and non-threatening society should be influenced by the individual's commitment to the ideal of offering service to Israel, as well as the desire for the fulfillment of one's Jewish commitments. In a free and non-threatening society this is a choice that is made by the individual, family or group. This was the point of view I stressed in my work with Young Judaea in the United States. It was the ideal which motivated me and my family to decide on Aliyah to Israel. Earlier, this commitment of giving service to the Jewish people influenced my career choice to become a Jewish educator.

The Process of Education — Formal and Informal

We turn now from philosophy and theory to the realities of the educational process. I view the school as an agent of change and character development, as well as a source of information and knowledge. A primary goal of Jewish education should be the transmission of the meanings of Jewishness. It is the task of this process to influence the free development of a system of commitments. These become the loyalties that form part of the moral conscience of the individual learner. This, then, would enable the learner to choose actions that reflect the meaning of one's Jewish commitments. The individual learns from experience the restraints of proper behavior which help develop a conscience.

The process of education includes both the formal and informal aspects of any school program. The home and family, the school, clubroom, peer, social and other associations are all part of the process of educational influence. The nuclear and extended family continues to be the major influence in defining meanings in life and developing commitments for children and youth. However, the significant changes brought about by the diversification in the functioning of the contemporary family structure are greatly affecting the traditional roles of the woman and mother. This has emerged through the major increase in the number of one parent families. A primary influence on the changing role of women has been the feminist movement. It has helped fashion new attitudes about the role of women in the family. It has opened new horizons in career opportunities and the family planning by mothers. The mother-father roles are in a state of flux and change. This requires a rethinking of some of the goals and methods usually accepted by schools and youth programs in the educational process.

Increasingly, caregivers are replacing working and active mothers and fathers. Therefore, they have to be reckoned with in our discussion of the family unit serving as a major influence in the development of children. Do the caregivers come with appropriate credentials to supplement the role of those mothers, and often the fathers? In the past, parents, as the role models, served as the major sources of influence in a child's arrival at an awareness and understanding of the meanings of things in life and the beginning of commitments. Is one of the criteria for selecting a caregiver the candidate's commitments to those meanings which are expected to influence the child's understandings and loyalties as a Jew?

I am a firm advocate of the educational theory and philosophy which describe the earliest years of a child as crucial to development, intellectually, morally and physically. In general, these caregivers are expected to replace the working and active mothers and fathers during the critical hours of the day and evening when their children need attention, and expressions of concern, warmth and love.

The family unit, whatever its human composition, continues to be the major educational influence of the young person living at home. This family unit is the primary influence on the development of children. Thus we need to view the family unit as the main source of a child's education. The family is directly involved in providing models for clarifying and displaying the Jewish meanings, commitments and loyalties that parents hope to pass on to succeeding generations. In view of the changing role of the mother in the family and the increasing place of the caregiver in the educational scheme of things, the importance of pre-school Jewish education, almost from the cradle onward, becomes imperative, if we are to be concerned with issues of Jewish consciousness, commitments and loyalties. The level, quality, educational preparation and training of the personnel dealing with these very young children in the home or in a child care facility then becomes of major significance.

The economic needs of families, especially in Israel, usually require two wage earners, so that most women have become an important part of the workforce. This is in addition to the motivation of many women today to go out into the working world as part of their desire for individual freedom, career choice and personal fulfillment. In Israel this question of the caregiver, his or her role, education and training, is therefore of major concern, whether dealing with the function of housekeeper, Mishpachton caregiver (baby group), or nursery teacher. In general, such caregivers are selected for their kindly and warm personalities, some basic high school education, and general commitments to those things which seem consistent with parental judgments about background and values. It is only in recent years that the required qualifications for kindergarten teachers in Israel have included a three-year certification from a teachers college, and in a growing number of situations, a four-year academic degree together with certification. I am particularly pleased that I have been able to further this development by the pioneer work we did at the David Yellin Teachers College in this area of early childhood teacher education.

In general then, the role of adults in the lives of children and youth can be viewed as twofold. In the first instance, adults, whether as parents, teachers or those who are the employees of parents, are all caregivers. However, from the perspective of adults serving as influences on these children and youth in the development of character and personality, the caregivers have to be considered as serving as role models. They become the models for children who are beginning to grapple with such questions as the meanings of life, the loyalties to be developed, and the character of their conscience that is being formed.

Curriculum Issues

The Jewish school, in the Diaspora and Israel, at all age levels, should be viewed as a youth community with a culture, both humanist and religious, and a social program. This concept of "community" and its program, reflects my beliefs and understandings of the meanings of Jewishness for Jews living in Israel or in the Diaspora. It is in this sense that we should view the transmission of information and subject matter as a means and a technique, not as an end in itself. As a cultural, religious and social community, the effectiveness of a school has to be measured in terms of the meanings it has established in creating the environment, the internal organizational structure and the goals of achievement for each classroom and the individuals within it. As pointed out by the American educator Philip H. Phenix:

> Since the object of general education is to lead to the fulfillment of human life through the enlargement and deepening of meaning, the modern curriculum should be designed with particular attention to these sources of meaninglessness in contemporary life. That is to say, the curriculum should be planned so as to counteract destructive skepticism, depersonalization and fragmentation, overabundance, and transience.[1]

In presenting fields of disciplined inquiry, the curriculum task is searching out the distinct logical types of human meanings contained in each of the disciplines to be studied. Curriculum content should be selected and presented so as to enable the learner to analyze each of the disciplines as to the meaning of its particular structure, basic concepts, and methods of inquiry. This, then, should be the way to organize and teach the basic subjects usually included in the curriculum of the Jewish school, whether in Israel or the Diaspora: Bible, literature, history, religious thought, math and sciences, civics, art forms, customs and ceremonies.

Before completing my tenure at the Forest Hills Jewish Center, I had the opportunity to design and develop an experimental program in curriculum development. This was a process of evolving the beginnings of a philosophy of Jewish education and a related theory of instruction for the Jewish school. The concept of a "Jewish School" as used here, applies both to the private Jewish school in the Diaspora, day and afternoon, and to the State Mamlachti (general public school) in Israel. It is my contention that the uniqueness of Judaism as the foundation and source of Jewish culture, religion and the meanings of Jewishness, requires a special theory of instruction in order to reflect this special quality.

---

1. Phenix, Philip H., *Realms of Meaning*, McGraw Hill, N.Y. 1964, page 5.

During my years at the David Yellin Teachers College, I did not have ample time to continue the development of what I had begun in Forest Hills. My major task here was administering the College and advancing the long struggle for academic recognition. However, during those twenty years at the College I did teach some courses on curriculum development and began to search out ways of relating my thoughts about Jewishness and the Judaic content for the general public Jewish schools in Israel. In addition, I managed to do some experimental programming in the Early Childhood Center in the demonstration school at the College, with children between the ages of three-four and seven.

We experimented with concept formation in the meanings of Jewishness for the young child and how that could be taught and learned. My colleagues and I worked with the materials found on such subjects as Bible, Jewish history and the Jewish and national civic holiday cycle. Aside from this limited successful experiment in curriculum planning for the young child, I had difficulty on the College level with the indifference and quiet opposition from some members of

Pesach model Seder in College Early Childhood Center: Schanin chanting the Kiddush

the veteran faculty. The student teachers also indicated an indifference to specifically Jewish and Judaic programming.

From the beginning of work in these areas, it was clear that we were entering a difficult area of curriculum development for the Jewish school in Israel. In general, there existed a lack of clarity concerning the meanings of Jewishness within the program of the general public school in Israel. The religious-secular conflict in Israel often confused the goals and curricular programs offered by the general public school for the Jewish child and student. This lack of clarity as to the meanings and relationships between Jewishness (specifically Judaism) and Israeliness, have only confused the issues and created many dilemmas in curriculum development for the Jewish school in Israel.

In trying to deal with such issues, I began exploring, earlier in the Diaspora and later in Israel, ideas which would be at the heart of a philosophy of Jewish education and a related theory of instruction. Such a unique theory of instruction is necessary in view of the special relationship between the Jewishness of the learner and Judaism as the major source of the culture of the Jewish people. The presentation of the pluralistic nature of Judaism as a culture (or religious civilization) would include Hebrew literature, Jewish history, religion, the arts and the differing ethnic folkways and mores of the Jewish people.

In developing such a special theory of instruction for the Jewish school in Israel and the Diaspora, the integrative focus is the meanings of Jewishness. In my view, Jewish education both in Israel and the Diaspora, is the process by which the individual experiences and develops an understanding of the meanings of Jewishness. The Jewish school should serve as a fabricated environment which functions integrally with the home and family, the peer group, the community and nation. The general purposes of the Jewish school ought to be expressed in terms of intended behaviors, as ways to think, feel and act. These behaviors should reflect the meanings of Jewishness for the individual and the Jewish people as an identifiable group.

To experience and understand the meanings of Jewishness requires the building of conceptual frameworks from key generative ideas, feelings and experiences. The school curriculum, as well as the teaching and learning acts, need to reflect the development of Jewish-Judaic conceptual frameworks.

Such frameworks explain, order and synthesize the relationships between content, ideas, feelings and experiences. The conceptual frameworks are to be derived from the teaching-learning act by each individual and group of students.

In viewing the school as a youth community, informal education during the hours when the formal school is not in session should be considered as an integral, complementary part of the educational program. Informal education would include clubs of varied types, non-political youth movements, and special interest groups. Hopefully, the informal educational program would also reflect the meanings provided by the conceptual frameworks developed during the formal school hours. From an economic point of view, utilizing school facilities during non-formal classroom hours for informal purposes is most desirable and cost-productive. Then, too, teachers available and interested in supplementing their income could become involved in leading and/or supervising the informal educational program during off-school hours. This availability of additional employment opportunities for teachers is another way of attracting more males to enter the educational system as teachers and youth workers. I developed and expanded on the significance of informal education for teenagers in an article that appeared some years ago in the magazine "Jewish Education."[1]

Community Responsibility

In Israel, the government assumes responsibility for public education in accordance with the legal obligation of parents to send their children to school until the age of sixteen. This international norm is generally accepted by most Western democratic countries. The problem of public education responsibility in Israel is compounded by the fact that there are several separate systems, some independent school networks, and others with supplementary and special interests. They function, to some extent with limited government involvement. The mainstream Jewish educational system in Israel is divided into Mamlachti (State public schools) and Mamlachti Dati (State public religious schools). In addition, there are Mamlachti Aravi (State Arab public schools) and also

---

1. "Jewish Education," Informal Education For Secondary Age Group, Fall 1961, Volume 32, Number 1.

independent, but officially recognized, school networks. The latter are conducted by ultra-orthodox Haredi groups (Agudat Yisrael and Shas) which receive governmental financial support largely on the basis of political coalition pressures. There are also private schools, organized by special interest groups such as Christian churches and foreign diplomats.

I cite these details in order to make the point that the Israel public educational system is suffering from the growing tendency of separateness along religious and ethnic lines. The public education system should foster and fulfill the essential requirement for unity among the citizens of Israel, Jewish and Arab. This need for unity in diversity is one of the primary needs of Israeli society as it strives for greater harmony among all its citizens. Seeking a solution for this situation should become one of Israel's major educational objectives in the twenty-first century.

For Diaspora Jewry, the need for unity and centralized authority and direction have been amply demonstrated by the United States and other large Jewish communities. Strengthening the unity of the Jewish people is crucial to its continuing existence in each community. Centralizing the control and development of a Jewish educational system, supplemental and/or full-time, formal and informal, is the responsibility of the leadership and membership of each community

Institutions and organizations offering private and separate small schools with limited community support and supervision cannot satisfy the educational needs for the continuity of the Jewish people. Denominational and other demands for separateness weaken the unity of the Jewish people and provide for inadequate educational opportunities lacking public support, guidance and supervision. When the Israel educational house becomes more orderly and less politically dominated by the ruling political groups, then it should be expected and required to offer educational resources of a significant nature toward preserving the unity and continuity of the Jewish people throughout the world. This has to become a primary responsibility for Israel in its concern for the continuous growth and well-being of Klal Yisrael (world Jewry).

Needed: A Moral Dimension for Jewish Education

As mankind has moved into the twenty-first century, the problem of establishing a moral dimension for living has intensified. The individual in democratic societies is experiencing a level of personal freedom unparalleled in human history. How to live with this freedom alongside others who have equal freedom has become the primary question as individuals seek maximum fulfillment and happiness. Can people with similar and diverse backgrounds and loyalties live together and create societies that are characterized by the absence of fear, hatred and violence? How are we to educate people to accept the limitations of personal freedom as we search for ways to live with others in peace, security and self-fulfillment?

In my view there is a great need to rebuild the moral dimension of our societies in order to encourage the individual to find and experience greater personal freedom. However this freedom has to be tempered by the acceptance and effective working of a moral imperative for controlling one's behavior. Such a morality will enable all people to live together on a local, national and international basis. I believe that a major part of the existing dilemma for the thinking, feeling and believing person is the need for a value system — an ideology and/or theology which will guide and act as a self-controlling element for human expression and experience. This is the great challenge for the process of education and the educator who seeks meaningful direction and hope for the future.

What has become clear today is that many individuals see themselves as the independent focus and ego-central force in the universe. This, then, raises many questions concerning the belief in the existence of God. For most men and women, God exists in different forms and in a variety of ways and beliefs. For many, God has a special place in their hierarchy of values, which is meaningful to them, and serves as the basis for faith in something that exists beyond human existence and experience. For others, God is the center of their personal existence — the Creator, the central commanding, demanding and omnipotent Force in their personal lives. And for yet others, God is dead or does not exist.

The troubling developments in the twentieth century reflect, on the one side, the outstanding and unusual discoveries of men and women which contribute to the common good. On the other side, there is the horrendous record of their continuing bestiality toward each other. The exceptional technological developments, medical advancements and the freedom achieved by people living in democratic societies, exist within a framework of continuing fear for personal safety. This condition has emerged from unrestrained terror, violence, atomic weapons, the everlasting possibility of another Holocaust and continuing genocide occurring somewhere in the world. This is the background for the search for meaning and defining the existence of man's spirituality and the moral dimension in his or her life.

The School's Role as a Moral Authority

Defining morality or the moral person is not as complicated as it may seem. Most definitions seem to include two aspects: to know what's right and wrong, and to behave in accordance with that which is right. The second aspect refers to relationships with other people, in keeping with the Hillel principle, "Do unto others what you would have them do unto you."

Moral education in the schoolroom is part of the hidden agenda and curriculum that reflects the organizational structure of the class, the school as an entity and the personnel involved. The school curriculum that emphasizes the teaching of the Jewish cultural heritage should include those values upon which Jewish civilization is built. As part of a common family heritage, every Jew shares these values to varying degrees. It is the function of the Jewish school, be it in the Diaspora or Israel, to develop the critical thinking and judgement necessary for examining the values which apply to every moral situation.

The school, which is one of the important influences in the development of the moral person, ought to be the place where students test the meanings of values and their practical application as ideals and standards of behavior. The school is the place where students live, work, and play with others. It is in such a situation that the individual tests his or her judgments, modifying and even changing them as required by this experience.

The school inculcates character education by means of the values exemplified by teachers and other personnel, as represented by the school as a whole. This, then, is supplemented by the content of Jewish civilization and the history of the Jewish people, as perceived and understood by the learner. It is influenced by the emotional attachments and responses developed within the school as an entity, with its personnel and curriculum. These cause the student to identify or imitate what those values exude, expound and demonstrate by all those involved. Young people are great imitators. Therefore, the school and classroom environment play an important role in behavioral influences. So do the demonstrated personality and character of the teacher, the choice of learning activities and content that help transmit the values considered important by those involved, at home and school, in the educational process.

The growing violence in schools, abroad and locally, is symptomatic of the lack of adequate value systems to influence the behavior of all those involved. Violence and belief in the sanctity of human life are two opposites that cannot co-exist.

Moral Imperatives (To Believe or Not to Believe)

In any presentation of the nature of meaning or meanings and their relationship to values affecting human behavior, there is a need to create a hierarchy of values which functions as a system of commitments and beliefs. Any hierarchy, to have meaning and direction, needs to be rooted in some foundation built on some higher idea or ideal, such as belief in God (Godliness), the idealization of such concepts as the supremacy of life, humanism, and the preservation of nature.

The significance and meaning of these roots in the life of the individual is that they serve as a means to push or pull that individual toward the realization or experience of the meanings of one's beliefs. If these beliefs become a real part of one's character, then they become more than beliefs; they become commitments and part of his or her conscience and personality. When consciously understood and accepted, the belief or value forms the basis of a loyalty to something, such as a cause, which reflects the active meaning of that belief. Loyalty to such a cause is what motivates the individual to actuate and fulfill or experience the true meaning or meanings of what he or she believes in.

In his very important and stimulating book, *The Disappearance of God: A Divine Mystery*, the biblical scholar, Richard Elliot Friedman, presents an intriguing alternative answer to a current question asked by many. Is God alive or dead?[1]

Friedman writes about the biblical development which he describes as the "disappearance of God" or the "hidden face of God." He presents his thesis within the context of biblical research and analysis reflecting the changing nature of the divine-human balance as indicated by biblical writers and editors. The God of miracles and direct contact with men and women in the book of Genesis gradually changes in the sequential development as presented in the latter biblical books, to the point where the name of God does not appear even once in the book of Esther.

This process of change in the gradual disappearance of God or the hiding of God's face, continues in post-biblical Rabbinic literature. It is debated ever more forcefully by great thinkers, philosophers and religious leaders of varied faiths over the centuries to this very day. The Jewish thinker-philosopher Martin Buber described this process of the disappearance of God as being the "eclipse" of God. To Buber, God is the Eternal Thou in the I-Thou relationship.

As the history and experiences of men and women continue to move forward at a phenomenal rate of change and development, the current knowledge explosion has raised questions, some old and others new, that challenge the very existence of the God idea. As a result of this knowledge explosion, a new relationship between religion and science has developed. This has taken place particularly in the field of cosmology, which seeks to understand the origins of the universe.

The "Big-Bang" theory of an expanding universe, which had a beginning somewhere in time, leaves room for a belief in a God who is *part* of the universe and not outside of it. Friedman also points out that there is much in Kabbalistic thinking and writing that deals with a conception of God which is similar in some ways to that found among cosmological thinkers. This is, in a sense, a reflection of the idea that mankind needs to rediscover the existence of God. In Kabbalistic literature there seems to be some basis for such discussions as a

---

1. Friedman, Richard Elliot, *The Disappearance of God: A Divine Mystery*, Little, Brown and Company, Boston, New York, Toronto, London, 1995.

legitimate part of Jewish tradition. This can, perhaps, bridge a new relationship between science and Judaism.

The continuing knowledge explosions have raised serious religious questions for many people, such as the basic question of whether one can believe in the existence of God or not. If the answer is positive, then the further question is asked, what kind of God to believe in. The possible answers to these questions are similar to still other important and related ones concerning the basis and nature of morality in human behavior.

As indicated, the idea of God is a human discovery. God's revelation came to the minds of thinking and feeling persons. God is not merely a human creation. The discovery and revelation of God is a process of knowing and feeling that has existed from earliest times when people believed in a deity that existed in things, and that which is unknown. Individuals and their groups have usually prayed to their deity or gods for help, guidance and intervention. Such a deity or gods was often thought to have anthropomorphic qualities. The process of discovery and the revelation of one God is an ongoing phenomenon that continues to occupy the minds of men and women. Historically, monotheism seems to have begun out of the experiences of the Jewish people following their exodus from Egypt. Monotheism, as we understand it today, probably emerged, or at least was crystallized, as a belief during the wandering of the Jewish people in the Sinai desert and their cataclysmic experience at Mount Sinai.

When everything else has been said and done, even as a result of the most scholarly research into the question of the monotheistic existence of a Deity, God remains a mystery, a hidden reality, and truly unknowable in human language and understanding. You either believe in God or you do not. I am convinced that every man and woman believes in some form of existence of the God idea, however they refer to it. God, or some other representative word or expression, is perhaps the highest human value, the most profound idea that gives completeness and meaning to human life and nature. It is this meaning and the resultant belief in what it represents that form the basis of commitment, and the formulation of conscience and loyalty. This understanding is often greater than the ability of man to fully comprehend and control. This is where the element of faith often becomes part of a belief.

Events in the twentieth century have wreaked havoc with the faith of many who believe in God. The question asked by many, including this writer, is where was or is this God we believe in, when the human suffering and horrors we have witnessed in our lifetime were permitted? Is God alive or dead? The very nature of such a question has undermined the belief that human morality is based upon the existence of a God, who is considered to be the source of authority and enforcement.

God is not dead, but understandings of former and old beliefs need to be changed for many of us, and reconstructed. They are no longer valid for many who want to believe, as well as for those who already call themselves atheists, secularists or humanists. Still others sometimes join groups which form the basis of newly-created cults and other often strange, exotic and intense expressions of passions — all in the name of a deity or the earthly representatives of a variety of gods.

This is my God

I believe in God. I believe that my God is the same One shared with my forefathers and their ancestors. However, this belief today needs to be understood differently in the light of accumulated human experiences, knowledge and history. But ultimately, God remains a mystery, the same mystery experienced by Moses on Mount Sinai and the Jewish people in the desert, that has to be rediscovered anew by every individual in his or her own way.

My God is neither omnipotent, imminent, nor corporeal. God exists within and as part of the cosmos, within man and woman, and beyond them. God is the creative energy in nature and the power within an individual and one's society that leads to salvation. Such a salvation is the ability to reach out and achieve meaning in life. For me, the spiritual achievement of Godliness, which is the experience of the meanings of God, is the highest value in my hierarchy of values.

The creation of a spiritual Godliness is life eternal. Every human being needs to be preserved, protected and offered the opportunity to advance him or herself in this world. This individual is to be remembered in the memory of others in the family group, and by friends and colleagues with similar dreams of fulfillment and the meanings of life. Godliness is form and content in human relations, in the work place, and in one's private dreams for a better world, for happiness and love, for creative expression and fulfillment.

As indicated earlier, Martin Buber spoke of God in relation to the individual as an I-Thou encounter. In spiritual terms, Thou refers to the Eternal God as an existence independent of the human mind. God is not only a projection of human consciousness. God exists both within and without the human mind. Thus God is not the creation of men and women, but rather mankind has discovered God's relationship to human beings. Even without the existence of an individual's belief in an Eternal Being, God remains in nature and the universe. The Power of God is involved in the creation and development of all men and women, and in nature. Perhaps this is the meaning of the term "Nature's God" as used by Mordecai M. Kaplan.

Buber expounded the thought that we cannot really talk to God. His God can only be experienced and understood in terms of an encounter. God can be inferred in the human mind and spirit. I understand the meaning of the term "encounter" as the experience of God in real-life situations.

There is another important dimension to Buber's Thou. This is the use of the term to explain and describe the nature of the human relationship between people. The I-Thou concept refers also to a personal relationship between the "I" and the "other"; one subject confronts another subject. This is a relationship between people in the present; it is a direct and spontaneous meeting. The "I" meets as an equal with the "other" human being.[1]

I understand my God as that power within me that is the source of my motivation. It is a moving internal force, the push and pull within me, that creates the desire and will to advance in directions suggested by my understanding of the meanings of Godliness. These provide me with the safeguards and controls to govern my behavior. Godliness works as a function of conscience. To me, God is the "soul" of the man who believes in such a deity.

The forceful drive of a planted seed within me and within nature to grow, to flower and create beauty, and new seeds, is the creative energy, the Godliness at work within both me and nature. God is not the Creator; God is the unlimited

---

1. Buber, Martin, *I and Thou*, translated from the German by Ronald Gregor Smith, N.Y., Charles Scribner's Sons, 1958.

energy source. When freed by belief and faith, God can generate beauty, love, art and meaning in life. God is that power and energy that needs to be released and nourished by discovery, by everlasting rediscovery and understanding.

Just as we can define God as the creative power in man and nature, so too are we able to find the role of the deity in human history. God is not the causal element in history. My God is the power source and direction of men and women that influence history. Such power can be utilized positively and purposefully by individuals, nations and societies searching for security, sustenance, peace and meaningful existence. Unfortunately, this power source is often misused and misdirected as a result of human ignorance and evil intentions. The historical record of social change is like the planted seed or the newborn infant struggling to survive. It develops in fulfillment of an inherent potential which can then be nurtured for the good of the individual and others who are part of the surrounding environment created by man and nature.

I have learnt from my revered teacher, Rabbi Mordecai M. Kaplan, the following: "Modern man must experience God's relevance to man. An authentic conception of God is relevant to the facts of human nature and to the contemporary world. God as the Power in nature and in the human species that makes for the salvation of men and nations gives purpose and meaning to their existence."[1]

Good and Evil; Reward and Punishment

Let me state categorically from the outset: I believe that individuals, not God, are the sources and causes of evil. Evil is the product of people and nature gone awry. The existence of evil marks the absence of God in any specific situation and experience. I believe that evil exists when and where there is lack of the good (or Godliness), which is represented by God. When the spirit and meanings of Godliness prevail in human beings and nature, there is God; when it does not, there is evil. Reward and punishment are a function of the existence or the absence of Godliness. There are no absolutes which guarantee reward and punishment. However, I do believe that when Godliness becomes an integral part of an individual's character, there is the achievement of greater meaning

---

1. Kaplan, Mordecai M., *The Religion of Ethical Nationhood*, MacMillan, New York, 1970, page 47.

and perfection. These, then, provide the sources of the good as well as rewards in life.

Kaplan uses the term "Godhood" to express my meaning of Godliness. He wrote: "The subjective experience of Godhood through moral responsibility or conscience presupposes a high degree of ethical development and requires lifelong and intensive education of conscience. The need to be needed — as true of nations as of individuals — is the objective psychological experience behind the need to be accepted and loved."[1]

The existence of good and evil is relative to each situation and experience. It is a matter of balance and degree. As stated earlier, there are no absolutes. The existence of God as portrayed here cannot be considered or understood in absolute terms. Neither can we view evil from the perspective of absolutism. Human beings and nature, even when imbued with the power and spirit of Godliness, are not and cannot be considered as perfect and complete within themselves. They can be improved and become ever closer to God by the interplay of the creative energies and forces within individuals and nature. These then drive them forward toward greater fulfillment, beauty and the meaningful use of the inherent qualities within each. This is the highest level of meaningfulness in life. This then becomes the Godliness of God. This is my God!

Prayer

And what of prayer? Individuals, theists and atheists alike, often express themselves in some manner or form of prayer, elucidating their personal hopes and aspirations. Prayer is a form of human expression, for some a dialogue with God. It may be verbalized or internalized in silence as a feeling, a want or an act of willingness and identification with something or somebody. Prayer is usually a reflection of one's belief in God, but sometimes it may be related to a person or object, without any direct association with the idea of Godhood.

For the religious person, prayer represents the efforts of the believer to express in words and song the meanings, the strength and power of one's belief in God. In this human fashion, the individual attempts to deal with his or her

---

1. ibid., page 49.

personal, individual and collective needs and wants. These reflect their experiences in association with others who may be members of some group or society, to which they extend their allegiance and identification. God is neither known nor exists for the individual unless sought after. Prayer is both a declaration of faith and belief as well as the expression of human feelings, intellect and loyalties. It expresses thoughts and words that imply an awareness of God, or the effort to achieve such an awareness.

The problem of individuals in every generation is to find the meanings and words which best express their needs and wants. Real prayer is an expression of one's hopes, needs and wants. Individual prayer may express the voice of our inner conscience. Consequently, it is a most arduous and difficult task to find the effective words and other forms of human expression, such as the arts and music, which give insight and meaning to one's longings. These usually express feelings and thoughts in the form of prayer for personal redemption and salvation. Individual and collective needs and wants often find expression and meaning in prayer. Such prayers serve as a true vehicle for achieving meaning and self-fulfillment for individuals. Further, they express the loyalties and identification shared with other group members.

One of the special problems of Jewish prayer in every generation, for those who believe in God or want to believe, is the legacy of several thousand years of accumulated words and ideas, poetry and song. These have expressed the needs and wants of individual Jews and the ethnic and communal groups to which they belong, spiritually and geographically, at a given time and place. For the Jew who considers this vast treasury as the words sanctioned by God rather than man-made, the problems of acceptance and change, as well as the creation of new materials, are manifold. Many such believers are not prepared to accept changes introduced or suggested by other men and women. For them, the word of God as written down in the past is binding.

Some will accept emendations and interpretations suggested by revered and honored teachers and preachers. Others will not. Therefore, any change, elimination and reinterpretation is difficult to suggest and accept unless the individual Jewish believer, or group of Jews, is prepared to accept prayer as a man-made response to a human need or want, or related to a particular situation. I do not have any problem with the idea that prayer is man-made, or

God-inspired. Therefore for me, prayer can be changed, eliminated or newly created in accordance with the changing needs and understandings of people. What is created by humans can always be changed by individuals and their groups. The original creation remains an honored part of the vast treasure house and heritage of the Jewish people. The experience of group prayer, such as in the Jewish Minyan, creates the release of collective energy or will to feel the presence of God.

I do not accept the idea that every word of prayer is poetry produced by past generations, or by others today, that it needs to be logically understood or explained. For me, the historical association or dimension of a given prayer, is often sufficient to override the need for intellectual understanding and significance. I offer two examples to amplify and illustrate this point.

One instance is the Kol Nidrei (All Vows) prayer on Yom Kippur. Its content and specific words may have lost their meaning and intellectual significance for many Jews today. But in terms of its historical and emotional significance, the words and the traditional haunting melody associated with this prayer, make it absolutely essential, in my view, to retain it in its traditional context and melody.

Similarly, I can sing and identify with the Hebrew song, Ani Ma'amin (I Believe) which is purported to reflect the sorrow and resignation of Jews going to their death in the gas chambers of Nazi Germany and its allies. This song, which concludes with the affirmation of the belief in the coming of a Heaven-sent Messiah, though He tarry, is a song I can accept and sing, because of its very specific historical associations. The fact that there are Jews who, in the depths of their despair, can accept this concept and the words as a profound belief, means that I can accept and sing this song, even though I reject intellectually the idea of a Heaven-sent Messiah.

Educational Significance

What has been said above also applies to the matter of the intellectual understanding and acceptance of the words of the Bible. I accept the view that the Bible is a series of documents produced by men, or even inspired by God. Nonetheless, these documents and the volumes of interpretations, emendations and amplifications that have appeared since their final codification contain the foundation and fundamental ideas of Judaism that need to be taught, learned, reinterpreted and expounded in every generation. The extraordinary and profound historical significance and associations of these documents override the importance of their significance as words and ideas to be accepted and understood even intellectually.

The educational significance of the above historical approach to prayer, poetry, song and the Bible is paramount to the capacity of an old or young person's intellect to understand and identify with the meanings inherent in these creations of human greatness, productivity and understanding. For contemporary people there is no educational alternative to transmitting the knowledge, understanding and love of such traditions in creating an atmosphere and environment of intellectual honesty. This will enable the learner to establish an emotional response and historical association with the facts to be learned and taught intellectually. In such a classroom environment, the teacher should feel free to deal with this material in such a way as to enable a variety of opinions to be expressed, even his or her own, without trying to convince the learner that only one position and point of view is correct.

After a process of intellectual search and research, many answers to the questions asked can be accepted without trying to indoctrinate in one direction or another. It is in the light of these understandings and a resulting methodology that the curriculum of the school for the Jewish child and student of all ages has to be fashioned. It is in this spirit that the continuing education of parents should be conducted. The role and accepted methodology of the teacher not functioning with such a methodology needs to be redefined and transmitted anew. This will require basic changes in teacher education programs and even the organization of compulsory in-service training for those already in the field.

To conclude these reflections on what I believe, the new freedoms and opulent materialism available to people living today in Western democratic countries have created generations of people, especially the young in age, who have adopted an "I-Me" juxtaposition as the primary motivation in life. This changing development began to emerge in the aftermath of World War II. During the past fifty years, the acceleration of this process of change has weakened and often replaced the I-Thou relationship that was primary earlier. It followed, firstly, with a new and stronger emphasis on an "I-It" connection with things. In the course of the last generations of the twentieth century, it changed once again to become a new emphasis on an "I-Me" relationship.

The "I" or "Me"-first syndrome has created the all-consuming need and desire for a kind of self-fulfillment, whose goal is to achieve personal success as measured in terms of wealth and power. To reinforce the centrality of the "I" relationship, there has also developed the dimension of an "I-We" connection. The "We" meaning all those others who agree and subscribe to the "Me" focus and who may join together in the pursuit of the wants of "Me." It would seem that we are educating our children and adults today to aim in the direction of the individual's taking full advantage of the extensive freedoms, opportunities and riches offered *now*. All this may be achieved in character development, but often at the expense of making commitments to the demands of traditional or cultural beliefs, ideologies and values, which were formerly shared with a larger group with a purpose or cause.

This change has weakened and in many cases destroyed the Buber I-Thou relationship between the individual and the other, and the "Eternal God." This alteration has moved even beyond the I-It (per Buber) impersonal relationship between persons and things, to a new juxtaposition which I identify as the I-Me syndrome, sometimes operating with modification as an "I-We" relationship. This latter position stresses the focus on the "Me" as being the primary element in human relationships with the other, one's family, heritage and origins, and the outside community.

This new relationship between "Me" and myself, most often comes at the price of commitments, real and spiritual, for something beyond the "Me first" ideal. This has led frequently to dysfunctional families and the psychological disorientation of one or more of its individual members. It has often expressed itself in violence, at home, in the school, the street, the business and professional arenas. It has led to political conflicts. This ideal seemingly encourages the use of drugs, the seeking out of exotic spiritual cults, and sexual cruelties and deviations. In the extreme, it has legitimized wars and other forms of organized human destruction, as well as that of nature's resources. Ethnic cleansing and national conflicts can often be traced to the "I-Me" syndrome when expanded to include the "We" as against the "Other" in human relationships.

The implications of these changes in human relationships as suggested by the above developments, require a new collective effort to protect the individual from the dangers of this new form of human slavery brought about by the I-Me and the I-We syndromes. These all lead to meaninglessness, and sometimes to self-destruction. The educational process has to be reexamined in the light of these developments and concerned with their effects on character development, especially for the very young. This should become a primary task of the Jewish educational establishment, since all of this reflects on the Jewishness of the individual learner, especially if we are to and deal with Jewish continuity. Membership in the Jewish people requires the individual to be concerned with and involved in issues beyond the I-Me syndrome. The Jewish educational process needs to focus on an I-Thou relationship with the idea of peoplehood and the required commitments and loyalties such a membership demands.

As I conclude and summarize these reflections, I wish to emphasize the implications for education in **general**, and Jewish education in **particular.** There is an ever-growing need for more responsive educational establishments, because educational establishments have in the past, perhaps unwittingly, become part of the above destructive processes through indifference and inaction. They have neither sought nor found new ways of coping with these changing realities.

For Jewish education, in Israel and the Diaspora, there is an even greater need to rebuild and reconstitute the concept of the Jewish people for Jews, wherever they may live, as the basis for educational direction. This will provide a unified meaning and central force for building and seeking new curricular content and ways. This process needs to occur in the home, the class and clubroom, and the outside world, where one develops relationships with others. Perhaps, then, we will be able to succeed in finding new meanings in the twenty-first century for a changed but renewed I-Thou relationship between the individual and the other, and with one's God and the Jewish people.

I believe that by moving in this direction, we can become a more forceful and positive partner in the human endeavor to fulfill the divine hope as expressed in the traditional prayer book:

עַל כֵּן נְקַוֶּה לְךָ.... לְתַקֵּן עוֹלָם בְּמַלְכוּת שַׁדַּי, וְכָל בְּנֵי בָשָׂר יִקְרְאוּ בִשְׁמֶךָ;

We hope for the day when the world will be perfected under
the dominion of the Almighty and all mankind learn to revere
Thy name;[1]

---

1. Translation from Bokser, Ben Zion, *The Prayer Book* (סידור), Hebrew Publishing Company, New York, 1961, page 80.

Chapter 7

Postscript:
Retirement and Kehillat Mevakshei Derech

During the months of our deliberations and preparations for Aliyah, we, like many others, lived in a post Six-Day War euphoria of security and tranquility with regard to questions of war and peace in Israel. We were moving there with a sense that peace was assured, now and in the future. Perhaps this was even the beginning of the Messianic Age for the Jewish people.

Amidst the excitement of our arriving at the port of Haifa on July 22nd, 1968, we disembarked from the Queen Anna Maria with tremendous expectation and joy. Our first encounter with real Israelis, non-officials, were the porters who helped unload our carry-on baggage. We had many suitcases and bundles. One of the porters, after sizing up our sons Jonathan and Hillel, exclaimed that they would make great paratroopers in the Israeli army. We laughed. Little did we know then that he was prophesying what was to come.

War and Peace

The period following our arrival in 1968 until the outbreak of the Yom Kippur War in 1973 was one of general tranquility for the Schanins in Israel. It was a time punctuated also with the day-to-day problems and tensions surrounding new immigrants and their adjustments to a new country. I settled into my work at the David Yellin Hebrew Teachers Seminary. After a year, Roslyn began working part-time at the Israel Museum, and later at the Hebrew University. The boys continued their schooling, Jonathan and Hillel in Jerusalem, while David had returned to his former school, Queens College in New York City. The shock of the Yom Kippur War in 1973 shattered all the euphoria and illusions that existed for all of us in the aftermath of the Six-Day War.

In a piece I wrote for relatives and friends entitled, "War Chronicle of the

Schanin Family in Israel — September 27th through October 31st, 1973," I included the following excerpts:

> For us it began when Hillel, the new recruit since late July, did not return home for Rosh Hashanah. We had hoped for him to sound the Shofar and perhaps to read the Torah. Jonathan (Yoni), who was serving twenty-five days on reserve duty, did come home. Hillel's unit was flown down to a military airfield near Eilat where he was on guard duty. Those in the army were on low alert. Since Yoni was taking a course, as part of his reserve duty, they sent him home for each of the holidays. We knew that there was an alert but thought it was by way of being ready for possible trouble during the holidays…
>
> On Friday, Erev Yom Kippur, October 5th, we became further aware of something happening… We expected both boys home, but since Hillel, did not appear for Rosh Hashanah, we decided that Yoni and not Hillel should prepare the Torah readings for our services on Yom Kippur. We felt certain that Yoni would be released from his course for the day… Hillel arrived home in the early afternoon but Yoni failed to appear. As the afternoon wore on, we began to realize that Yoni would not be coming home and so Hillel sat down to prepare the Torah reading for Shaharit and Minchah, as a replacement for Jonathan…
>
> Kol Nidrei services were moving and still we were not aware that war was imminent. On the way home from Synagogue that evening, we noticed an Egged bus parked on the corners of Rehov Hanassi and Keshet. It was picking up soldiers. As no radio or T.V. function on Yom Kippur, we had no news. We heard other vehicles on the road that evening, which was very unusual, since Yom Kippur is very quiet, [with absolutely no traffic except for an occasional ambulance]. The city is either asleep or at prayer. At 7 a.m. on Yom Kippur morning the stillness was sharply broken by a swift flight overhead, at a low altitude, of one or two Phantom planes — an ominous sign. On the way to synagogue we also

noted the larger than usual number of vehicles, army and civilian, picking up people and then speeding on their way. We understood at once that the reserves were now being called up. We assumed this was part of serious precautionary measures....

Hillel read the Torah beautifully and the morning Yom Kippur prayers were as meaningful as ever. With the added and uneasy feeling of something in the air, we completed Musaf at about 1.20 p.m. and headed home for the two-hour break before Mincha. Hillel and his friends decided to stay around at the synagogue and to visit other friends. As we walked home, we noted the increase in vehicle activity. It was clear something serious was taking place. While walking home, Hillel, with his friends Danny Pins and Michael Laufer, both of whom were spending Yom Kippur with us, came up to us. Hillel decided to remain at home for any reports that might come through or any phone calls that he would receive. We had just settled down in chairs to rest when the first air raid sirens went off. We were startled into sudden awareness that we had to move down to the shelter. I ran to open the shelter and people began to go down, including our next door neighbors. A second air raid siren sounded and we were somewhat confused as to whether this was an all-clear or not. We turned on the radio and Israel radio began to broadcast for the first time, breaking the Yom Kippur silence. We were told that Egyptian and Syrian Armies had crossed the cease-fire lines, attacked our forces and war had begun. The broadcast was punctuated by code announcements which apparently were mobilization instructions for army reservists and civilian defense units...

As indicated, when the war broke out that afternoon in 1973, Hillel was on leave from the army and at home with us. Jonathan had returned to his army course relating to the artillery. David was living, studying and working in Boston, completing his university education and career preparations. The date of October 6th, 1973, coincided with David's 24th birthday.

We learned later on that Jonathan, together with the others in the course, were rushed up to the Golan Heights on Friday, October 5th, 1973, just before they were to embark on holiday leave. This was still a precautionary move on the part of the army high command, who were now aware that something militarily very serious was about to happen.

War erupted and Jonathan was now part of a group of soldiers on the Golan Heights moving in a converted Sherman tank equipped with a Howitzer 155mm gun. They were ambushed by the Syrians, and Jonathan, soon after, found himself alone, separated from his group. After some personal fighting encounters with Syrian soldiers who spotted him among the rocks where he had taken shelter, Jonathan managed to reach the evacuated settlement of Nahal Geshur. He found a radio, some food and ammunition. He then took up a position in one of the observation towers of the settlement. Jonathan remained there, alone, for two nights, hoping to spot the returning Israeli troops. He was eventually picked up by an Israeli tank unit returning to the offensive. Before Sukkot, he called us from Tiberias to say that he was well and to disregard any possible notification that he was missing in action.

Later, Jonathan unexpectedly appeared at the entrance to our Sukkah on the eve of the Sukkot holiday as we and our guests were sitting down to dinner. He had been given leave before he could be reassigned. He was dirty, tired, with his uniform torn from crawling over rocks and thorns. Needless to say, our gratitude was overwhelming as we heard him retell his story. It wasn't until several days later that we heard from Hillel, who as a new and still untrained recruit, had been sent south with his unit to provide protection for an oil field at Abu Z'neimeh in the Sinai peninsular. They stood as a second line of defense, should there be a breakthrough from the Suez Canal and Sinai fronts. He subsequently went over into Africa, with a unit assigned to guarding the air base at Fayid, Egypt. Jonathan returned to a new artillery unit on the Golan and was part of the Israeli effort to successfully fight back the Syrian Army and bring about the cease-fire on that front.

A year later, in the aftermath of the war, Jonathan volunteered for, and then completed, an army officers course. Hillel continued on with his basic training as part of his three years of compulsory military service, including paratrooper's training. Jonathan had completed paratrooper's training during his regular

Yom Kippur War Reunion
David visits soldier brothers Jonathan and Hillel in the Jordan valley, 1973

military service. David came to visit his parents and brothers shortly after the cease-fire arrangements, when civilian travel to Israel became normalized. Needless to say, this became a very warm and important family reunion.

The trauma of the Yom Kippur War, the great sorrow and sadness shared with friends, neighbours and colleagues who had suffered the loss of loved ones, and the wounding of many others, left a permanent mark and greatly compromised the hopes for peace and tranquility in Israel. The atmosphere in the country had been unsettled, negatively affecting the attitudes of all its citizens and inflaming the passions of many Israelis against our Arab neighbors. The sense of permanent security was lost, even for us today, many years later. The internal turmoil brought about in the aftermath of the war has continued to disturb the atmosphere in the political domain and in human relationships. Our Zionist dream suffered a setback that has yet to be regained.

The peace and security so desperately desired by all in Israel, have continued to be elusive as we strive for a positive response and some understanding with our Arab neighbors. Again, in 1982, war erupted on our northern borders with Lebanon, involving indirectly the Syrians who had occupied part of Lebanon. Lebanese Moslems, together with Palestinians living amongst them, continued to make life dangerous for Jews in the Northern Galilee. Hence the name for this new war, Sh'lom HaGalil (Peace for the Galilee).

Both Jonathan and Hillel, as reservists, were once again called to active duty. Jonathan in the artillery and Hillel in a paratroop unit were actively involved in the fighting up to Beirut and the Beirut-Damascus Highway. On the Eastern Front, Hillel's unit sustained heavy losses in killed and wounded in the battle at Ein Ze-Chaltah. The unit was then withdrawn, reorganized and later called back for the assault on Beirut. They trained in the Lebanese city of Damur, for house-to-house fighting in high-rise buildings. Fortunately, a cease-fire was called, and then the Palestinian forces were forced out of Lebanon to North Africa by sea. This was another very difficult and sorrowful experience for Israel. Securing a real peace with Syria, Lebanon and the neighboring Palestinians is still a very elusive reality.

As I describe Israel and our family in times of war and peace, I cannot refrain from reflecting on the continuing issues that have sorely divided the Israeli population, politically, economically, culturally, religiously and socially. The problems of war and peace continue to disrupt internal harmony in Israel. The fragile base of human relationships has been disrupted by ideological conflicts on issues of peace with our Arab neighbors, of the separation of religion and state, social, ethnic and gender equality, as well as cultural and pluralistic differences. During the past two decades, Israel has accepted the influx of some one million Jews from the former Soviet Union, Ethiopia and elsewhere. Not all have been pulled by the significant meanings of emigrating to the Jewish State, nor have many been coming with adequate Jewish and Zionist backgrounds and understandings.

Our Zionist dream of a Jewish State flourishing in Israel and serving as "a light unto the nations" needs to be advanced, protected and reconstituted in the light of the demands of moving into the twenty-first century. All of us, citizens of Israel, aided by the reinforcement of Diaspora Jewry, need to give some form of more active and positive *personal service* to the process of the continuity and reconstruction of the Jewish people.

In Retrospect

Recently, two significant events in our family life have brought to fruition much of what we have dedicated our lives to and hoped for. These very important and joyous occasions express the full and true meaning of these memoirs. I refer, firstly, to that very happy occasion in December 1996 when Roslyn and I celebrated our fiftieth wedding anniversary together with family and friends. The second event was also a fiftieth anniversary, in 1998, that of the State of Israel. Despite all its difficult problems, Israel has been created as the independent, democratic and sovereign state of the Jewish people in the land of our forefathers.

Roslyn and I share a deep and fundamental commitment to the ideal and need of family as the foundation and fulfillment in the lives we share together.

Our Fiftieth Wedding Anniversary Celebration, 1996
The entire Schanin family together in the Jerusalem mountains

Consequently, our family hopes and loyalties have always been uppermost in our minds and endeavors. The idea of creating a "Jewish" family was a priority we tried to fulfill. This was an ideal we wanted to experience and by personal example transmit to our children and grandchildren throughout all our marital years.

The concept of a family has undergone many significant changes during our lifetime. The process of radical change in family structure in the Western democratic world is still going on. These changes are emerging as a reflection of the variation of roles played by modern liberated women in the lives of the family, particularly as they affect child-rearing and career planning. Then, too, the notion of authority in a democratic society, especially in the family setting, is still in a state of flux. What are the roles and rights of the father and mother, the child, other siblings, and society at large? And what about long-term family traditions and such fundamental questions as values and belief in God? To what extent do these traditions and beliefs have any authority in determining what is good or evil, reward or punishment, for individuals living in a contemporary family setting?

In such a period of radical changes, it is often very difficult to make decisions affecting the lives and relationships between individuals even in the family setting. But true parenthood demands answers, even on a temporary and relative basis, to many urgent family questions. It would seem to me that the personal example set by parents, older siblings and authority figures in the community and school is one of the primary ways by which members of a given family can arrive at some answers to the questions that are asked and remain open for further consideration.

On an individual basis, behavioral guidelines need to be defined and presented in response to developing situations. Hopefully, the accompanying education, formal and informal, that we all experience, will help reinforce family guidelines. In extreme and problematic family situations, other institutions and interested personnel can often provide alternative models which can be useful in helping the learner of whatever age to adjust to one's personal situation and find new and more stable models to emulate and affect behavioral choices.

However, when everything else has been said and done, it remains within the power of each individual also in the family setting to make choices as to how to think and act. This freedom to choose is one of the major human accomplishments and characteristics of the past century, and probably the next. This personal freedom is a right that needs to be defended and preserved. Unfortunately, individual freedom is still far from being fulfilled as a universal norm or value. However, the limitations to experiencing the full and unfettered extent of personal freedom, are part of the answers to an individual's quest for meanings in life, as one translates them into commitments and loyalties to others, and to those things which are beyond one's full grasp and control. Let us hope that this is the message we are transmitting to our children and grandchildren.

As indicated above, it has been a major goal in our family life to create and transmit the ideal of a "Jewish" family. The Jewishness of our family is what gives it the meaning and warmth we want so much for ourselves and our offspring. As defined earlier, Jewishness means membership in the Jewish people and acceptance of Judaism as the religious civilization and culture of this people. This culture with its religion contains the value system, knowledge and traditions we so admire and wish to experience and transmit to others.

The Jewishness of our family is a given. Yet each member is able to choose those elements which he or she desires to emphasize and share with others in and out of the family. But the framework of peoplehood and Judaism remain the key elements which we trust will continue to contribute to life's achievements and understandings. Our clear identification as a Jewish family, which has accepted much that is part of the content and traditions of Judaism, has led us to settle in Israel in what we considered to be an act in fulfillment of the meaning of our Jewishness.

Adjusting to life in Israel has not been easy. All the members of the family have had their own difficulties with it. At times, life in Israel seems to be in a constant state of adjustment. Israel is a new creation of an old idea, and the realities of daily living are ever changing. We are in an ongoing process of reconstituting our Jewish peoplehood as citizens of a democratic country located in an unfriendly area of the world. The ever-present national conflict and wars with our neighbors, and the continuing absorption of significant numbers of new immigrants with different cultural baggage, affect our daily lives.

As a society still in transition, we have many problems of forging a new

Roslyn and Norman,
Jerusalem, 1998

national identity. We have yet to resolve the issues of understanding the meanings of our Israeliness, redefining Jewishness and the content of Judaism, in the light of our new national identity. We pray that our family will remain committed to Israel and our Jewishness, and all its members will do their part in expressing these identifications and loyalties by means of offering personal service, each in his or her own way, to the fulfillment of these ideals.

I can therefore happily conclude that I have much to be thankful for in being able to fulfill many of my life's aspirations and commitments. May I be granted to continue to function in the years ahead in the service of my family, my friends and neighbors, my people, and my God.

On Retirement

I retired from the David Yellin Teachers College on August 31st, 1988, after twenty years of service advancing teacher education in Israel and reconstructing the College programs, campus and status. The years had literally flown by and here I was at sixty-five years of age.

As I recall, I received the notice of my pending retirement with mixed feelings. On the one hand, I had expected it and was ready to accept such notification, but on the other hand, I was actively involved in advancing and completing the academic process of turning the College into a full academic institution and reconstructing the College campus. However, there is much that can be said in favor of a planned and scheduled retirement after many years of fulfilling yet tiring service in the same institution. And so I accepted the retirement notification as something that was expected and even welcomed.

In preparation for my retirement years, one of the first things I wanted to do was write about the experiences I had as the College Director. It was especially important to me to record the details of the battle that was fought and won to turn the two-year David Yellin Teachers Seminary into a four-year academic College. Our struggle was a pioneering effort that resulted in changing the character and quality of teacher education in Israel and opened the doors for many other similar institutions to enter the academic process. Too often such major achievements are forgotten or incorrectly remembered over time.

I began to assemble materials for that project and to complete the process of reorganizing the College archives. This was a slow and arduous process, due to the archival neglect of years and the poor quality of the existing materials. I described earlier in the chapters on the College, how we discovered lost historical materials and restored them for normal use. In addition to preparing the archives for this project, I was able to turn an unused nurse's office in an adjacent small building into a working area for myself. This workroom was ideal, since it was near the archives and yet away from the hustle and bustle of daily College life. Shortly after retiring, I began to work on assembling and categorizing the materials that would be useful in preparation for the writing of a book about my experiences and developing philosophy.

During the first two years of my retirement, my time was divided between working on the book and assisting the Chairman of the College Board in the public relations and fundraising efforts of the College. I had been invited by the Board Chairman, Judge Elazar Halevi, to accept a part-time assignment, at least until the transition period instituting the new college leadership would be completed. At the end of the two-year period, I asked the new chairman, Rehavam Amir, that I be relieved from the assignment. I wanted to concentrate on preparing the book which was now ready to be written. The book was completed in 1996 and published soon after by the Magnes Press of The Hebrew University of Jerusalem.

One of the best parts of my retirement years has been the travel program that Roslyn and I have been able to accomplish. We increased substantially the time available for visiting our children and grandchildren living in Haifa and Rehovot. We also have been able to travel abroad more frequently, spending more time with our son David and his family in California. We also wanted to visit friends and relatives living in the United States. In addition, we began to travel more extensively to countries and cities in Europe that we had always wanted to visit but had never had the opportunity to do so. And so, each year we visited different European countries.

In 1990 we traveled to Leningrad. There, for the first time, we met relatives from the Schanin side of the family. I had several cousins and children of cousins living there with whom we were in written contact for several years, but whom we had never met. In the years immediately following our visit there, many of our Russian relatives emigrated to Israel. Though we assisted in their settling in Israel, the decisions to come here were taken by each family in its own way and time.

Kehillat Mevakshei Derech

As part of our settling into life in Israel we gravitated toward experiences which had meaning for us in our former lives in the United States. Both Roslyn and I were thoroughly involved in the synagogue center we grew up in Brooklyn, and then in Forest Hills, where our synagogue affiliation became both avocational and vocational. Even for our growing family of children, the synagogue facilities had served as a house of worship, assembly, and community center for much of their social and recreational activities. Therefore, upon settling in Israel, we naturally sought out a similar kind of institution which could provide for our religious, cultural and social needs. The place for us was Kehillat Mevakshei Derech, where some of our old and new friends were active.

Kehillat Mevakshei Derech has been trying to develop a new religious concept for Israel. The idea of a Kehillah (Community) is that of an institution which functions with a synagogue as its center and a program to meet the cultural, educational and social needs of its members. Since this was to be a family-oriented program, it had to be developed for all ages of children and adults. Such a program required appropriate facilities, enabling it to develop in the fullest sense. This concept of a Kehillah could serve as an Israeli model similar to the synagogue centers functioning in many places abroad.

At the time of our arrival, the Kehillah met in a rented hall in a building owned by the League of Jewish Women in Rehavia. There were some sixty to eighty families and singles who could be identified as members. The program and activities at that time were largely centered around the Sabbath and holidays. The Kehillah functioned on a voluntary basis and, originally, with no professional employees. There were several rabbis and well-informed members who took turns as volunteer leaders of the religious services and the various organized programs. A central part of each religious service and gathering was the presentation of a d'var Torah (an informed talk), by different members of the Kehillah. Our conception of a religious service highlighted reading from the Torah in a three-year cycle, and a d'var Torah, usually based on the Torah reading. On the Sabbath and holidays there were morning and evening services.

The early founders of Mevakshei Derech were largely influenced in their thinking and religious practices by the Reconstructionist movement and its revered founder, Rabbi Dr. Mordecai M. Kaplan. During the long periods that Rabbi Kaplan lived in Jerusalem, he was an active and participating member of the Kehillah. He was not happy with the choice of the name of the Kehillah — Mevakshei Derech — which means Seekers of a Way. He maintained that we had already found a way, as enunciated in his writings and the existing Reconstructionist movement, whose principles served as our guiding lights. He was often critical of some of the content of our religious services, which did not directly reflect all of his philosophy and teachings.

The meaning and very existence of the Kehillah were predicated on the acceptance of the ideal of religious pluralism in Israel. In a pluralistic society, individuals and their groups should be granted the freedom and opportunity to express their Jewish religious beliefs and practices in accordance with their own intellectual and emotional needs and expressions. The founders and original members of the Kehillah comprised both Jews recently arrived from the Americas and veteran Israelis. Many of the latter had spent time in Diaspora Jewish communities, where they experienced the meaningful existence of more liberal streams of Judaism as alternatives to the Orthodoxy dominant in Israel.

Orthodox synagogues and institutions were the only ones to receive the official stamp of approval and support from the governments of Israel. This development has remained part of the status quo maintained by the various coalition governments formed during all the years since the establishment of the State as the national home of the Jewish people. The political power retained and enforced by the Orthodox and ultra-Orthodox groups precluded creating an atmosphere and legal status guaranteeing Jewish religious freedom for other, more liberal, religious streams. Consequently, the non-Orthodox religious groups and their institutions were forced to provide for their own facilities, programs and financial needs.

During 1975-1976, the Kehillah entered into a period of conflict and negotiation with the League of Jewish Women about our continuation as tenants in their facilities. The management of the building demanded an exorbitant increase in the rental costs for the facilities used. After much negotiation, it became apparent that the League really wanted us to leave the premises, hence the inordinate demand which was above our ability to fulfill. We had the feeling, though unsubstantiated, that other issues were involved, such as pressure from Orthodox circles for us to leave. In any case, the new situation created required some serious considerations by the leadership of the Kehillah as to future directions.

An additional pertinent and serious factor had entered the picture. As part of the aftermath and shock of the Yom Kippur war, Israelis began to reexamine many fundamental political, religious and social issues, including the status quo situation with Orthodox groups and political parties. There also seemed to be the beginnings of an awakened interest to reexamine the Judaic roots of Jewish life in Israel. Meanwhile, other liberal Jewish religious streams, as represented by the Conservative and Reform movements in Judaism, developed in Israel, emerging as new religious forces that needed to be heard and recognized. We, as a Kehillah, also felt the need for a reexamination of our existing situation. I was asked by the leadership to prepare a working paper as to possible alternative directions. The directions I recommended in my paper were generally accepted by the leadership Board and subsequently approved by the membership at large, at a special meeting held on August 21st, 1976.

The directions approved and adopted were to guide the Kehillah as it developed during the period from the late 1970's until the mid 1990's. Primary among them was the need to provide for a permanent facility to house our synagogue and enable the Kehillah to conduct a program for cultural, educational and social activities — in short, to build a synagogue center similar to the American model. To do this, we understood that we would have to break out of our isolated and totally independent position. We accepted that we would have to approach outside public and private sources for assistance to build and provide funding needed to function as a recognized communal religious, cultural and educational entity, with a permanent address. At the same time, we wanted to become part of the liberal religious efforts and streams of Judaism who shared the need to change the status quo situation and strive for greater Jewish religious freedom and equality in Israel.

Our initial major building project was designed to be completed in two major stages. The first was to include facilities for the sanctuary, a library, office and one classroom. The second stage (that would eventually have to be built) would provide more adequate facilities for an educational, cultural and social center. One of our first actions was to begin to find property we could buy or rent. We had begun to set aside a building fund for this purpose. However, it soon became clear to us that to buy a suitable piece of property with the amount of funds then available, or that we might be able to raise, was not a realistic option at that time.

The leadership of the Kehillah decided to proceed in two other directions. Firstly, to turn to the Jerusalem city authorities for assistance in finding a new place to hold our services and programs on a temporary basis, until a permanent solution were to be found. We were encouraged by the responsiveness of the

Jerusalem municipal authorities. This was the period that Mayor Teddy Kollek and his assistants were firmly established in the city government. With the help of these able assistants — Joseph Gadish and later Tamar Eshel — we found a temporary solution in being able to transfer our activities to a neighboring high school, the Gymnasiya Halvrit.

At the same time as we negotiated with the city authorities, we turned to the Jerusalem Religious Council, an Orthodox-controlled body, for financial assistance. They receive government funds for use in support of the synagogues of Jerusalem. It was during this period of transition and negotiations that I served as the Chairman (President) of the Kehillah (1977-1979). Our reception by the Council was not very promising. They stated that as a condition of receiving assistance, we would need recognition by the Chief Rabbinate of Israel that we were an acceptable and recognized synagogue. They required this after we indicated truthfully during the discussion in answer to their questions, that we were an egalitarian synagogue. Women had equal rights and were permitted to perform all the same duties and responsibilities as the men. We, of course, understood from the tone and nature of their questioning, that there was little chance of receiving such recognition from the Chief Rabbinate.

We therefore decided instead to apply directly to the Ministry of Religions, the governmental body which sponsored local Religious Councils and provided them with the funds to carry out their funding and services to "recognized" religious institutions. We argued that, as taxpaying citizens, our synagogue membership was entitled to receive financial support from governmental sources for a basic facility and for programming. We were told by the Ministry that it did not directly support local institutions, since this was the responsibility of the city Religious Councils. However, they indicated that, should we need some small assistance for stocking a library or for a cultural activity, they would consider the request on the basis of the principle of matching funds for the library or activity.

Our Kehillah used this argument of representing taxpaying citizens and the negative response received from existing governmental religious bodies when we turned to the Ministry of Finance for intervention with the Ministry of Religions. In the meantime, we decided to ask Mayor Teddy Kollek for his assistance in obtaining a suitable piece of land from the city municipal authorities for building our synagogue center. Mayor Kollek readily agreed to support our request.

We endured a long and arduous period of negotiation with the city authorities, building committees and sub-committees in the years 1977 through 1979. During this time, many Orthodox-influenced groups and individuals fought against the idea of granting the Kehillah public city land. We were then awarded ground for a synagogue building on Shai Agnon Boulevard. Details of this period of difficult negotiations appear in an article I wrote on the history of this experience that appeared in the souvenir booklet issued in 1987 by the Kehillah on the occasion of the dedication ceremonies for our newly-completed building.

It took more than two years to complete the plans for the new building and have them approved finally by the several city building committees involved in issuing a building permit. By 1982 we were ready to begin building. Nonetheless, we had still not succeeded in finding enough donors or other private financial sources for all the funding necessary to complete the building project. We held a very meaningful ground-breaking ceremony, appropriately on the afternoon of lighting the third Hanukkah candle, on December 12th, 1982. We began the actual building in 1983. Since raising the total amount needed continued to be a problem, we were forced to build slowly and in stages. We began to use the incomplete but structurally enclosed building for the High Holidays in 1986. We spent a cold winter in the new building, since for financial reasons we were unable to install the heating system.

The problem of raising funds for our Kehillah has remained with us from the very beginning of the original building program. This was one of the high prices the Kehillah had to pay for remaining independent, egalitarian and liberal, and not affiliating with any of the non-Orthodox movements then beginning to develop in Israel. The needs for building and program funding forced us to turn also to governmental sources. We had refrained from doing so as a matter of policy, since we fervently believed in the importance of issues related to the separation of religion and state.

Since our original application to the Ministry of Religions for building assistance had been rejected, we decided to appeal to the Ministry of Finance which provided all the government ministries with their funding. The Ministry of Finance responded positively to the Kehillah's request that they intercede with the Ministry of Religions, since our appeal was based on the argument that, as taxpaying citizens, we were entitled to support for a project that fell within the jurisdiction of that ministry. As a result of the intervention by the Ministry of Finance, the Ministry of Religions reluctantly agreed, in a letter dated April 17th, 1979, to commit itself to providing the Kehillah with $50,000 in matching funds and a one-time grant of $25,000 for construction of the needed building.

When the Kehillah finally raised the additional $50,000 requested, we turned to the Ministry of Religions for the promised matching funds and the one-time grant. After much effort, letter writing, telephone calls and meetings, we were told, to our dismay, that no funds were available, since this was a period of economic distress and governmental funding had been reduced for all the ministries. The Kehillah leadership then decided to seek legal advice about what to do with the commitment in writing that we had from the Ministry of Religions. It was decided to take that ministry to court in order to demand and receive the allocation due the Kehillah.

After a short period of time, the Ministry of Religions decided on an out-of-court settlement with the Kehillah. They would provide the $50,000 in matching funds but pleaded inability to add the one time grant promised. The Kehillah accepted the compromise and received the promised matching fund allocation. This was an important precedent for all other non-orthodox institutions to receive a more positive response for funding assistance from the Ministry of Religions. We were very fortunate, indeed, to find a major benefactress, Sue Brecher, a friend of several veteran members, who contributed substantial funds to enable the Kehillah to complete the sanctuary part of the new building.

The other important recommendation that I presented in my special report to the Kehillah in 1976, which I referred to earlier, concerned the relationships with the other non-Orthodox and liberal religious movements in Israel. I advocated developing a joint program of activities, and appearing together with other liberal groups before the Israeli public on issues of religious freedom and pluralism. During my term as President, I was able to organize a joint conference on the subjects of pluralism and religious freedom together with the

Israeli leadership of the conservative and reform movements. Our Kehillah was able to serve as a kind of catalyst on this occasion to bring together the two movements. This was a role we wanted very much to play, since it was not our intention at that time to affiliate with either group. The conference was successful as a conference, but it did not serve as any breakthrough for bringing the two larger movements together with our Kehillah as a kind of continuing joint body.

Both the Conservative and Reform movements have been primarily interested in developing a strong independent Israeli stance, each going in its own direction, especially on issues of religious practices, observances, and public reaction to the politicization of Judaism in Israel. We were too small to compete with or influence these larger bodies to become part of a common effort on behalf of Jewish religious freedom and pluralism in Israel. Both movements were very interested in our Kehillah and invited it to affiliate with one or the other of them.

During the 1980's and into the 1990's, the Kehillah continued to remain independent, even though it meant going it alone in Israel, programmatically and financially, and having to constantly seek private assistance from abroad. We continued to have difficulty in obtaining financial assistance from the organized fund-raising programs of American Jewry. We were not known and did not succeed in convincing large donors and the organized funds that we were worthy of their support. It was easier for donors and the various available private funds to deal with the local representatives of recognized national and international institutions and organizations existing in Israel.

One of the negative developments asociated with our having a central building and facilities, and the resulting need for a minimum professional staff to operate the facility, was the changing role of the membership. In the past, members conducted all the activities of the Kehillah on a volunteer basis. Gradually, it was assumed and expected that the professional staff would take over the direction and operations of the Kehillah, while the volunteer membership and their elected officers would oversee the management aspects and formulate policies. The process of reducing the operational involvement of the membership meant a lessening and weakening of volunteerism. This, in turn, placed more responsibility and involvement on staff, resolting in increased staffing needs. This then created an additional circle of financial problems, since the annual membership dues were no longer able to adequately fund the operational requirements of the Kehillah.

By the middle of the 1990's, the Kehillah leadership became acutely aware of the growing problem of providing adequate resources, financial and physical, for programming, and the staff essential to develop and implement it. The leadership was forced to turn more frequently to the membership for personal contributions in order to deal with growing budgetary needs. The response from the native Israeli population was particularly limited. The younger generation had not been taught to recognize the obligation for more serious personal giving to others and the causes they believed in. This lack stemmed from the early history of Israel, when the native population was on a much lower economic level than is the current situation. Moreover, many of the younger members were not yet financially able to give more substantial contributions. Consequently, the sums actually raised from local contributions, though growing in significance, were not large enough to meet the developmental needs of the Kehillah.

The continuing problem of finding outside public and private funding in Israel and abroad remained a serious stumbling block to solving the financial problems of the Kehillah. Membership growth was limited, and there was the continuing pressure to find replacements for the aging and slowly diminishing ranks of the founders and other veteran leaders. We had to engage in a more effective and expensive publicity program in order to attract new members, especially young families and singles.

While the above problems were becoming more acute, a new and important development took place, affecting the overall picture. Since the days of my presidency of the Kehillah, I continued in the role of chairman of the building committee, which eventually also became a fundraising committee. As indicated earlier, the vision of the future of the Kehillah that I presented to the leadership and membership in 1976 was divided into two stages. The first was concluded at the dedication ceremonies of the new building held in 1987. The second stage featured the addition of an educational and cultural center to be built on a plot of land adjacent to the existing building. Such additional new construction was very important, in order to provide programming facilities not

Kehillat Mevakshei Derech
Jerusalem, 1997

available in the existing building. During the first half of the 1990's, the Jerusalem political situation began to change. Mayor Kollek was considering retirement and the Orthodox population, particularly that of the ultra-Orthodox Haredim, was growing substantially and becoming a strong political power in Jerusalem.

The vacant area adjacent to the Kehillah's building had been earmarked for a public building. Construction of an elementary school had been completed at one end of the area, and we understood that another plot had been made available for the orthodox scout movement. This left the plot alongside our building as the only one still available for public use. Despite the fact that the Kehillah was not in the financial position to undertake a major building project, it was decided to apply for rights to obtain use of this last existing plot, so as to provide space for the Stage II project we had planned to undertake in the future. Then, too, we were not certain as to how the political situation would develop in Jerusalem. And so we turned to Mayor Kollek, and through his efforts the municipality approved the Kehillah's application in 1993 to receive this last remaining parcel of land (one dunam, or a quarter of an acre) for the construction of an educational and cultural center.

We engaged an architect and began to plan for the new building. We had accumulated about $100,000 and, with some additional small-scale fundraising efforts, internally and abroad, the Kehillah managed to provide sufficient funding for completing the plans and obtaining a building permit.

The projected new two-storey building would provide enough classrooms, meeting rooms and operational facilities to enable the Kehillah to offer a rich program of study, and activities which would reflect our concept of a synagogue center for all ages. For three years after it received the land, the Kehillah was unable to find enough donors to enable it to begin the actual construction. We were looking for a serious benefactor and others to start a major fundraising campaign. The experience over the years indicated that many potential donors were hesitant to be the first or among the first to contribute large sums of money until they felt confident that the project was real, significant and progressing. This was, again, the penalty for being an independent institution, largely unknown abroad.

With the changing political situation in Jerusalem and the defeat of Mayor Kollek for reelection, the building project was now in danger of being canceled. The Kehillah had not been able to fulfill its obligations in terms of the contract with the city which called for building within a two to three-year period from the date the contract was signed. After much deliberation and action-planning, the leadership of the Kehillah decided to mount an emergency fundraising effort and lay the foundations for the new building so as to protect our rights to the property. The Kehillah instructed the project managers to go forward and engage a construction company for building only the foundations. Meanwhile, we proceeded to raise funds internally and to seek additional support from friends abroad.

After several months of effort to obtain approval for starting the building, we began to understand that the delays encountered were largely political. The Haredi-controlled city building committees were not content with the earlier decision to grant the Kehillah additional choice land. It was reported that our application and the file could not be located at that time. It turned out that the

Haredi chairman had taken the file to his office in order to reexamine it personally and probably to find ways to cancel it. When this situation became known, we turned to others with influence to try and unlock the situation with the file.

As chairman of the building committee, I finally succeeded in communicating directly with the city building chairman, in order to determine whether or not the Kehillah would have to take legal action to free the file and enable it to start the construction work, since we had complied with all the requirements for obtaining a building permit. I was pleasantly surprised to find that the chairman was very cordial and explained that after studying our file, he was now prepared (after my telephone call) to approve the issuance of a building permit. We finally received the permit in 1997.

Though we had still not managed to raise all the funds necessary for completing the foundations, we decided to proceed slowly, using only those funds which had already become available. By the beginning of 1998, work on

Building the foundation for the new Cultural and Educational Center
Norman with construction supervisors, 1997

Kehillat Mevakshei Derech- Educational and Cultural Center

Architect's simulated presentation of the Cultural and Educational Center, 1998

the foundations was completed. While we were unable to cover the immediate costs, the builder extended us credit until we were able to find a potential donor prepared to give or lend us sufficient funds to cover our obligations for completing the foundations. To this date, the Kehillah has fenced off the area of the foundations and continues to seek a donor or donors to enable it to complete the building project.

During this same period of the mid-'90's, the Kehillah continued to suffer from budgetary limitations for programming and staff. It was clear to the leadership, that unless the membership at large was prepared to contribute substantial sums above the membership dues, the Kehillah would be faced with several serious and immediate internal financial problems. Public support proved to be elusive, and the Kehillah's approach to foundations, trusts, major private philanthropists and the large fundraising instruments abroad, were not very successful. This situation of having to deal with internal budgetary needs and fundraising for completing the new building forced the Kehillah leadership to reassess the situation and seek immediate and long-term solutions.

As mentioned earlier, periodically voices were heard in the Kehillah, and among the leadership, which questioned the advisability of joining with one of the existing liberal non-Orthodox movements in Israel. The two movements that then existed in Israel were Masorti (Conservative) and Progressive (Reform). Both of these were very interested in our affiliating with them. It was argued that such an affiliation would provide the Kehillah with greater exposure and involvement with efforts to establish Jewish religious freedom and pluralism in Israel. It could possibly provide the Kehillah with additional budgetary sources for internal operations and for completing the new building now standing only with a foundation.

The Kehillah had simultaneously been trying to establish meaningful ties with the secular humanist movement and the College of Pluralistic Judaism, which shared some of our basic ideas about cultural pluralism. This had not been very successful. The latter groups were not prepared to accept our position with regard to religious pluralism on the one hand, and the centrality of the belief in God in our conception of Judaism on the other.

We continued to seek ways of organizing a cooperative and joint effort with all these and other groups interested in working toward advancing Judaism as the national culture of Israel and civilization of the Jewish people. We advocated a type of federated relationship between such groups. This, then, could enable the Kehillah to become part of a much larger group or groups, rather than selecting one specific ideological group for affiliation. But there was little positive response to our efforts from all these movements.

Finally, during the latter half of the 1990's, the Kehillah leadership, with membership approval, began to negotiate with the Masorti and Progressive movements in Israel. We made a point in our negotiations of stressing that we were considering affiliation with the Israeli side of those movements, even though we were not always in agreement with religious positions taken by both movements in the Diaspora. It soon became obvious that there were ideological difficulties in considering affiliation with the conservative and secular humanist groups. The Conservative movement defines itself in Israel as an Halachic religious group and the secular humanist movement as a non-religious group, unaffiliated to any synagogue body. Clearly, these ideological positions did not mesh with the Kehillah's conception of itself as a non-Halachic but tradition-oriented and liberal group. The Kehillah attempts to adapt, select and develop new ideas and practices from the Halacha and Jewish traditions, in keeping with the religious needs of our times. While negotiations were taking place with these other two movements, we also turned to the Movement for Progressive Judaism (Reform), to explore possibilities of affiliation with them. They proved to be the most forthcoming of all the movements consulted and were prepared to accept our ideological and internal independence as an affiliate. We were considered by them to be a highly desirable group for affiliation, coming as we would with important human and physical resources.

While these final negotiations were taking place, the Reconstructionist movement in the United States, after many years of delay and indecision, began to appear on the religious scene in Israel. Contact with our Kehillah was naturally established, and we also began to investigate the possibilities of an affiliation with that movement. This was a new and attractive possibility. Some of the founding members of the Kehillah had an ongoing ideological relationship with the teachings of Rabbi Dr. Mordecai M. Kaplan. Preliminary efforts were undertaken to explore the meaning and obligations of serving as the base or Israeli address for this newer movement in Judaism. As chairman of the affiliation committee, I became quite involved with all these contacts and negotiations.

The Kehillah leadership recognized the need for an affiliation, but was concerned about the possible loss of independence that it would bring about. Then, too, there was the uncomfortable feeling, expressed by some, of joining a movement that locally in Israel may be considered a foreign import. The question of affiliating with the Reconstructionist movement was rejected because it did not exist in Israel. After much internal debate and ideological considerations, the membership of the Kehillah, at a special meeting held on December 10th, 1998, decided to affiliate with the Movement for Progressive Judaism in Israel. In essence, however, many of us continue to consider the Kehillah as being the Reconstructionist wing of the Progressive movement. The Reconstructionist movement has been a part of the World Union for Progressive Judaism for many years.

By way of temporary conclusions, since the affiliation development has yet to be fully realized, it is important to acknowledge that Kehillat Mevakshei Derech has entered a crucial period in its history. I have changed my thinking about the advisability of affiliation with the Progressive movement. This was brought about by the final realization of how necessary it was in order to meet the programming, building and operational needs of the Kehillah. I am now convinced that the time has arrived to come out of the narrow and impossible confines of trying to function as an independent group. Hopefully, the Kehillah will now be able to find its rightful place and voice as a major institution, part of a larger framework engaged in the ongoing struggle for Jewish religious freedom and pluralism in Israel.

The Kehillah has progressed historically from a synagogue offering primarily religious services, to an Israeli model of a communal institution, a synagogue center, with a religious, cultural and national ideology for all of Israel — a Kehillah.

The civilization and peoplehood ideology espoused by the Kehillah needs to be offered and presented more effectively to that majority in the Israeli Jewish population which still defines itself as traditional (non-Orthodox) or even secular, but not anti-religious. This should be the vision, and the goal, nay the obligation, of the Kehillah, to persevere in its efforts to bring this message and direction for developing a national ideology before the Jewish people in Israel.

By Way of Conclusion

Writing these pages has been a wonderful and exciting opportunity for me to relive many beautiful and meaningful experiences. I am appreciative of, and content with, the knowledge that I have fulfilled my commitment of giving dedicated service to my people, the Jewish people. These memoirs and reflections are the result of my satisfying career and fulfillment as an educator and devoted Jew.

I have been rewarded by many years of happiness, a wonderful wife and mother, our three sons, their wives and our lovely grandchildren. I have written these memoirs and reflections primarily for them. May I be blessed to witness our offspring moving in a similar fashion, each in his or her own way, but motivated toward the common goal of serving and transmitting our Jewish heritage to those who follow after us. I conclude with the words from the Passover Haggadah which speak of the obligation of each generation to renew the Covenant made at Mount Sinai:

בְּכָל דּוֹר וָדוֹר חַיָּב אָדָם לִרְאוֹת אֶת עַצְמוֹ כְּאִלּוּ הוּא יָצָא מִמִּצְרָיִם.

In every generation, every man should feel as though he himself took part in the Exodus from Egypt.

This is my legacy to all those who will follow in similar directions.

Index

547th Signal Corps Depot Company, 30 ff, 38, 52; its facilities in Manila, 46-47

5th Replacement Depot, 66

A

A History of the Jewish People, by Margolis and Marx, 57

AACA, *see* Association of Americans and Canadians for *Aliyah*

AACI, *see* Association of Americans and Canadians in Israel

Abu Z'neimeh, a location in Sinai Peninsula, 223

Ackerman, Dr. Walter, co-editor of *New Insights into Curriculum Development, Part I*, 108

Adar Investigating Sub-Committee, 156

Agranat, Hillel, 170, 171

Agudat Yisrael, *Haredi* political party in Israel, its school system, 204

AJDC, *see* American Joint Distribution Committee

Aliyah (immigration to Israel), 82, 84, 85

Alon, Yigal, 152

American Friends of Israel, 127

American Joint Distribution Committee, 53, 56, 57

American Zionist Council, 127, 128

American Zionist Youth Commission, 72, 77, 80; its constituent groups, 80-81; 83-84;

Amir, Rehavam, DYTC Board Chairman, 142, 231

An Introduction to Prayers and Holidays for the Student, by Norman Schanin (1960), 108

Ani Ma'amin (I Believe), Jewish song, 215

Ardennes Forest, 35

Army Cooks and Bakers School, 28, 29

Army Signal Corps Clerk School 28, 30

Arranne, Zalman, Israeli Minister of Education, 125;

Association of Americans and Canadians for *Aliyah*, 126-129; established, 127; elects Schanin as chairman of its executive committee, 127; develops its program for *Aliyah*, 127, 128; its first *T'nuat Aliyah* Conference, 128; changing leadership, 128; its demise, 129

Association of Americans and Canadians in Israel, 126, 127

Avon, NJ, Signal Corps Warehouse, 31

AZC, *see* American Zionist Council

AZYC, *see* American Zionist Youth Commission

B

Baguio, Philippines, 64

Bank Street College, NYC, 139

Bar Ilan University, 149

Bardin, Dr. Shlomo, Executive Director, AZYC, Brandeis Camp Institutes, 80, 93

Base X (in Manila), 49, 50, 54, 66

Batangas, Luzon, Philippines, 55

Batkin, Ruth, 168

Batkin, Sanford, Friends of DYTC President, 7, 167, 168

Battle of the Bulge, 35

Benderly, Dr. Samson, camp director, 14

Ben-Gurion, David, 145

Berlove, Manuel, 54

Bet Hakerem Hebrew Teachers Seminary, (*see*

also David Yellin Hebrew Teachers Seminary; *see also* David Yellin Teachers College) 125, 132 ff, 145

Bet Hakerem, Jerusalem neighborhood, 137

Bethlehem, NH, 106

Big-Bang theory, 208

Bnai Brith, 96

Board of Directors of DYTC, 157, 167, 169

Bokser, Dr. Ben Zion, Rabbi of FHJC, 101, 104, 106, 183, 219

Brandeis Camp Institute, 72, 80; its three sites, 93; 94

Brecher, Sue, 237

British Mandatory authorities, 19

Brooklyn Jewish Youth Council, 25

Brooklyn Zionist Youth Commission, 72

Bruckenstein, Joseph, 124, 128

Buber, Martin, Jewish philosopher, his I-Thou relationship to God, 208, 211, 217

Building Association (of DYTC), 134-136, 141; reorganized as Board of Directors, 141, 142;

Burger, Henry, FHJC School Board Chairman and Friends of DYTC President, 7, 101, 167, 168

Burger, Lottie, 8, 167

Burger, Paul and Asnat, 8

Byelorus(sia), 10

C

Camp Achvah, 14

Camp Cejwin, Port Jervis, NY, venue for founding Reconstructionist Institute for Jewish Youth Leadership, 75; 115

Camp Crowder, MO, 30

Camp Edison, NJ, 31

Camp John Hay, Philippines, 64

Camp Lown, ME, 115

Camp *Tel Yehudah*, 86 ff; its establishment, 86; its objectives, orientation and policies, 86-88; its weekly "Town Hall," 87, 88; polio scare at its Hendersville, NC site, 88, 89; overcomes *kashrut* problems, 89; its camp program, 89-92; its *Bikkurim* Festival, 91-92; its Tel Noar Lodge, Hampstead, NH

site operated jointly by Young Judaea and Eli and Bessie Cohen Foundation, 93; 97, 106

Camp Tevya, Brookline, NH, 77

Canaanites, 195

Cassel, Margot, 57, 59; describes *Kvutzat Chaverim* outing, 62-63; marries Arnulf Pins, 67

Cassel, Sol, 57

Chaplaincy in Manila, its organization and functions, 49-51

Charleroi United Service Organization, 37

Charleroi, Belgium, 36-39

Chazan, Barry, Asst. Education Director of FHJC, 123-125, 128

Chazan, Naomi (*née* Harman), 124

Chief Rabbinate of Israel, 235, 236

Cohen, Bessie, 93

Cohen, Eli, 93

Cohen, Gerson, Chancellor of JTS, 118

Cohen, Rabbi Jack J., 15, 95

Cohen, Sandy, FHJC Youth Director, 106

Cohen, Shirley, FHJC Early Childhood Department Director, 103

College Board of DYTC, 231

College of Pluralistic Judaism, 244

Columbia University Teachers College, 105

Commitment to values and ideals, 184, 185; educational implications, 192, 195, 196, 205, 207

Committee to Promote Western *Aliyah*, 124; sponsors *Aliyah* conference, 126; its policy of independent identity, 126, 127

Community Centers, contrasted to Synagogue Centers, 99

Conscience, 80, 185-188, 196

Council for Higher Education, 149, 152, 153; process of receiving academic recognition from, 155, 156; 159

Courcelles, Belgium, 35-38, 40

Curriculum and educational issues, 190-192, 199-203, 215-219

Cysner, Cantor Joseph, 51, 53, 59

D

Damur, city in Lebanon, 225

Dan Committee, 155

David Yellin Hebrew Teachers Seminary (see also David Yellin Teachers College, Bet Hakerem Hebrew Teachers Seminary), appoints Schanin as its Director, 127; its relationship with Ministry of Education and Culture, 132 ff; its academic level and physical facilities in 1968, 133, 134; its Mechina Pedagogic High School, 135-138; public elementary school on its premises, 136; Israeli Army facilities on its premises, 136; its Early Childhood Center, 138-141; its relationship with HU, 144; becomes part of HU School of Education 1952-1956, 145, 146; its upgrading from Seminary to College, 146-150; professional advisory committee formed, 149; receives approval as a college, 153; 220, 231

David Yellin Teachers College (see also David Yellin Teachers Seminary, Bet Hakerem Hebrew Teachers Seminary) 72; 132 ff; long-range plan, 143; Yom Kippur War's effect on, 150-152; receives recognition to award B. Ed. degrees, 154; proceeds towards full academization, 154-157; adopts Schanin's views on early childhood education, 157-159; introduces new teacher education models, 159-160; its interaction with HU on Special Education, 160; its Institute for Remedial Education, 160, 161; institutes Arab teacher training program, 161, 162; Jewish identity and Judaic studies, 162-164; its campus development, 164-166; is supported by "Friends of the David Yellin College," 166-168, 199, 201, 231

Davis, Rabbi Moshe, JTS Rabbinical School Registrar, 28

Dayan, Miriam, Special Education Teacher Trainer at DYTC, 161

Diaspora, Jewish education in, 199, 200, 202; function of the Jewish school in, 206-207;

Dinur, Prof. Ben Zion, 142, 144; as Minister of Education, 145; 166

Dushkin, Prof. Alexander M., 94, 95; heads HU B.A. program, 144

DYTC, see David Yellin Teachers College

E

Early Childhood Center at DYTC, established, 140, its functioning described, 141; 166, 201

East Midwood Jewish Center Religious School, employs Schanin as part-time teacher, 71; 72; Young Judaea Youth House held at, 86; 97, 167

East Midwood Jewish Center, its Religious School, 13, 18, 25; 65; its Junior Congregation, 13-14, 16; its Hebrew High School, 14; its Parents Association, 16; its Rabbi Harry Halpern Day School, 16; strike by its Religious School teachers, 16-17; its Junior Congregation, 18;

Eden, Miriam, Early Childhood Teacher Trainer at DYTC, 140, 141

Educators Assembly of the United Synagogue of America, research and curriculum development, 16, 108, 116-118, elects Schanin as president, 119

Eisenberg, Azriel, Principal of East Midwood Religious School, 13, 14;

Eisenstein, Rabbi Ira, 24

Eisenstein, Judith, 24

Eli and Bessie Cohen Foundation, 93

Ellenbogen, Abe, 42, 46

Eshel, Tamar, 235

Ettenberg, Sylvia, Dean, JTS Teachers Institute, 114, 118

European Theater of Operations, 39

F

Fabry, Dr. Joseph B., 186

Fayid, air base in Egypt, 223

Feinberg, Sheldon, 18, 23, 24

Feldbin, Chaplain Abraham, 66

Feldman, Estelle, FHJC Early Childhood Department Director, 103

FHJC, see Forest Hills Jewish Center

Fishman, Jacob, maternal grandfather of Norman Schanin, 12

Fishman, Lilly, aunt of Norman Schanin, 12

Fishman, Rose, maternal grandmother of Norman Schanin, 12

Fishman, Sam (Jimmy), uncle of Norman Schanin, 12

Fishman, Yetta (Bobby), aunt of Norman Schanin, 12

Fleischer, Louis, father of Roslyn Schanin, 12

Fleischer, May, half-sister of Roslyn Schanin, 12

Fleischer, Murray, half-brother of Roslyn Schanin, 12

Fleischer, Roslyn (Rahel), *see* Schanin, Roslyn

Fleischer, Sophie (née Rothbaum), mother of Roslyn Schanin, 12

Forest Hills Jewish Center, its Junior Congregation, 13, 14; appoints Norman Schanin as its Educational Director, 72, 97; 98 ff; its facilities and activities, 99; developing an integrated school system, 103, 104; its Junior Congregation, 103. 104, 106; its Youth Activities Program, 105, 106; its Youth Committee of laymen, 106; developing a new curriculum design, 109 ff; background material on its history, 111; its Parents Association, 111; its School Board, 111; outcome of new curriculum project reviewed, 114-116; its efforts to assist Israel in Six-Day War, 119, 120; 122, 130, 138, 167, 200

Forest Hills Jewish Community, background material on, 111

Forest Hills Tennis Club, 98

Forest Hills, description of, 98, 99; 231

Formal and informal education, the blending of, 19, 20, 72, 73, 114, 197-199, 203

Fort Bragg, CA, 68

Fort Dix, NJ, 69

Fort Monmouth, NJ, 32

Frank, Avraham, Director of Israel *Aliyah* Center, 124

Frankel, Prof. Binyamin, 149

Frankl, Prof. Viktor E., 183, 185, 186

Freund, Dr. Miriam, 94

Friedman, Prof. Richard Elliot, 208

Friends of the David Yellin Teachers College, 167, 168

Fuld, Ernst, 62

G

Gadish, Joseph, 235

Galut (exile), 82

Gannes, Abraham P., American Jewish educator 14

General Zionist *Halutziut* Commission, 80

General Zionists (political party in Israel), 83; its youth group in the US, 83; its *Halutziut* Commission, 83, 84; 96

Gibson, Chaplain Thomas M., 41-46

Ginsburg, Sammy, 37-38

God (Godliness), Schanin's view of, 187, 193-194, 205, 207 ff, 210 ff, 212-215

Golan Heights, as battlefield in Yom Kippur War, 223

Goldberg, Henry R., Principal of East Midwood Religious School, 13, his role in Schanin's Jewish education, 14-16; 18, 24

Good and evil, 184; 212-213

Gothelf, Jeanine, 37; her son Nicolas, 38; 69

Gothelf, Joseph, 37, 38

Gothelf, Marja, 37; receives visits from the Schanins in 1990, 38

Greenberg, Prof. Moshe, 149

Greenwald Accompanying Committee, approves academic recognition of additional DYTC educational programs, 156, 157

Gymnasiya HaIvrit, Jerusalem high school, its premises used by *Kehillat Mevakshei Derech*, 235

H

Hadassah, 72, 80, 83, 93, as sole sponsor of Young Judaea, 94; its partnership with ZOA, 97

Halacha (adj. *halachic*) (Jewish religious law), 175, 176, 180, 244

Halevi, Judge Elazar, DYTC Board Chairman, 142, 168, 169, 231

Halkin, Prof. Abraham, 149

Halpern, Harry, Rabbi of East Midwood Jewish Center, 13, 15, 16

Halpern, Minnie, 94

Halutziut (pioneering), 82-85

Hammer, Zevulun, Minister of Education, 152

Hancock, NY, 72

Hanoar HaTzioni (Zionist youth group in Israel), 83

Haredim (adj. *haredi*) (ultra-orthodox Jews), 180, 195, 204, 241

Harman, (Avraham), Israeli ambassador to US, 124-127

Hashomer Hatzair (Zionist organization), 42

Hassidism (adj. *hassidic*), stream in Judaism, 179

Hebrew Arts Committee, 80

Hebrew University, *see* The Hebrew University of Jerusalem

Hecht, Manfred, 65

Heiferman, Solomon, FHJC School Board Chairman, 101

Hellman, Rosie, 59

Herman, Prof. Simon, 177, 178

Hever Madrichei Yehudah Hatzair (Young Judaea Leaders Association), 85, 86

Hevra, Society to promote personal service, 85

Histadrut Ivrit, 80

Holabird Army Signal Depot, Baltimore, MD, 31

Hollandia, New Guinea, 44

Holocaust, 18, 39, 195

HU (Hebrew University), *see* The Hebrew University of Jerusalem

Hugei Aliyah (groups for *Aliyah*), 84

I

I and Thou, by Martin Buber, 208, 211, 217, 218

Igorot people (Philippines), 64-65

Institute for Remedial Education, *see* Rachel Shazar Institute (of DYTC), 161

Intercollegiate Zionist Federation of America, 80, 93

Internal Academic Committee of University Professors, 149

Ish-Shalom, Mordechai, 168

Israel Aliyah Center, 121, 123, 126

Israel Ministry of Education and Culture, 95

Israel, State of, 82; religious and ethnic politics in, 180-182; day of rest in, 181-182; Jewish education and curriculum planning in, 199-203; *Mamlachti* (public) schools in, 200; 203; non-government school systems in, 204; function of the Jewish school in, 206-207; post-Yom Kippur War atmosphere in, 224; 50ᵗʰ anniversary of, 226

Israeliness, 181, 191

J

Jerusalem City Council, 235

Jewish Agency, its Israeli *Aliyah* Center, 121, 123, 126; 127; its American Section, 128; 135

Jewish consciousness, 15, 19, 182, 191

Jewish Education Committee of New York, 116

Jewish Education, magazine, 109; Schanin's articles in, 192, 203

Jewish Educators Assembly, *see* Educators Assembly of the United Synagogue of America

Jewish identity, 163, 176-182; educational implications, 190-191

Jewish National and University Library, Jerusalem, 76

Jewish National Fund, 18, 167

Jewish Reconstructionist Foundation, 25, 109

Jewish religious observance in the military, 42-43

Jewish School, concept of 200

Jewish Teacher, magazine, 191

Jewish Theological Seminary of America, 15; its Teachers Institute, 15; its Israel Friedlander adult education courses, 17; awards BRE degree to Norman Schanin, 17; 27; Schanin resumes studies at its Teachers Institute, 71; awards Doctor of Pedagogy *honoris causa* to Schanin, 71, 119; 111; invites Schanin to teach courses at its School for Jewish Studies, 114; invites Schanin to teach courses at its Teachers Institute, 115; its Melton Research Center, 117

Jewish Welfare Board, 43, 57

Jewish Welfare Board Club in Manila, 48-50

Jewishness, meanings of, 110, 174-177, 180,

181, 184; educational implications, 191-195, 199-202, 228

JNF, *see* Jewish National Fund

Joplin, MO, 30

JTS, *see* Jewish Theological Seminary of America

Judaism as a Civilization, by Mordecai M. Kaplan, 15

Judaism Faces the Twentieth Century: A Biography of Mordecai M. Kaplan, by Mel Scult, 191, 192

Junior Hadassah, 80, 93

Junior Young Judaea program, 80

JWB, *see* Jewish Welfare Board Club

K

Kabbalism (adj. *Kabbalistic*), Jewish mysticism, 208

Kane, Nat, FHJC Youth Activities Chairman, 101

Kaplan, Rabbi Dr. Mordecai, his Reconstructionist philosophy, 15-16; 22, 42, 73, 78; his view of Jewish Peoplehood, 81, 102; 191, 193; his term "Nature's God," 211; 212; his term "Godhood," 213; as member of *Kehillat Mevakshei Derech*, 232-233; 245

Katamon, Jerusalem neighborhood, 137

Katzburg, Fred, 52, 54, 59

Kehillah (community), defined, 232

Kehillat Mevakshei Derech, 220, 231 ff; its beginnings, 232; its underlying principles, 232, 233; branches out in new directions, 233; its search for a new location, 234, 235; turns to religious and other authorities for assistance, 235-237; breaks ground for its building on Shai Agnon Boulevard, 236; its problems with Ministry of Religions for allocation of funds, 237; its relationship with other non-orthodox bodies, 237, 238; the changing role of its membership and the resulting financial problems, 238, 239; acquires land for educational and cultural center, 239-241; receives building permit, 242; its attempts at affiliation with a religious movement, 243-246; affiliates with Movement for Progressive Judaism in Israel, 245; its progress from synagogue to synagogue center (communal institution), 245, 246

Kelman, Prof. Herbert C., 178

Kertzer, Rabbi Morris N., 73

Kibbutz Hulda, Israel, 95

Kirshblum, Rabbi Mordechai, 128

Kogen, Rabbi David, 118

Kol Nidrei (*Yom Kippur* prayer), 215

Kol, Moshe, General Zionist leader, 96

Koleynu, Camp *Tel Yehudah* newspaper, 91

Kollek, Teddy, Mayor of Jerusalem, 161, 235, 236, 240, 241

Krasner, Norman, FHJC Youth Director, 106

Krauss, Adolph, FHJC Exec. Director, 101

Krauss, Muriel Goldberg, Assistant to Director, Young Judea, 76

Kvutza, 15; group to help Jewish survival and advancement, 19 ff; its role in Norman Schanin's becoming an educator, 19-20; its motto, goals, activities and organizational principles, 20-26; its Oath of Membership, 22; its uniqueness on the American Jewish scene, 22-23; its *Va'ad* (Executive Committee), 23; its *Keren Tarbut* (Cultural Fund), 24; its anniversary celebration, 24; its Junior *Kvutza* and *Kvutza* Bet, 24; its *Kvutza Gimmel*, 25; *Kvutza's* activities ended, 25; *Kvutza* program in Manila modeled on, 25; 72, 88

Kvutzat Chaverim, 56 ff; its opening meeting described, 59-60; preamble to its constitution, 60-61; its activities, 61-66; its children's group "Stars of David," 63, 65, 66; its Purim Carnival, 65; its activities ended, 67; 88

L

Lake Taal, Philippines, 62

Lam, Prof. Tzvi, chairman of three Lam Committees, 152

Lapson, Judah, American Jewish educator, 14

Laufer, Leo, 42, 52, 54, 59, 64

Laufer, Michael, 222

Lavine, Chaplain Bernard H., 54, 66

League of Jewish Women, *Kehillat Mevakshei Derech* located in premises of, 232, 233

Lebanese war, *see Sh'lom HaGalil*

Lewin, Prof. Kurt, group dynamics 78-79; 177

Logotherapy, 183, 186

Loyalty, 78-80, 187-190, 196, 207

Lyon, France, 41

M

Magnes Press of The Hebrew University of Jerusalem, 170, 231

Mamlachti (public) school system in Israel, 200; its subdivisions, 203

Man's Search for Meaning, by Viktor E. Frankl, 183

Manila (Philippines), 25, 44, 46, 47, 49, 50, 55, 62, 64-69, 88

Manila Jewish Community Center, 51; its post-war condition, 56

Manila Synagogue, its Temple Emil Congregation, 46; its Bachrach Wing, 46; used by Japanese as munitions dump, 46; its rebuilding, 51 ff; Memorial Service held in, 53; 54, 56

Manila, its Jewish community, 48 ff; 63, 67

Manila, Jewish life in during and after Japanese occupation, 56-57

Marseilles, France, 40, 46

Masada, 93

Masorti (Conservative) movement in Israel, 244

Mechina Pedagogic High School, located at DYTC, 135; its funding and operation, 136; is relocated to Katamon area of Jerusalem, 137, 138, 140; its program and *raison d'être* described, 137

Mehlman, Dr. Israel, 142

Messiah, 180, 195, 215

Meyouhas, Josef, 95

Meystel, Sid, 59

Ministry of Education and Culture, its involvement in DYTC, 133-135; its Teacher Education Department, 133, 152, 156; its involvement in Mechina Pedagogic High School, 136; 137, 139, 146, 148, 152, 153; 157-159, 161, 162, 164; its financial support to DYTC, 166, 167; notifies Schanin of his reaching retirement age, 169

Ministry of Finance, 235-237

Ministry of Religions, 235-237

Mishael, Esther, Asst. Director at DYTC, 150

Mishpachton (baby group), 199

Mitzvot (commandments), 175

Monotheism, 209

Moral education and character development, 192, 195, 196, 199, 205-207

Moses, 210

Mount Sinai, 209, 210, 247

Movement for Progressive (Reform) Judaism in Israel, 244, 245

N

Nahal Geshur, Golan Heights settlement, 223

National Council for Jewish Education, 116

National Library, 171

National Young Judaea, 77, 80, 81, 85

Navon, Yitzhak, as Minister of Education, 168

Nazi Germany, 18, 215

Netzorg, Morton I., Manila Jewish community leader, 48; as AJDC representative, 53; 57, 59, 67

New curriculum design for the Diaspora Jewish school, 107 ff

New Guinea, 43, 44, 69

New Insights into Curriculum Development, Yearbooks edited by Norman Schanin, 108, 109

New York University, 27; Schanin resumes studies at, 71; awards B.A. and M.A. degrees to Schanin, 71; awards Ed. D. degree to Schanin, 71, 76

Novozybkov, Byelorus(sia), 12

NYU, *see* New York University

O

Olim (immigrants to Israel) 82

Open School concept, 139

Ornan, Prof. Uzi, 149

Orthodoxy, in Israel, 233

P

Pacific Theatre of Operations, 41, 54, 67

Palestine Song and Dance Group, 15, 18, 21

Palestine, 18, 19

Palmach, Israel fighting unit, 171

Panama Canal, 41-43

Park Avenue Synagogue, NYC, 73, 116

Passover (Jewish festival) 36, 37, 68

Passover Haggadah, 247

Peace for Galilee, *see Sh'lom HaGalil*

Peoplehood, 15-18, 81, 102, 176, 181, 193-195

Permanent Committee for Academic Programs in the Teachers Colleges (Dan Committee), 155

Phenix, Prof. Philip H., 200

Philippine Islands, 25, 43, 44, 46, 54-56, 66, 67, 69

Philippinews, Manila Jewish military personnel newsletter, 54

Pins, Arnulf M., 66; marries Margot Cassel, 67

Pins, Danny, 222

Plugat Aliyah, General Zionists' youth group in the US (also affiliated with *HaNoar HaTzioni*), 83-84

Prero, Rabbi Amram, Executive Director, AZYC, 93, 94

Protest movement among military personnel in Philippines, 54-56

Purim (Jewish Festival), 65

Q

Queen Anna Maria, Greek flagship, transports the Schanins to Israel, 129, 220

Queens College, New York, 220

R

Rabbinical Assembly, 127

Rabin, Yitzhak (as Israeli ambassador to the US) addresses AACA's *T'nuat Aliyah* conference, 128

Rachel Shazar Institute (DYTC), 161

Ramah Camps, 106, 129

Realms of Meaning, by Philip H. Phenix, 200

Reconstructionism, its influence on Norman Schanin, 15-18; 22, 42; its relationship to Conservative Judaism, 73-74; 193

Reconstructionist Institute for Jewish Youth Leadership, 75

Reconstructionist movement, 232, 245

Reconstructionist, article by Norman Schanin published in, 109

Rehavia, Jerusalem neighborhood, 232

Rehovot, Israel, 95

Resolving Social Conflicts, by Kurt Lewin, 78-79

Robbins, Dr. Morton, J., 94, 95

Rosenberg, Bert, FHJC Youth Director, 106

Rosenfeld, Jacob, Young Judaea club leader, 15, 17

Rosenwald, Harry, half-brother of Roslyn Schanin, 12

Rosh HaShanah (Jewish New Year), 44-46

Royce, Prof. Josiah, 78-79, 188-190

S

Samentevich, Byelorus(sia), 10

San Francisco, CA, 67, 68

Santa Mesa (suburb of Manila), 62

Sarid, Yaakov, Director General, Israeli Ministry of Education, 125

Schanin family, moves to Forest Hills, 98, makes *Aliyah*, 129, 130, 132, 220; their Yom Kippur War experiences described, 220-221;

Schanin, Charles, father of Norman Schanin, 10

Schanin, David Jacob, son of Norman and Roslyn Schanin, 7, 220, 222-224, 231

Schanin, Evelyn, sister of Norman Schanin, 12

Schanin, Hillel Avram, son of Norman and Roslyn Schanin, 7, 220-222; as a soldier in Yom Kippur War, 151, 223; in the Lebanese war, 225

Schanin, Jeane, mother of Norman Schanin, 10

Schanin, Jonathan, son of Norman and Roslyn Schanin, 7, 220, 221; as a soldier in Yom Kippur war, 151, 223; in the Lebanese war, 225

Schanin, Nisan, paternal grandfather of Norman Schanin, 10

Schanin, Norman, his objectives in writing this book, 7; his motivations for becoming a

Jewish educator, 10; his family background, 10-13; his early Jewish education, 13-15; influence of East Midwood Junior Congregation on, 13-14; at Camp *Achvah*, 14; his introduction to Reconstructionism, 15-16; as President of the Educators Assembly, 16; attends Israel Friedlander adult education courses at JTS, 17; admitted to JTS Teachers Institute, 17; receives B.R.E. degree from JTS, 17; collects funds for JNF, 18; helps organize Palestine Song and Dance Group, 18; helps organize *Kvutza*, 18; his activities on behalf of *Kvutza*, 18 ff; meets his future wife, Roslyn, 19; his professional and personal development influenced by *Kvutza*, 19-20, 23, 25-26; writes article for *The Reconstructionist*, 20; his continuing contacts with *Kvutza* members, 25; receives B.A., B.R.E. and M.A. degrees, 27; inducted into the US Army, 27-28; his experiences in Cooks and Bakers School, 28, 29; enters Signal Corps Clerical School, 28, 30; assigned to 547th Signal Corps Depot Company, 30, 35, 36; on staff of *The Depot Digest*, 31; transferred to Holabird Army Signal Depot, Baltimore, MD, 31; at Avon, NJ, Signal Corps Warehouse, 31; becomes engaged to Roslyn Fleischer, 32; assigned to overseas duty, 32 ff; aboard USS Mount Vernon, 32, 33; with the US Army in England, 33-34; with the US Army in France, 34-35; with the US Army in Belgium, 35-40; hospitalized in Charleroi, Belgium, 36; spends Passover in Charleroi, Belgium, 37; (with wife Roslyn) visits Marja Gothelf in 1990, 38; at staging area in Marseilles, France, 40-41; his reaction to Holocaust revelations, 39; aboard USS Sea Flyer, 41-46; organizes religious services aboard the USS Sea Flyer, 42, 45, 46; as Chaplain's Assistant, 49-54; assists in rebuilding Manila Synagogue, 51-52; edits *Philippinews*, 54; his efforts to help Manila Jewish community, 56 ff; organizes Jewish youth group in Manila, 57 ff; ordered back to the U.S., 65; reviews his Manila activities, 67; named Lifetime Honorary Member of Manila Synagogue, 67; celebrates Passover aboard USS General Langfitte, 68; his demobilization, 69; reviews his years of military service, 69-70; resumes studies at NYU and JTS, 71; his efforts to support himself during his studies, 71 ff; is offered position of Director of Brooklyn Zionist Youth Commission; 72; begins to formulate a philosophy of education, 72, 73; as Assistant Principal and Youth Director of Park Ave. Synagogue, 73; defines himself as a "Reconstructionist Conservative Jew," 73; as co-founder of Reconstructionist Institute for Jewish Youth Leadership, 75; as co-editor of *Tehiyah*, 75; his doctoral thesis, 76; his research in the field of group dynamics, 78; influences on his Jewish educational thinking, 78-80; as National Executive Director of Young Judaea, 75 ff; 80-86, 106; expounds on Young Judaea's position on *Halutziut* and *Aliyah*, 84, 85; as Director of Camp *Tel Yehuda*, 86-92; describes camp life and its objectives in "*Koleynu*" (camp newspaper), 91; plans visit to Israel to set up permanent young Judaea summer program, 95; is asked to postpone visit to Israel, 95; his visit takes place one year later, 95; makes arrangements for first Senior Judaean Summer-in-Israel, 95; participates in *Tsofim* training center dedication, 95; his return trip to USA, 96; his motivation for leaving his position at Young Judaea, 96, 97; his view of partnership between Hadassah and ZOA, 97; appointed Educational Director of FHJC, 97; as Educational Director of FHJC, 99 ff; 115; his efforts to educate a lay leadership towards a Kaplanian philosophy of Jewishness, 101, 102; his efforts to provide a program of family education, 101, 102; is instrumental in opening Solomon Schechter Day School in Queens, 104; enrolls as post-doctoral student at Columbia University Teachers College, 105; his efforts to strengthen school children's ties with Israel, 105; develops Youth Activities Program, 105, 106; his summers in New Hampshire, 106, 107; completes doctoral dissertation, 106; develops new integrated curriculum design for school and youth activities in American Diaspora, 107 ff; prepares teaching material on "The Weekly Torah Portion" and Prayers and Holidays, 108; prepares Yearbooks for Educators Assembly of the United Synagogue of America, 108, 109; publishes articles on developing ideas for Jewish education, 109; tries to apply his philosophical and pedagogic principles to Israeli education, 109; his Jewish educational concepts explained, 110, 111; prepares classroom and resource materials for Jewish education, 111; writes "The World of the Bible," 111; publishes progress report on new curriculum project in *The Message,* 111-114; reviews outcome of curriculum project, 114; invited by JTS to teach courses in group work and education and to serve as Teacher Trainer, 114, 115; head of Leadership Training in summer camps, 115; as group leader for United Synagogue teenage pilgrimage to Israel, 115, 116, 119; his contacts with other Jewish educators, 116-119; invited to join Executive Committees of two educational organizations, 117; writes memorandum for Educators Assembly Executive Committee, 117; asked to serve as chairman of its research committee, 117; elected president of Educators Assembly, 119; elected secretary of National Council for Jewish Education, 119; awarded Doctor of Pedagogy degree, *honoris causa,* 119; his Zionist commitment, 119 ff; his reaction to Six-Day War, 120, 121; pros and cons of *Aliyah* for Schanin family, 120 ff; prepares for *Aliyah* to Israel, 121 ff; prepares list of educators interested in Aliyah, 124; as part of delegation to explore employment opportunities in Israel, 125, 126; serves as chairman of Aliyah Conference, 126; elected chairman of AACA executive committee, 127; appointed Director of David Yellin Teachers Seminary, 127; makes Aliyah with his family, 129; his parting from parents and friends in US, 129, 130; publishes farewell statement in FHJC's *The Message,* 130,131; assumes position as Director (Dean) of David Yellin Hebrew Teachers Seminary, 132, 133; period of adjustment, 133; describes physical and academic conditions in 1968, 134, 135; unexpectedly finds himself to be head of Mechina Pedagogic High School, 135-137; his views on early childhood education, 138; his educational goals at DYTC, 138-140; establishes Early Childhood Center, 140, 141; presents long-range plan for restructuring David Yellin Hebrew Teachers Seminary as a Teachers College, 143; his long-range plan for

upgrading the Seminary to a College, 146 ff; his philosophy of early childhood education, 146; his vision of the Seminary's serving Jerusalem's needs, 147; institutes practical steps in that direction, 148-150; reorganizes study structure and curriculum, 150; his sons serve in Yom Kippur War, 151, 152; achieves partial academic status for DYTC, 153; concludes development of DYTC from Seminary to College, 155; new academic models, 155-162; oversees the process of full academization of DYTC, 154-157; his theories on early-childhood education put into practice at DYTC, 157-159; institutes program for training Arab teachers at DYTC, 161, 162; attempts to intensify Judaic studies at DYTC, 163-165; oversees campus development program, 166, 167; organizes "Friends of the David Yellin Teachers College," 167, 168, reaches retirement age, 168; passes the reins to new Director, 169, 170; on Executive Committee of Board of Directors, 170; looks back on twenty years at DYTC, 170-172; his *The Academic Development of Teacher Education in Israel,* 170, 171; his final report as Director of DYTC, 171, 172; reflects on the meanings of Jewishness, 174 ff; compares Jewishness in the Diaspora to that in modern Israel, 174-176, 190; reviews the many facets of Jewish identity, 176-182; ponders conflict between different sectors of Israeli society, 180-182; reflects on the meanings of Jewishness, 174 ff; compares Jewishness in the Diaspora to that in modern Israel, 174-176, 190; reviews the many facets of Jewish identity, 176-182; ponders conflict between different sectors of Israeli society, 180-182; his views on: the meaning of life, 182-184; commitment to values and ideals, 184-186; conscience, 186-188; loyalty, 188-190; the educational implications of his views, 190-192; the many shadings of the meaning of Jewishness; 192-194; Zionism, 194-195; commitment and loyalty leading to service, 195-197; informal education in the family setting, 197-199; the role of caregivers for young children, 198-199; Jewish education curricula, 199-203; his earlier experimental curriculum program at FHJC, 200; discusses the difficulties of Jewish curriculum planning in the Diaspora and in Israel, 201-

203; his article in *Jewish Education*, 203; his recommendations for effective Jewish educational systems, 204; his views on: education towards morality, 205-207; moral imperatives and God (Godliness), 207-213; prayer 213-215; educational significance of the historical approach to Bible and prayer, 215-219; describes his family's Yom Kippur War experiences, 221-222; reflects on issues dividing Israeli society, 225-226; his 50th wedding anniversary, 226; his views on the values of Jewish family life, 226-229; describes his early retirement years, 230-231; his book on the history of DYTC, 230-231; his travels after retirement, 231; meets relatives in Leningrad, 231; his involvement in synagogue life, 231-232; leads *Kehillat Mevakshei Derech* in new directions, 233-235; as Chairman (President) of *Kehillat Mevakshei Derech* oversees various projects, 235-238; as Chairman of Building Committee initiates attempts of enlarging *Kehillat Mevakshei Derech*'s premises, 239-243; as Chairman of Affiliations Committee, 245; sums up his life and work, 246, 247

Schanin, Roslyn (Rahel) *née* Fleischer, 7; her family background, 12; 13; 16; as a leader in *Kvutza*, 19-25; meets future husband, Norman, 19; 24; 26; dates Norman, 29; becomes engaged to Norman, 32; visits the Gothelf family, 38; 68, 70, 72, 93, collaborates with husband Norman on preparing teaching materials, 108; as group leader for United Synagogue teenage pilgrimage to Israel, 115, 116; 119; her reaction to Six-Day War, 120, 121; prepares for *Aliyah* to Israel, 121 ff; makes *Aliyah*, 129; 130, 151; works at Israel Museum and Hebrew University, 220; her 50th wedding anniversary, 226; her travels after retirement, 231; her involvement in synagogue life, 231-232

Schanin, Sarah Breyner (née Raskin), paternal grandmother of Norman Schanin, 10; her demise, 12

Scheinin, Dora (nee Raskin), great-aunt of Norman Schanin, 12

Scheinin, Harry, uncle of Norman Schanin, 10

Scheinin, Hyman, cousin of Norman Schanin, 12

Scheinin, Jack, uncle of Norman Schanin, 10

Scheinin, Joseph, cousin of Norman Schanin, 12

Scheinin, Nathan, great-uncle of Norman Schanin, 12

Schiffrin, Harold, 52-54

Schwarz, Rabbi Joseph, 53, 59

Scult, Prof. Mel, Kaplan biographer, 191

Secular humanist movement in Israel, 244

Seder (Passover ceremony) 37, 68

Senate Military Affairs Committee, 55

Senior Young Judaea, 25; 78 ff; its program and goals, 78; its National Convention, 1950, at Camp Shor, Indiana, 81-82; preamble to its constitution, 81-82; 83; its *Hugei Aliyah* and *Garin Aleph*, 84; its Summer in Israel program, 84; its National Council rejects establishment of *Hevra*, 85; votes for *Hevra*'s abolition in 1951, 85; its National Senior Convention approves *Hevra*'s dissolution, 85; 86; its Summer-in-Israel program, 95

Service to the Jewish People, 19, 81-85; educational implications, 196, 226

Servicemen's Committee to Aid the Jewish Community of Manila, 52; its fundraising, 53

Sh'lom HaGalil (Peace for Galilee), Israel's war in Lebanon, 225; battle at En Ze-Chaltah, 225

Shabbat (Jewish Sabbath), 181

Shas, haredi political party in Israel, its school system, 204

Shazar Rachel, Israeli president's wife, 161

Shazar, Zalman, President of Israel, 161

Shlichim (emissaries from Israel), 82-83; their work with potential Western immigrants to Israel, 121-123

Shlilat Ha-Golah (negation of the Diaspora), 82

Shofar (ram's horn), 43, 45, 46, 221

Shtetl, ghetto-like Jewish community, 179

Signal Corps Depot S-858, 36

Sinai peninsula, 223

Six-Day War, 119, 161, 220

Solomon Schechter Day School in Queens, NY, 104

Solomon Schechter Day Schools, 16

Stars and Stripes (American Army newspaper), 39

Steinberg, Rabbi Milton, 73

Styer, Lt.-General, 53

Sub-Base "R" in Batangas, PI, 55

Suez Canal, 223

Synagogue Centers (in US), 96, 97; contrasted to Community Centers, 99

Synagogue Religious Schools, their aims and activities, 102

T

T'nuat HaMagshimim (self-realization for Aliyah), 127, 128

Teachers Union, 158, 159

Tehiyah (Renaissance), bulletin published by Reconstructionist Institute for Jewish Youth Leadership, 75

Tel Noar Lodge, Hampstead, NH, site of 1951 National Senior Convention of Young Judaea, 85; site of Camp *Tel Yehudah*, 93

Temple Emil Congregation in Manila, 46

The Academic Development of Teacher Education in Israel, by Norman Schanin, 170

The Disappearance of God: a Divine Mystery, by R.E. Friedman, 208

The Hebrew University of Jerusalem, its teacher training program, 143; its relationship with DYTC, 144; its early development, 144; offers B.A. program, 144, 145; establishes School of Education, 145; incorporates David Yellin Hebrew Teachers Seminary into its School of Education 1952-1956, 145, 146; 148, 149; its involvement in DYTC's academization 152-157; its interaction with DYTC on Special Education, 160

The High Holiday Prayer Book, edited by Ben Zion Bokser, 183

The Leader, Young Judaea publication, 84; Young Judea's position on *Halutziut* and *Aliyah* explained in, 84-85

The Message. FHJC's bulletin, publishes progress report by Schanin on new curriculum project, 111-114; publishes farewell statement by Schanin, 130,131

The National Council for Jewish Education, 109; elects Schanin as secretary, 119

The *Philosophy of Loyalty*, by Josiah Royce, 190

The Prayer Book, edited by Ben Zion Bokser, 219

The Pursuit of Meaning, by Joseph B. Fabry, 186

The World of the Bible, by Norman Schanin, 111

Torah (Pentateuch), 45, 221, 222

Tsofim (Israel's Scout movement), 83; its relationship with Young Judaea, 94-96; undergoes changes, 93 ff; asks Prof. Alexander Dushkin to investigate political affiliation of *Tsofim*, 94, 95

U

United Church of Manila, 48

United Israel Appeal, 120

United Jewish Appeal, 120

United Service Organization in Charleroi, 37, 39; in Manila, 43

United Synagogue, 115

United Synagogue Youth, 106

USO, *see* United Service Organization

USO-JWB in Manila, 48-50, 53, 57, 59, 61, 65

USS General Langfitte, 67

USS Sea Flyer, 41, 44-46

V

V-E Day, 36

W

War of Independence, 170

Weinberg, Chaplain Dudley, 47, 49, 51

Weisberg, Edward L., 54

Welisch, Doris, 59

Welisch, Gitta, 58, 59

Welsch, Capt. Glenn A., 49

Whartman, Leonard, 52

White Rock, NC, 88

Winter, Nathan H., 48

World Union for Progressive Judaism, 245

World Zionist Organization, 123

WZO, *see* World Zionist Organization

Y

Yadlin, Aharon, 152

Yadlin, Yehoshua, 125

Yafeh, Emanuel, Director of Dept. of Teacher Education, Ministry of Education and Culture, 125, 127, 133, 152

Yakir, Moshe, Director of Immigration Department, WZO, 124, 125

Yellin, Prof. David, 144, 155, 166

Yom Kippur (Day of Atonement), 44; services held in Manila stadium, 47; 215

Yom Kippur War, 147, 151, 161, 167, 220-224; Schanin family's experiences in, 221-222; Golan Heights battles in, 223

Young Judaea, Zionist youth movement, 17, 25, 71; its 1947 Conference of Leaders and Seniors in Spring Valley, NY, 76, 77; establishes Senior Young Judaea, 77; its National Convention of teenagers in Brookline, NH, 77, 78; adopts national constitution for Senior Young Judaea, 77; 79, 80; its Senior Young Judaea program, 78 ff; its Junior Young Judaea program, 80; its National Young Judaea Committee, 80-81; its national program identified, 82; its attitude towards the State of Israel, *Aliyah* and *Halutziut*, 82; its relationship to the American Jewish community, 82; its relationship to *Shlichim* from Israel, 82-83;
its ideological position vis-a-via *Halutziut* and *Aliyah* clarified by Schanin, 84, 85; his personal philosophy on Jewish values, etc., 84, 85; proposes establishment of *Hevra* (Society) to promote personal service in US and Israel, 85; its National Leaders Conference, 1951, establishes *Hever Madrichei Yehudah Hatzair*, 85, 86; its Camp *Tel Yehuda* for teenagers, 86ff; its Youth House at East Midwood Jewish Center, 86; its relationship with *Tsofim*, 94-96; raises funds for Tsofim encampment, 95; 96; Norman Schanin vacates his position as its Director, 96, 97; 106, 114, 116

Young Judaea: A Survey of a National Jewish Youth Movement in 1951-1952, Schanin's doctoral thesis, 76

Z

Zimran, Dr. Etai, succeeds Schanin at DYTC, 169

Zionism, 17 ff; 176, 180, 193-195

Zionist Archives, New York and Jerusalem, 76

Zionist Organization of America, 72, 80, 83; its partnership with Hadassah, 97

ZOA, *see* Zionist Organization of America

Zussman Accompanying Committee, recommends full academic recognition, 155, 156

Zwitman, Chaplain Coleman A., 49, 51, 54, 66, 67, 69